AF521924

SANDY SKOGLUND

Reality Under Siege

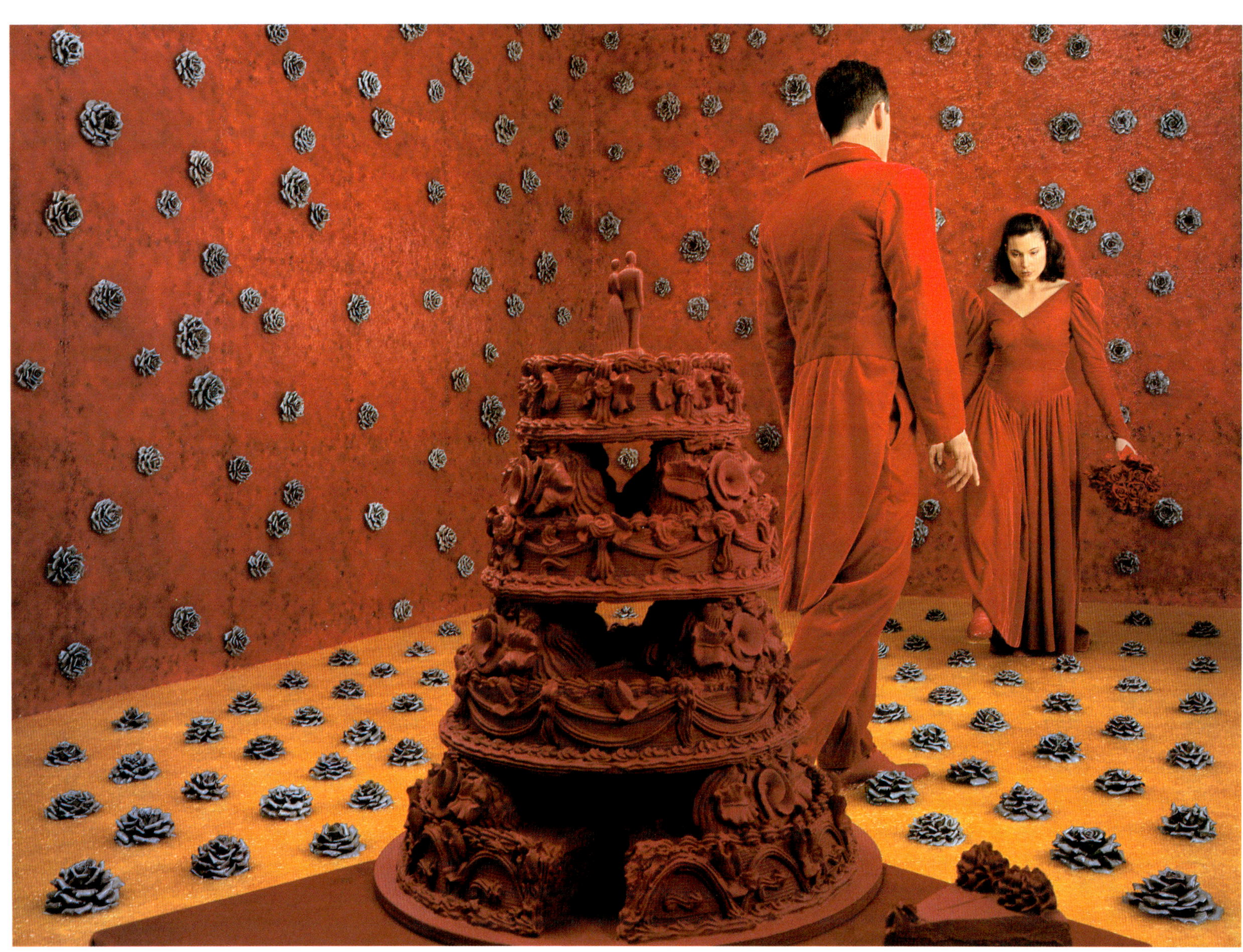

SANDY SKOGLUND

Reality Under Siege

A Retrospective

Smith College Museum of Art, in association with Harry N. Abrams, Inc., Publishers

Published on the occasion of the retrospective *Sandy Skoglund: Reality Under Siege* at the Smith College Museum of Art, Northampton, Massachusetts. Exhibition organized by Linda Muehlig, Associate Curator of Paintings and Sculpture, and Ann H. Sievers, Associate Curator of Prints, Drawings, and Photographs, Smith College Museum of Art.

Partial funding for the exhibition was provided by the National Endowment for the Arts. A portion of the museum's general operating funds for fiscal year 1997–98 has been provided through a grant from the Institute of Museum and Library Services, a federal agency that strengthens museums to benefit the public.

Page 2: *The Wedding,* 1994 (cat. 44)

PHOTOGRAPHY CREDITS:
Gamma One (cat. 21); Rudolph Nagel, Frankfurt am Main (page 65); William O'Connor (cat. 35); Stephen Petegorsky (cat. 4–6 and pages 73, 86, 87); Photograph copyright © 1997: Whitney Museum of American Art (page 64); Gayle Gleason (page 29)

EXHIBITION ITINERARY:

Smith College Museum of Art, Northampton, Massachusetts
March 12, 1998–May 24, 1998

The Cincinnati Art Museum, Cincinnati, Ohio
June 27, 1998–August 23, 1998

The Columbia Museum of Art, Columbia, South Carolina
October 12, 1998–January 3, 1999

The Toledo Museum of Art, Toledo, Ohio
February 14, 1999–May 2, 1999

The Jacksonville Museum of Contemporary Art, Jacksonville, Florida
September 10, 1999–November 7, 1999

Editor: Robert Morton
Editorial Assistant: Nola Butler
Designer: Robert McKee

Library of Congress Cataloging-in-Publication Data
Skoglund, Sandy, 1946–
Sandy Skoglund : reality under siege : a retrospective.
p. cm.
Catalog of an exhibition entitled "Reality under siege" to be held at the Smith College Museum of Art in the spring of 1998.
Includes bibliographical references and index.
ISBN 0–8109–4185–6 (clothbound). — ISBN 0–8109–2785–3 (mus. pbk.)
1. Photography, Artistic—Exhibitions. 2. Photography of art—Exhibitions. 3. Skoglund, Sandy, 1946– —Exhibitions. 4. Installations (Art)—Exhibitions. I. Smith College. Museum of Art. II. Title.
TR647.S56 1998
779'.092—dc21 97–36229

Published in 1998 by Harry N. Abrams, Incorporated, New York

Printed and bound in Japan

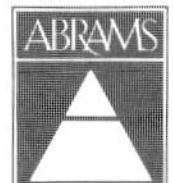

Harry N. Abrams, Inc.
100 Fifth Avenue
New York, N.Y. 10011
www.abramsbooks.com

CONTENTS

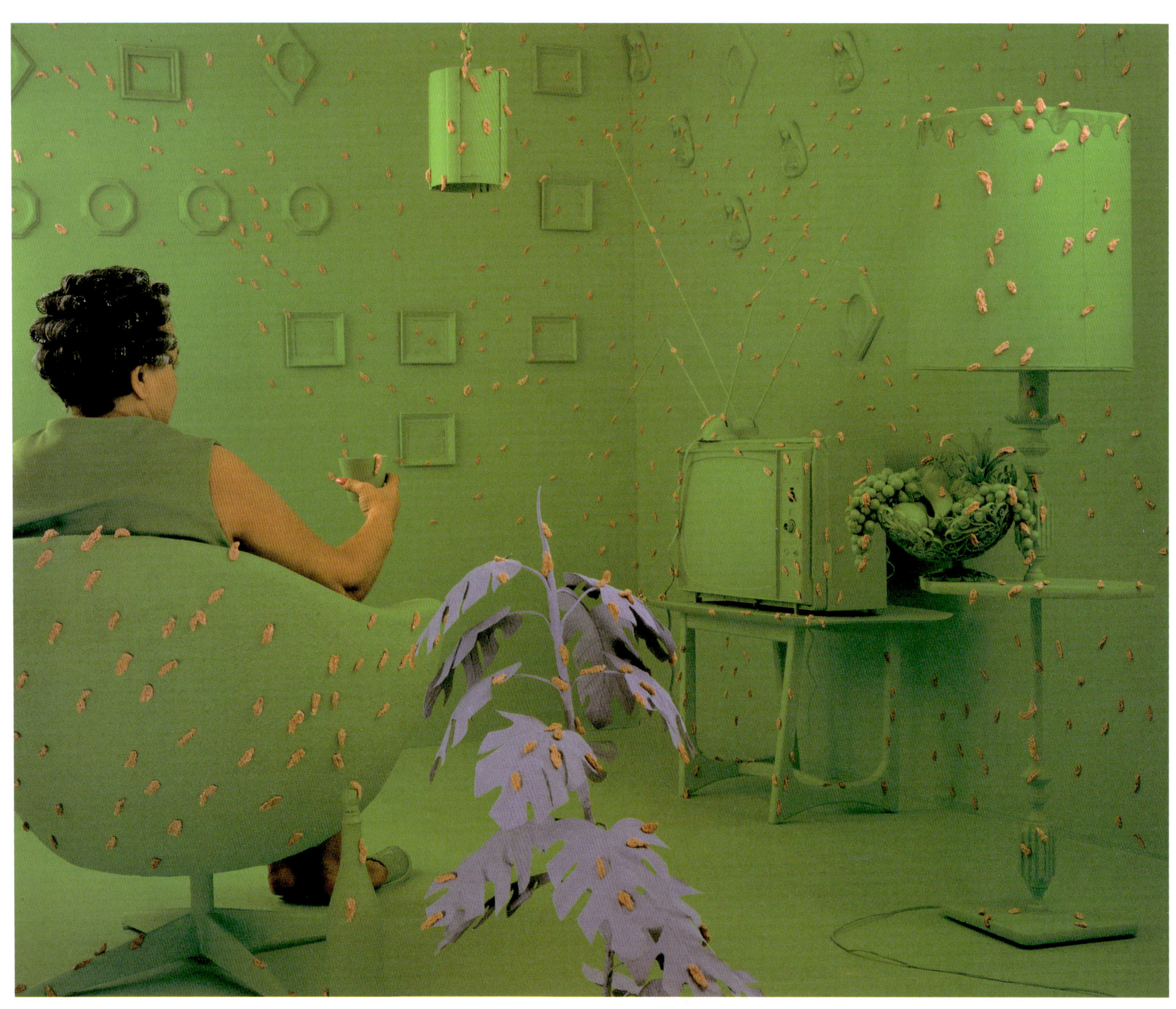

Germs Are Everywhere, 1984 (cat. 31)

INTRODUCTION

Well beyond the initial planning stages of Sandy Skoglund's first mid-career retrospective, we realized that the exhibition still had no title other than the artist's name. As the organizing curators, we felt a responsibility to give the retrospective not only a suitable title, but a memorable one that reflected Skoglund's work and at the same time avoided dry description or jargon. Our own imaginations proved too dull for the task, and we turned to the artist for help. Among the titles on the list she gave us, "Reality Under Siege" was our unanimous choice, perhaps for different reasons, none of which was a commentary on the great pleasure of working with Sandy Skoglund herself. There is no artist more skilled, better organized, or more unswervingly dedicated to her work.

Like Skoglund's work, the title, *Reality Under Siege*, resists easy explanation. Perspective on both the evolution of her work and the exhibition title was provided by the constantly changing landscape of Skoglund's studio during the time we were preparing the exhibition. There, thousands of whole, empty eggshells, snake and rabbit pinups, various bathroom fixtures in the process of being cast into paper, as well as hundreds of taxidermy glass eyes, were being assembled in preparation for her newest installation, *Walking on Eggshells*. Another insight into the appropriateness of the exhibition title had been furnished by the spectacle of a procession of Smith College students carrying Skoglund's oversize blue and pink baby sculptures down to the banks of Paradise Pond on the college campus in late March 1995. Skoglund deployed the toddling and crawling sculptures among the live student models in the grass, in a rowboat, and on the island in the middle of the pond for the photography session that would eventually result in the lithograph *Babies on Paradise Pond*, the first of the three new works created for the exhibition.

Reality Under Siege opens at the Smith College Museum of Art in spring 1998, the year of Skoglund's thirtieth reunion at her alma mater, and then departs on a national tour. Preparations for the exhibition began years earlier, when the museum's curatorial staff first approached the artist about the idea of a retrospective.

Surprisingly, although many people know Skoglund's most famous image, *Radioactive Cats*, a photograph of a gray apartment interior overrun by glowing green felines, they are not equally aware of its author. A review of Skoglund's extensive bibliography and exhibition history reveals that her work has been discussed and shown nationally and internationally. Most exhibitions, however, have centered either on a single sculptural tableau or on the large-scale Cibachrome photographic prints based on her installations. Many of the reviews, while admiring, have not discussed her work in depth. This retrospective was conceived as a way of redressing these shortcomings, by surveying the artist's career from its beginnings in performance and conceptual art to the three new works created for the exhibition: the installation *Walking on Eggshells*, the Cibachrome based on it, and the 1996 lithograph *Babies at Paradise Pond*. It was also an opportunity to extend the literature on Skoglund's work, with an interview of the artist by the distinguished art historian Robert Rosenblum, an essay by the photography critic Carol Squiers, and our articles on Skoglund's installations and lithographs.

While it is difficult to convey a complete picture of this complex artist, it is our intention to offer readers of this book and visitors to the retrospective an opportunity to assess and compare the interrelationships of her work in various media. Her sculptural installations, featuring domestic environments populated by figures, animals, and objects, are represented by *Revenge of the Goldfish* (1981), *Fox Games* (1989), *The Cocktail Party* (1992), and *Walking on Eggshells*, her most recent tableau. The Cibachrome photographs based on these and other installations are also included. This more familiar body of work is placed in perspective by a survey of her career, beginning with her little-known conceptualist "dot" pictures and realist drawings of the mid-1970s, as well as photographs from *Resemblance and Difference*, a suite of New England motel façades. Her photographic *Food Still Life* series, which playfully subverts conceptualist principles as well as advertising art, marks new directions at the end of her first decade as a mature artist. Skoglund's *True Fiction* paintings and photographs of the mid-1980s reflect the influence of her installations, but they explore exterior as well as interior spaces in a palette based on the color-separation dyes of photography and four-color-process offset printing.

Marshaling a project as large as this has been a challenging but highly rewarding task. Many people must be acknowledged for their help and assistance. We extend our thanks to the lenders to the exhibition for their generosity: private collectors Lita Hornick, Jenette Kahn, and Alvin D. Hall, and our sister institution at Amherst College, the Mead Art Museum. We are especially grateful to the Denver Art Museum, in particular Dianne Vanderlip, curator of contemporary and modern art, and Michelle Assaf, registrar, for lending the *Fox Games* tableau. Our colleagues at the museums to which the retrospective will travel deserve to be acknowledged for their persistence and hard work in making *Reality Under Siege* a reality at their institutions. In particular, we wish to mention Barbara K. Gibbs, director, Dennis Kiel, associate curator of photography, and Mary Ellen Goeke, head of exhibitions and registration, at the Cincinnati Art Museum; David W. Steadman, director, Christine Swenson, curator of graphic arts, and Davira Taragin, exhibitions team leader and curator of nineteenth-and twentieth-century glass, at the Toledo Museum of Art; Salvatore B. Cilella, director and CEO, and William B. Bodine, Jr., deputy director and chief curator, at the Columbia (South Carolina) Museum of Art; and Henry Flood Robert, Jr., director and CEO, at the Jacksonville (Florida) Museum of Contemporary Art.

Our thanks also go to the contributors to the catalogue, Robert Rosenblum and Carol Squiers, and to Robert Morton, director of special projects at Abrams, who shepherded this very handsome catalogue through the publication process. Janet Borden, director of Janet Borden, Inc. (and also an alumna of Smith College), facilitated the retrospective in every way. The exhibition and catalogue were supported, in part, by a grant from the National Endowment for the Arts and by the Institute for Museum and Library Services, a federal agency offering general operating support to the nation's museums.

A number of our colleagues and friends in the Smith College community deserve our thanks. We are grateful to Smith College's Jerene Appleby Harnish ('16) Visiting Artist Fund for underwriting both the photoshoot for *Babies at Paradise Pond* and the subsequent Smith College Print Workshop, where the lithograph was proofed. For their crucial roles in the success of this project, we express our warm appreciation to Professor Dwight Pogue, director of the Smith College Print Workshop, and master printer Maurice Sanchez, who editioned the print. Thanks are also owed the Smith College students, too numerous to name here, and the lone Hampshire College student who transported baby sculptures and posed with them for the photoshoot or took part in the print workshop.

All of the members of the staff of the Smith College Museum of Art have put their shoulders to the wheel for the exhibition and catalogue. In particular, we thank Edward Nygren, former director, who supported the project in its beginning stages and encouraged the idea of a retrospective; Charles Parkhurst, interim director, who sustained it in his turn; and Director Suzannah

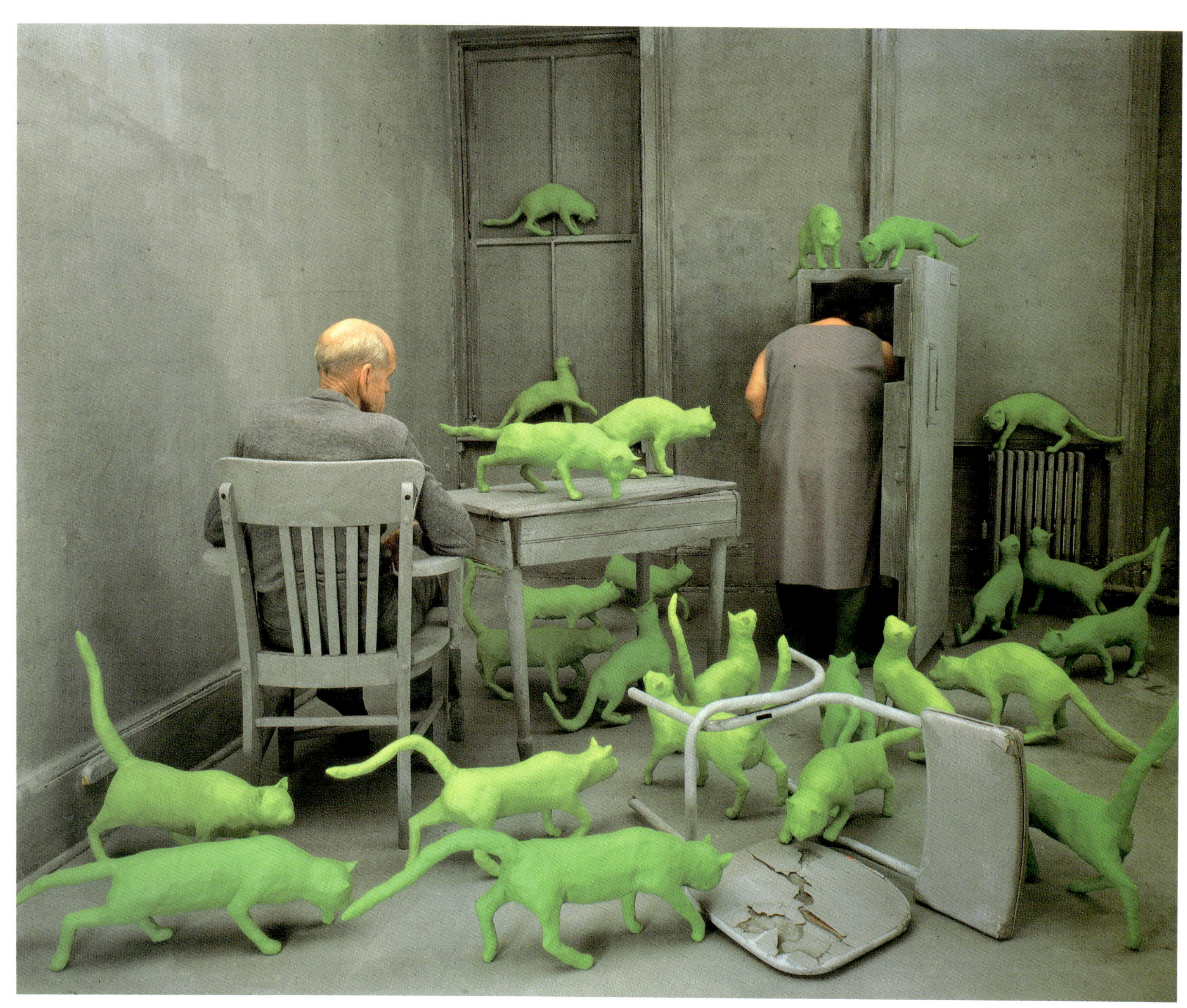

Radioactive Cats, 1980 (cat. 27)

Fabing, under whose leadership the retrospective was realized. Other key staff include Michael Goodison, archivist/program coordinator; Louise Laplante, registrar; and David Dempsey, preparator/conservator. Former graduate interns Kristen Erickson (who subsequently became special curatorial projects assistant) and Alona Horn were invaluable to the project. Ms. Erickson helped to organize the *Babies at Paradise Pond* photo-shoot as well as assisting in arranging the tour venues, and then passed the baton to Ms. Horn, who assisted with compiling the catalogue bibliography and exhibition history. Graduate students Gwen Allen and Nancy Noble tracked down missing information.

Last, and certainly not least, our heartfelt thanks go to Sandy Skoglund, who not only created the art in the exhibition but whose patience, good will, and professionalism have left us in her debt and made us her friends and admirers. We join her in thanking her studio assistant Jennifer Wiener, Sal Perrotta at Sculpture House Casting, and the staff at Dieu Donné Papermill (New York City), especially Pat Almonrode for his expertise in paper casting.

Linda Muehlig
Associate Curator of
Paintings and Sculpture

Ann H. Sievers
Associate Curator of Prints,
Drawings, and Photographs

ARTIST'S ACKNOWLEDGMENTS

My husband, Al Baccili, has been an unwavering source of support and inspiration through thick and thin. Many generous friends and family members have been willing participants in projects, especially Paul and Chris Skoglund, Diane Skoglund, Mike Starr, Nancy and D. J. Hallowell, Ann Baccili, and Frank Luis. My parents, Dorothy Bowes Skoglund and Walter Skoglund, gave me more than they'll ever know. Marvin Heiferman deserves special thanks for introducing my work at Castelli Graphics, and for his continuing friendship. Leo and Toiny Castelli are appreciated for their help early on. I am deeply grateful to all those who made this exhibition and publication possible, especially Beth Hinckley of SuperStock Inc., sponsor of the exhibition in Jacksonville, Janet Borden, Suzannah Fabing, Linda Muehlig, Ann Sievers, Robert Rosenblum, and Carol Squiers.

Sandy Skoglund
New York, June 1997

AN INTERVIEW WITH

by Robert Rosenblum

Edited transcript of an interview recorded May 17, 1996.

RR: Sandy, when I see your work, my eye and my mind move in so many different directions that I hardly know the first, not to mention the last, question to ask you. One thing has to do not only with you but with a general issue about the nature of boundaries. That is, when I think about your art, well naturally one says it's photography, but it isn't photography. It connects with a million other things. It's like installation art. It's like theater. It's like film. It's like painting. It's like pop sculpture. How do you define yourself? I mean, if you had to put yourself in a pigeonhole, an "ism," a classification, a medium . . . where would you locate yourself?

SS: I would say that it falls within the idea of a theme park . . . almost nonart. If the work offends, it offends more on the level of high art than on the level of low art. It's deliberately made to have a lot of different means of access . . . just as you've said, so it's distracting in terms of any kind of central focus. And then photography . . . I consider myself fortunate that photography exists, because otherwise I'd be stuck in the tragedy of ephemeralness that can come with installation art.

RR: Well, that's another interesting blur in your art. I've always wondered about the connection, or lack of connection, between, on the one hand, your installations which are there as things to see and, on the other hand, the photographs of the installation which seem to be what endures. But I mean, does your heart lie more squarely with the physical fact of the installation or with the artful photographic record of it? There are two sides to this coin.

SS: I think that I am most fond of the unseen part. I mean that the various cultural experiences that I go through, and the behavioral aspects of getting the work done, are just as important as the installation and the photograph. So, for me, the relationship between the two is more about hybridism and the search for an ideal form that I'm never going to arrive at. The installation and the photograph are mere approximations of this ideal.

By itself, I see photography as a medium within our culture that is really about control. No photograph is neutral. It is always about pointing and shooting, including and excluding. Expanding on that, I use a heightened photographic awareness to try to obsessively control the installation so that it appears a certain way. At the same time, I am dedicated to resurrecting experiences for myself as an artist that have been more or less jettisoned by modernism and postmodernism. In particular, I am thinking of mimesis. The making of representational sculpture within a postmodern strategy is important to me. So, I'm not happy to think of the installations as disposable.

RR: Well, what happens to them . . . I mean, are they preserved? Are they just scrapped after they're photographed? Are any of them around still, alive and well, or . . .

SANDY SKOGLUND

SS: Some of the work has involved materials with a very short shelf life, such as food products, and in that case the sculptural stuff doesn't exist except as a photograph. In the early work where the storage of it was financially impossible, such as two tons of black aquarium sand in 1983 for *Maybe Babies* (page 83), the sand doesn't exist anymore, but all the baby figures that I sculpted for the piece do. I think there's an important difference between going out and getting things as found objects, and sitting down to make them from scratch, sculpting them. At the very least, I always hold on to the handmade sculptures from each installation.

RR: But has any museum or collector ever acquired one?

SS: The Denver Art Museum bought the installation of *Fox Games* (page 14).

RR: Oh, that's right, and it's still there?

SS: Yes.

RR: I mean, it would seem just in terms of the practical reality of preserving your work—the real 3-D things as opposed to the photograph—I don't know why museums, and everybody else, couldn't consider acquiring them since there are so many installation pieces now in the repertory of every museum collection. So, that's another wavelength. But being an art historian, I, of course, want to situate you in terms of other artists—older and younger or the same generation. I know that in general, artists don't like comparing themselves to other artists, but I remember that, just for starters, you said something about how you wanted your work to be like reality but also interfere with it like Magritte's, and that set off my mind. Well, of course, you have connections with Magritte. But what about your feelings toward the whole world of sixties American pop art? You seem to wallow in its both terrifying and fascinating aspects . . . the ugliness of American assembly line products, the colors of American kitsch, etc., but is this something you were nurtured on? Is the sixties something that was important to you in terms of the pop explosion? You really came into being as an artist in the seventies, but what mark did this leave on you?

SS: Well, pop art had to be digested by anyone going through school in the seventies. I can remember being in sculpture class and one of my professors coming in with a photograph of the fur-covered teacup by Meret Oppenheim. Of all the pop artists, I've always been more inclined toward Claes Oldenburg. His early work especially seems to be on the cusp of attraction to the American landscape as well as the horror of it, and I would say that is where I am as well.

RR: It's funny that you mentioned Oldenburg, because when I was asking you about permanent acquisition and installation, I was thinking in the back of my head of that big Oldenburg bedroom ensemble installation in the National Gallery of Canada, which, in many ways, is a preview of your American suburban fantasies . . . an immaculate bed-

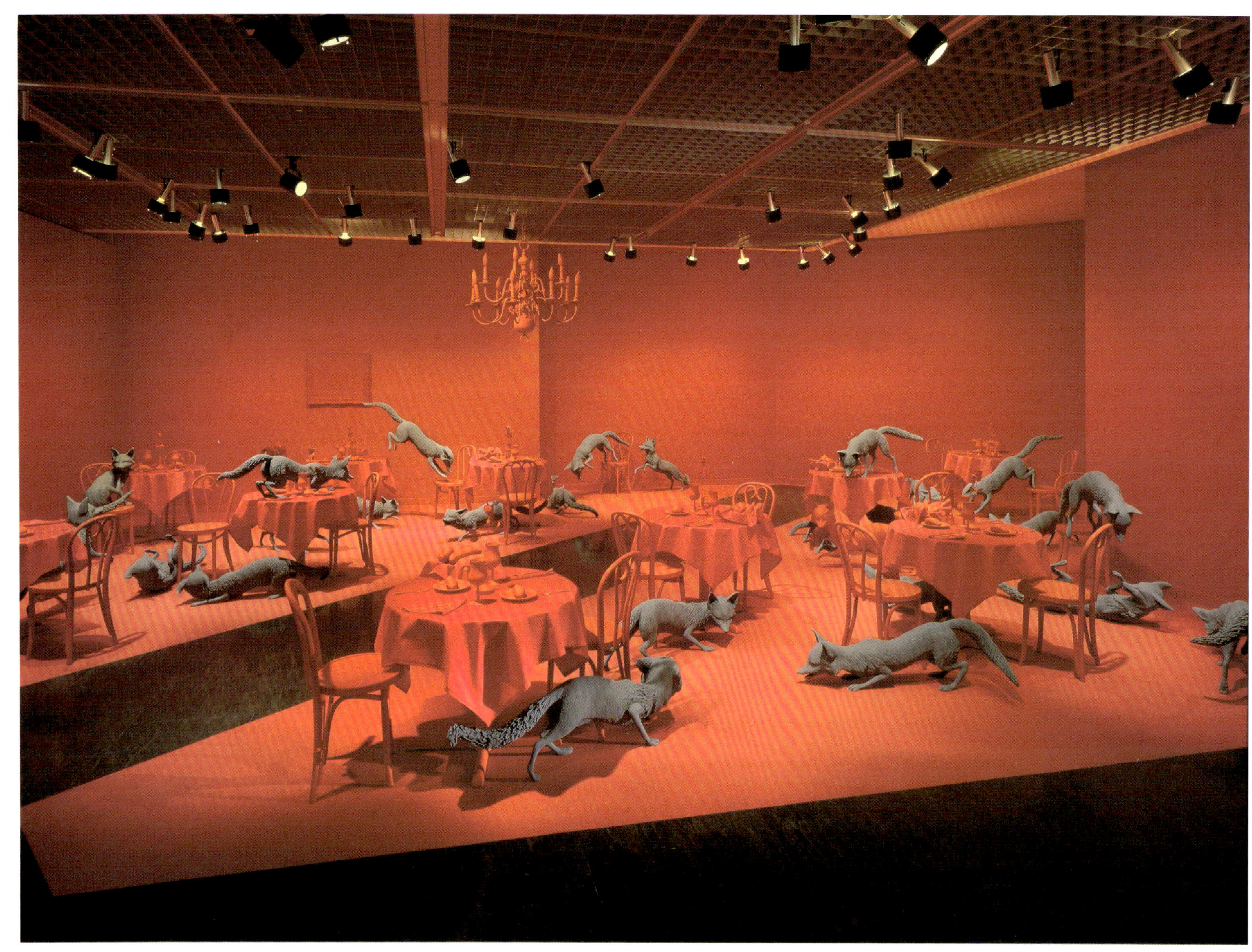

Fox Games (installation at Denver Art Museum), 1989 (cat. 35)

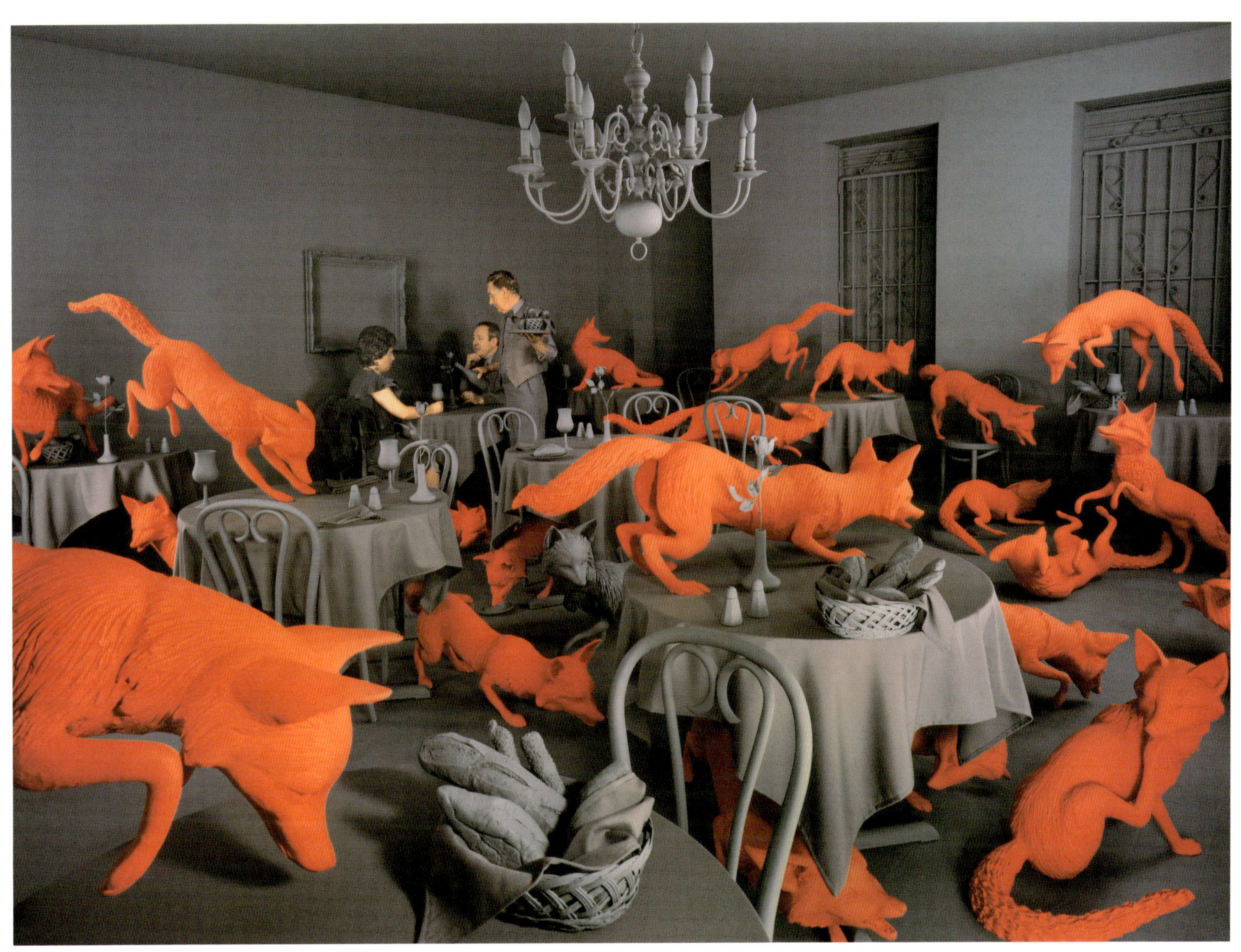

Fox Games (photograph), 1989 (cat. 36)

room with all kinds of weird things going on, in this particular case the strange, synthetic camouflage fur materials for the furniture and bedspreads. That seemed a kind of preview of what you would be doing in the seventies and eighties. But your relationship to the ironies of American culture is fascinating because like so many other American artists, you have a kind of attraction and repulsion syndrome; in other words, all of this hideous stuff that we see around us, the synthetic colors and materials, the kitsch toys, et cetera, are supposed to be hideous and crossed out of good taste. On the other hand, just because they are forbidden fruit, you are tempted to wallow in them and just enjoy their presence. "If you can't lick it, join it" is the message, I guess. But you clearly are on that wavelength. I'd love to hear more about it.

SS: Well, I think that it's not only the objects but also the surfaces. American ideologies of pleasure and beauty are embedded in our common objects, as they are in any culture. My attraction to these objects is kind of like that of being a stranger to myself, looking at the iconography of pleasure and how we are supposed to experience it in our culture.

In my early years as an artist, I went through a full circle in terms of how education worked its ideology on me, distancing me from my own culture in order to critique it. Some of the American aesthetic comes from profound cultural infantilism as well as Jungian or Freudian yearnings for things soft and cuddly. Snakes, for example, suffer from enormous prejudice against reptilian, hard surfaces. You can see these surfaces and forms integrated in popular-culture figures as monsters and signs of negativity. They are almost always lizardlike, with scaly surfaces. It's so simplistic yet revealing, like the cowboys in the fifties with the white hats for good guys and black hats for the bandits.

So, as I'm sculpting something, I'm really going through that whole process of the prejudices aimed against it by our culture . . . I'm reexperiencing the meaning of it in our culture. With *Radioactive Cats* (page 10), for example, the purpose there was to undermine the stereotype in our culture of the cute, domesticated pet. The cats are meant to dominate the scene as survivors in a postnuclear situation because they've adapted by turning green. In some ways, the piece proposes that the ultimate postapocalyptic, postcolonial situation would be the triumph of the animal world that we've manipulated for so long.

RR: Well, that's one aspect of your work that certainly separates it from either sixties-style pop art à la Oldenburg or Lichtenstein. You really seem to have this scenario of terror and apocalypse . . . something like a science fiction movie. I remember reading some reference to your work as resembling Hitchcock's *The Birds*. This seemed absolutely on target to me in the sense that what is ordinary about the American scene can suddenly turn into the craziest nightmare, but I'd be eager to know your connection with this whole American culture of horror films and science fiction, and especially explosions in terms of infinite number because this is something that seems so important in your art: the idea of an endless assembly line production of this or that product.

SS: It's got so many facets to it. Just as one aspect of this question, I've only recently noticed that as I start a new piece, my studio slowly turns into a quasi factory. I can't help but think that this goes back to my childhood working during the summers in a variety of factories. I had a summer job decorating cakes that came down an assembly line.

RR: Oh, my God. Well, that says it all, doesn't it?

SS: What fascinates me about the artmaking process is the endless mystery of it, the continuous unfolding of knowledge about yourself, yourself in the world, and the world separate from you as well. My own background is middle class, and class perceptions in terms of taste are at the root of a lot of the choices I make.

But let me get back to your question about horror films and science fiction. Science fiction presented a landscape that reflected the depth of my experience of suburban life in

America because it's a landscape of openness, of empty space, and a lot of anxiety going on in that open space. I was more interested in science fiction and horror before the cult of blood and gore in special effects took over. Bloodthirst and violence represent a cultural need that I am struggling to understand.

RR: Would you prefer the hygienic kind of science fiction without the guts . . . just the terror of suburbia?

SS: Right. To me terror is more terrifying if it relates closely to ordinary life. If it's more plausible, it's more terrifying.

RR: But I remember learning that you were once contemplating going into film.

SS: I was.

RR: How far did you get?

SS: I made a film as an undergrad that was a clay animation thing, and when I graduated from Smith, I got into NYU Film School. But I couldn't afford to go, so I went home and taught junior high school art for a year.

RR: Oh.

SS: Then I went on to graduate school at the University of Iowa, where I took some film courses. Being interested in Hollywood narrative structure, I took the courses in the theater department rather than in the art department, although I was a graduate student in painting. Then I came to New York and began a seesaw between conceptual art and traditional filmmaking. I would go into the studio and do this self-conscious high-art kind of stuff that frustrated me by its disconnection from society. So, to counteract that, I would run out and make a little film. The last one was a documentary that put me in debt, and left me feeling emotionally bankrupt from all the struggles with other people trying to get it done.

I look at the art object partly through the eyes of an art historian, so I'm plagued by questions like "who is going to consume this image, and why?" Filmmaking answers those questions easily when it's a Hollywood film because it's made for the person on the street . . . there's no confusion about that. It's the exact counterpoint to the most rarefied kind of high-art practice. So ultimately, I had to struggle to pull the two together.

RR: I take it it worked, because one of the facts about your art is that it obviously can appeal to the broadest possible audience which would never find itself in an art gallery or museum. Who wouldn't be enchanted by any one of your installations: looking at the attack of the Cheez Doodles, conquering the world with raisins, or what have you. But, on the other hand, it also plugs into a much more elite group of references to contemporary art. So, in a sense, you have it both ways. You've got the broadest and narrowest audience. But I would love to get back to the factory experience you had with decorating . . . was it cakes, or . . .

SS: Yes.

RR: I mean, this actually seems to be a primal experience for your later work. So, you were just mesmerized by these cakes . . . were they all the same pattern or did you have to do variations on them?

SS: They were patterns with variations. It was the night shift from around 11:00 P.M. to 7:00 A.M. in Detroit, and it paid pretty well because of that.

RR: Oh.

SS: They had assembly lines. You would stand there and the cake would pass in front of you, and you would do the decorating as it went by. There were three jobs: the edges around the top of the cake, the buds and roses, and the words Happy Birthday. You would get one of those jobs and do it all night.

The workers were all women in this part of the factory. Part of the job was to pick up these heavy trays full of cakes and put them on a rack. Because I had a little bit of paralysis from polio as a child, it was a struggle for me to do that. One day the supervisor came over and told me I wasn't strong enough for the job. Rather than let me go, she trained me to do the "Baby Face Cakes." They were cakes ordered for baby showers, and the face of the baby was a cartoon that was customized in terms of hair color, race, and gender. You painted the face in a transparent manner with food coloring onto the hard surface crust of boiled vanilla icing like the kind you see on petits fours. You had to have a very light touch, or the brush would break through the surface and cause it to crack, ruining the cake. It was a little like working on traditional gesso. Eventually, I was pretty good with that technique and they had me do portraits on cakes. Customers could send in a photograph and I would paint it onto the top of a birthday cake.

RR: Well, I hate to sound like a psychoanalyst, but don't you think this is really deep down at the root of a lot of work now?

SS: Yes. Well, the assembly-line aspect of it . . .

RR: Like nonstop repetition . . .

SS: Nonstop. Kind of hard work, you know.

RR: Conquering the world, and . . .

SS: More so . . .

RR: Can work and factory work.

SS: The culture of it was fascinating. The woman who was in charge was this powerful, militarylike person who had been there for many years. The fact that my talent had been functional within that context was rather rewarding.

RR: It was also a kind of psychological scenario of your being regimented into this factory system and at the same time wanting to explode it by letting everything go amok.

SS: Yes, the repressed rage from the regimentation is really something I never considered before. And the creepiness of working at night. . . . I also worked as a salesgirl, selling all sorts of products: perfume, shoes, notions in a variety store, and so on. Again, the consumerism . . .

RR: And in a restaurant in Disneyland.

SS: It wasn't a restaurant, it was just a hot-dog stand.

RR: Even better. More of the same.

SS: Yes.

RR: I'm curious about your connections with this surfeit of Americana. When you contemplate new work, do you go around looking, say, at supermarkets, at racks of candy, at tacky gift shops? I mean, do you study the stuff and are you fascinated by the synthetic colors and textures, choosing these jelly beans over those, or this kind of cheese doodle over another one.

SS: Oh, yes.

RR: I mean, do you spend a lot of time looking at the real thing?

SS: Definitely. That's part of the unseen part of the work that can become compellingly bizarre, too, as a parody of the scientific method and industrial practice. I always go through a research-and-development phase. I like to have the stuff in front of me, and live with it while contemplating it. So I'll buy all the different kinds of whatever thing I'm interested in, like every brand of puffed-cheese snack, and then choose one based on color, texture, and so on. When I worked with raisins doing *Atomic Love* (opposite), I ended up going to Raisin University before I was through with that piece.

RR: What is that?

SS: I ended up learning about how relative the size, shape, color, and availability of raisins are because we ran out of the particular kind we were using halfway through the piece. When I called up the wholesaler to order more raisins, he sent me cases of raisins that were totally different in appearance. It turned out to be virtually impossible to find the same raisins again, especially at that time of the year. At one point I was sending sending assistants all over New York with handfuls of raisin samples, trying to match the original ones. It's like learning more than you ever wanted to know about something of absolutely no consequence in the world of normal values, but ultimately this knowledge says something about how our world works.

RR: And apart from the particular objects, you must love the colors of synthetic America, but what's your favorite repertoire of colors, I mean, I don't even know that we have words for

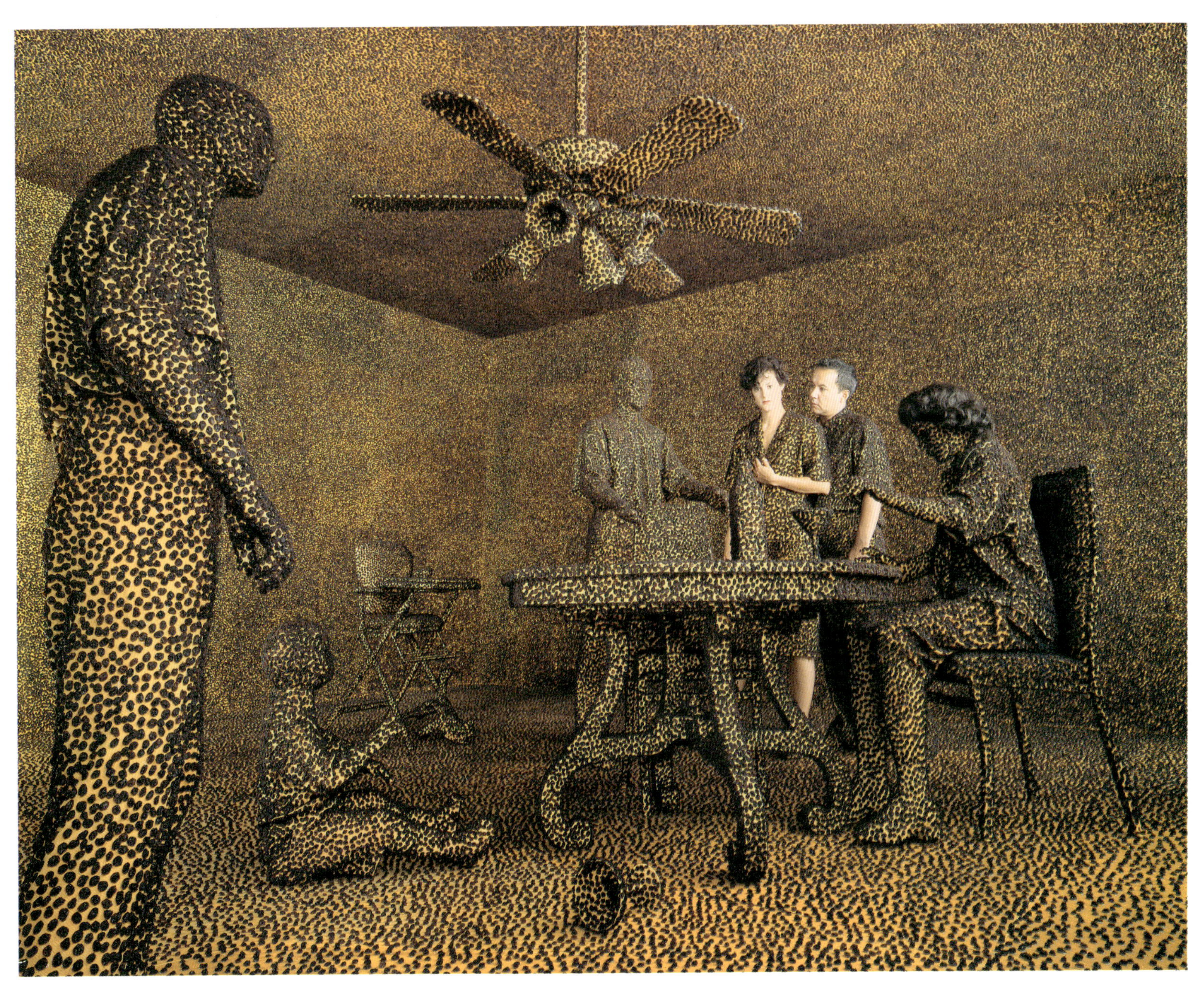

Atomic Love, 1992 (cat. 41)

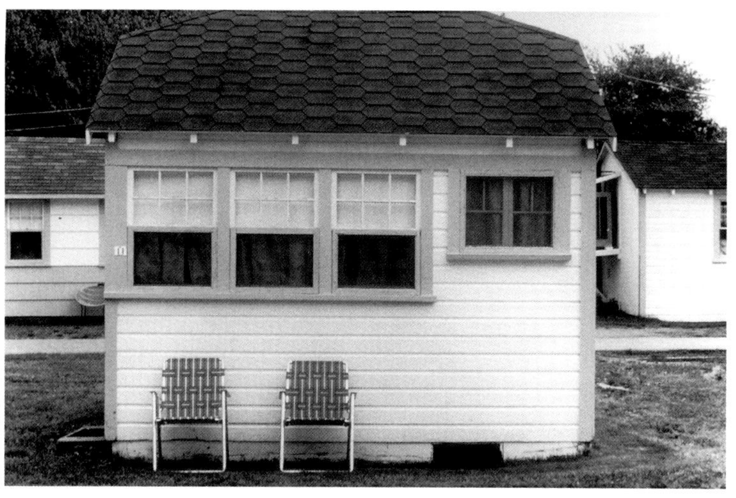

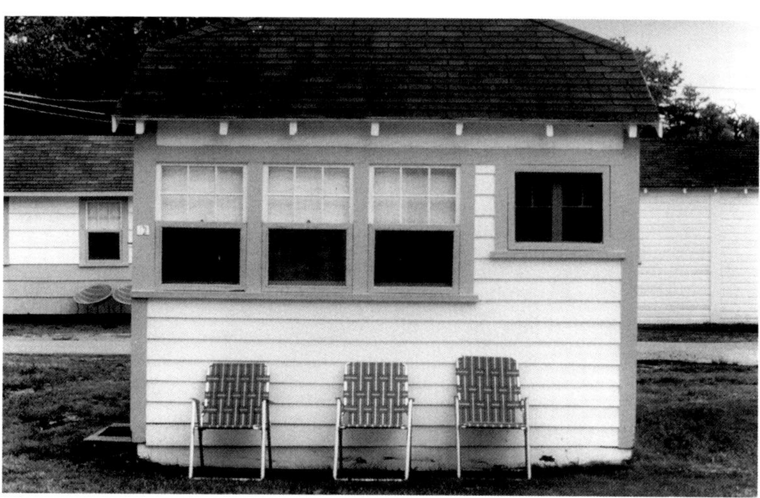

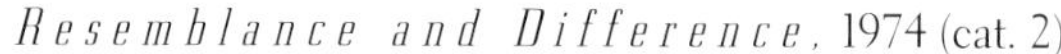

Resemblance and Difference, 1974 (cat. 2)

the kind of yellow or orange or green that you use. Can you name them?

SS: I don't have any favorites, really. In the early eighties, the use of color for me was pretty strategic. It had to do with challenging the black-and-white norms of fine art photography in the seventies, and just wanting to be bad, in poor taste, and make something that was aggressive on the wall.

RR: When did you begin to develop the idea of camouflage, I mean the kind of horrific conversion of infinitely small things suddenly blotting out humanity . . . it's such a fascinating mix of supermarket abundance and the extinction of us poor individuals, but it also has a visual aspect to it as almost a kind of op art, in which "now you see it, now you don't," and things just keep wobbling into focus and out of it. How long have you been doing this? What triggered it? I mean, it's not in your earliest work, but seems to have developed more recently.

SS: Right. Well, the sculpture is deliberately trying to be a pattern . . . if that's what you mean . . .

RR: Yes.

SS: For example, in *Gathering Paradise* (page 67), the many squirrel sculptures are meant to be breaking up the pictorial space, flattening it and therefore disguising or camouflaging its depth. In some ways, I think of the sculptures as crawling across the surface of the photograph. Now I'm trying to combine found objects with the made objects, and the found stuff tends to have that plethora of abundance you might find terrifying. But I'd say the beginnings go back to the early conceptual process work I did in the seventies, which had to do with the sheer display of labor. I mean, I would cover a canvas with zillions of dots, one by one. That kind of presence is back in the images, only done with things like cheese puffs.

RR: I remember that at the beginning of your career, in the seventies, a lot of your work seemed to connect with what used to be called "New Image" artists like Neil Jenney, and you'd

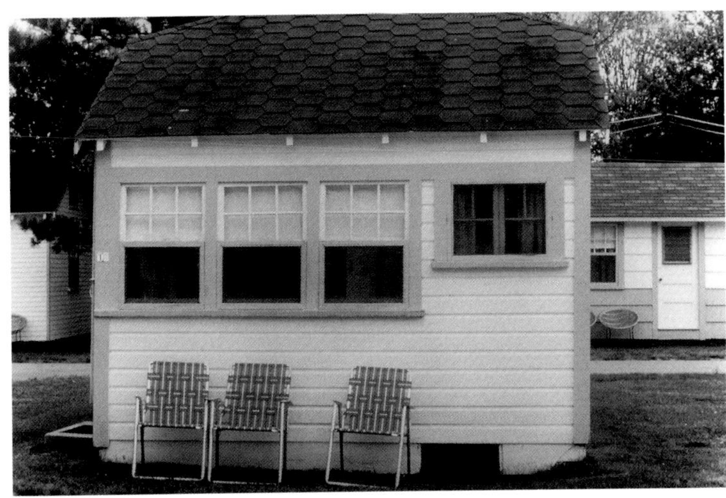

have combinations of something like knobs and kitchen pots: just comparing and contrasting very simple things (page 36). But were you in tune with the painting of the time, with this isolation of images and this scrutinizing of ordinary objects, seeing just basic similarities and differences? I know you did a series of motel façades, no?

SS: Yes.

RR: But did you do this work in the context of photography and painting in the seventies?

SS: Oh, absolutely.

RR: Thinking of the Bernd and Hilla Becher photos, for instance?

SS: Definitely. I was looking at all art that was being produced at that time. Minimalism was examining minute differences in things through repetitive structures, as in the Bechers' work, and there was also pattern and decoration.

RR: Yes, that's something else I was thinking about, I mean that's one of the elusive things about your work because it seems to fit into one current but then immediately slips into something else. But I was also thinking about that fascination with, for instance, quilt patterns in the seventies, the pattern and decoration artists, and how sometimes you . . . I remember your peas . . .

SS: Yes . . .

RR: They almost look like something by Miriam Schapiro or . . .

SS: Right. *Peas on a Plate* (page 49), *Two Plates of Corn*, and so on. That body of work was certainly within the context of pattern painting and food still life commercial photography. I was looking a lot at the style of commercial photography . . . what makes an image look commercial? I was deconstructing the commercial strategy as a way of achieving visual impact. I was working within the paradox of being commercially uncommercial, which can only be done in photography. There is no mainstream cultural look that one would call commercial painting the way there is the look and feel of what we call commercial photography.

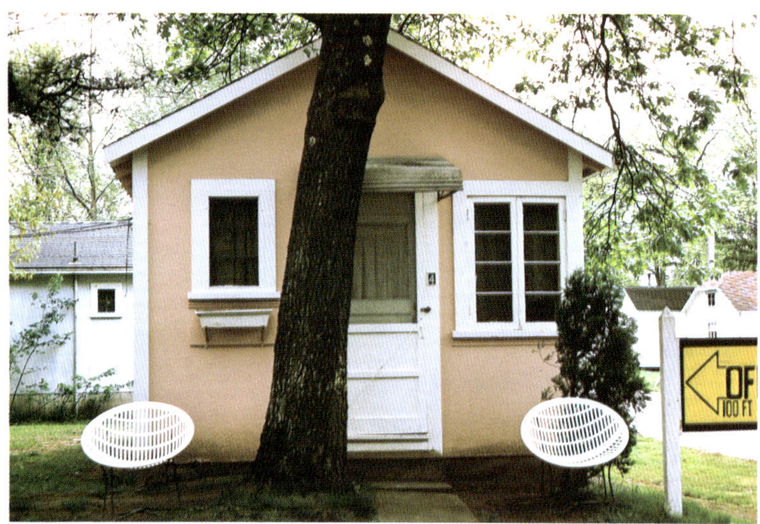

Resemblance and Difference, 1974 (cat. 3)

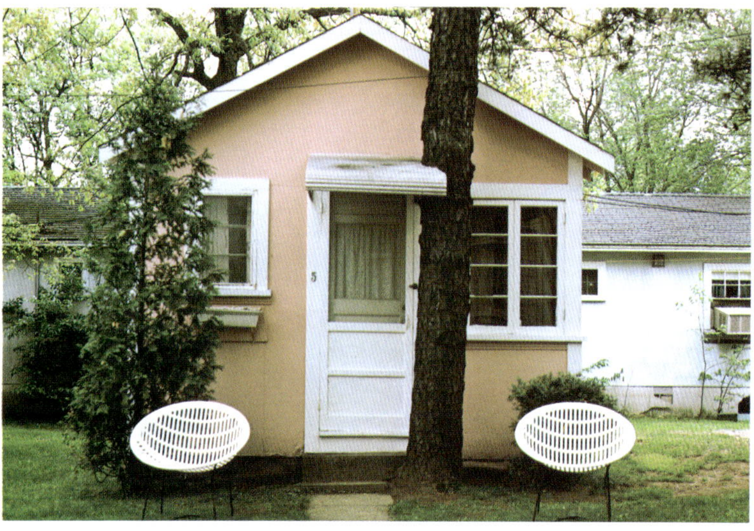

Resemblance and Difference, 1974 (cat. 3)

There are elements in commercial food still life photography that reflect inversions of reality in American culture. For instance, we enhance everything we depict. For the sake of a better photograph, we change the subject itself through synthetic means so that it appears better on film. The subject becomes like phototropic sculpture. But it's not only the insatiable cravings of American culture that cause this, but also the deficiencies in the medium of photography itself. The camera does not, unassisted, communicate exactly what we human beings see. For example, we think of a tomato as red. In fact, relatively speaking, real tomatoes aren't that red when compared to pure pigment. So, we make the tomato redder with dyes so that the photograph of it looks like what we think a tomato looks like, really.

RR: Are your favorite foods frozen foods? I bet Bird's Eye packages are your ideal . . .

SS: I prefer Stouffer's.

RR: Are they frozen peas in *Peas on a Plate?*

SS: Yes.

RR: I mean they look exactly like that.

SS: Yes, they are . . .

RR: . . . immaculate.

SS: That's right. They are.

RR: I can see that that's your level of food consumption. That's the ideal Sandy Skoglund presentation: a frozen brick of peas.

SS: Perfect.

RR: How large have your works been? I mean, you seem to be moving into ever larger dimensions and . . .

SS: I am.

RR: . . . height, width, and depth . . . how big have they gotten? How big will they get?

SS: About five hundred to a thousand square feet on the floor. I'm also trying to incorporate more of the process of performing for the camera. After all the work I go through to arrive at the perfect photo, one of the few accidents that can

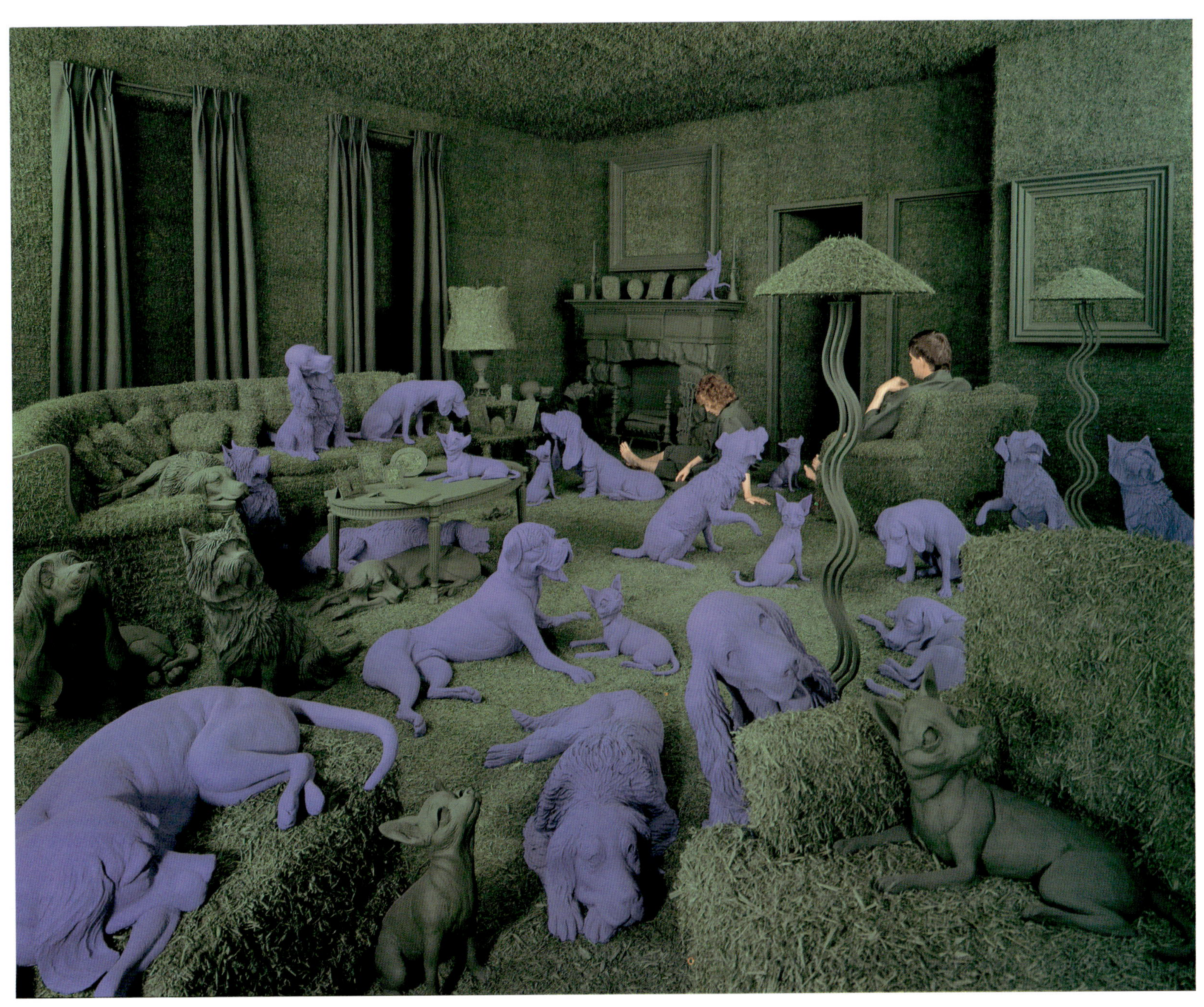

The Green House, 1990 (cat. 37)

occur is what happens when the models enter the installation. So, I'm trying to work with what the installation is made out of, and the interactive performance possibilities that exist in the materials. I especially like the idea of the model destroying or disturbing some of the carefully arranged installation components as he or she walks into it. For *Walking on Eggshells* (page 59), the plan is for the model to walk on top of the eggshells that are on the floor, crushing them and making tracks that the camera will record. I have no idea what it will look like.

RR: But how involved have your audiences been with your work? I mean, physically, that is, how many walk-in things have you done and also, what are the dangers? Has anyone ever damaged your work . . . picked it apart?

SS: I made two walk-in pieces. One was *The Green House* (opposite), and the other was *Gathering Paradise*. The wearing process of people walking into and through a piece was both fun and difficult. I'm not sure that the viewer's experience is enhanced by it. Somewhere there is a line between visual art and a carnival funhouse. I'm primarily interested in the eye and how the eye experiences, and giving the eye as much as I can to experience.

RR: So, it's better to see it behind a proscenium, as it were, as in a theater.

SS: Well, I went to see Elvis's house, Graceland. Have you been there?

RR: No.

SS: It's very interesting.

RR: That's what I've heard. Why?

SS: Well, for me I think it's because it's not the display of an enormous amount of wealth at all. It's a large house that anyone in the upper middle class might have. Only the columns in front make it really mansionlike. Inside, the rooms aren't very big, and Elvis had such a lugubrious, disconnected sensibility. Each room is decorated with a totally different kind of scheme. Since, like many performers, he was awake mainly at night, all the windows are closed up so you don't have a sense of the time of day. I'm bringing this up in the context of "walking on" because you can't walk into the rooms. You can look at them, but you can't go in.

RR: Well, my instinct is that that's a better way to do it: to be on the outside looking in, like a movie or like a theater experience. You don't want to touch it because then it loses its magic.

SS: Some of the photographic opinion on my work has been that the installations work negatively to demystify the photograph. In the sense that they unravel how the photograph was made, I think that's good, because the installation actually then informs and contributes to the understanding of the photograph. Without the installation, you might think that the photograph was merely computer generated.

RR: Well, the other answer is why choose when you can have both? I mean, when you have both it's inevitable to make a comparison and ask "which do you prefer?" But they are alike and different and there is no reason not to be able to juggle them simultaneously, so why not have your cake and eat it too? Have you ever—I'm not sure any longer what the difference between art for art's sake and art for commerce's sake might be—but have you ever been involved with the commercial art world? That is, making setups for advertising photos? Is that part of your repertory, or would you want it to be?

SS: I think there's a big difference between art for art's sake and art for commerce's sake. The difference may not be in how the work looks, but in how it feels to make it. There are only a few occasions where I've done commercial work for a client. I recently did a piece for *Life* magazine, where they asked me to do something that would embody life in the sixties, for a special issue dedicated to the aging baby boomer generation.

RR: What was your idea of the sixties?

SS: I saw Mod, blobby-shaped, designy furniture determining

the space. I saw black walls, then psychedelic shapes created by the bright-colored furniture, floating in the space. Then to further break up the space I used yellow peace signs everywhere. As for the models, the young couple in the room are the age that the baby boomers would have been, like undergraduates in college. In addition there are, of course, the requisite icons: a lava lamp, red bandanna, fringed vest, miniskirt, long hair, guitar, and so on.

RR: So, when will this appear?

SS: In June 1997, I think.

RR: Oh. So it'll all be past tense soon.

SS: Yes.

RR: Have you ever done, or have you ever thought about doing window display? I mean, supposing Barneys wanted you to do a set of windows.

SS: I did a window for Barneys. The piece *Sock Situation* (page 26) was done during the Christmas season of 1986.

RR: Oh! Well . . .

SS: In terms of commissions, I've found working with museums to be the most rewarding. I also support my work by teaching.

RR: Is that Ohio or Smith . . . or . . .

SS: No, Rutgers University in Newark, New Jersey.

RR: But you're there now?

SS: Yes.

RR: I didn't know that.

SS: The danger, of course, is that it can be a drain and distraction from your art.

RR: Do you have students who try to imitate you? That's usually the temptation.

SS: If I saw anything like that, I would discourage it.

RR: Nip it in the bud.

SS: I like to focus on the students' ability to think for themselves. So, no, I haven't seen my own work being done by my students.

RR: Well, you're so singular that it would be found out immediately as a big rip-off.

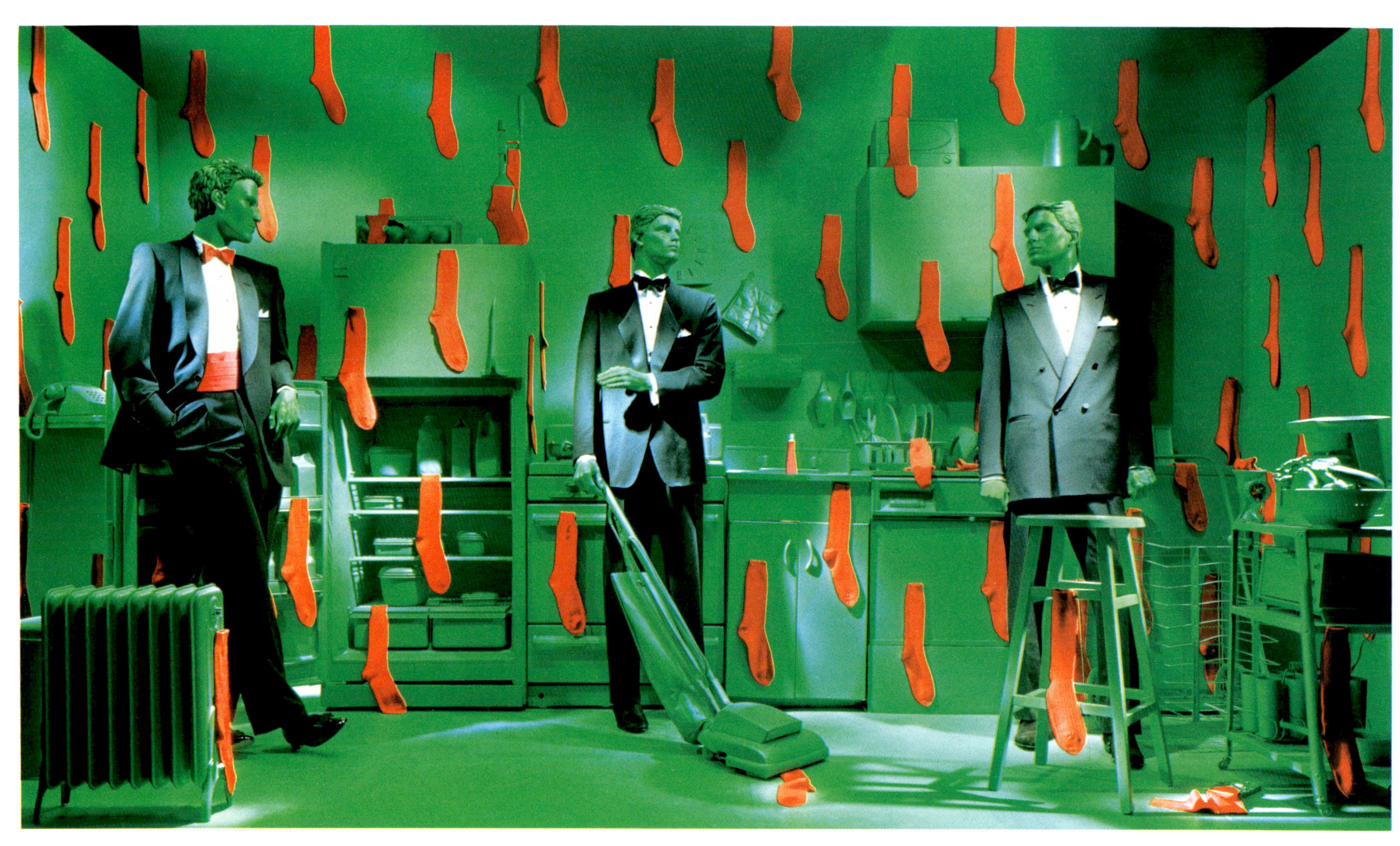

Sock Situation, 1986 (cat. 32)

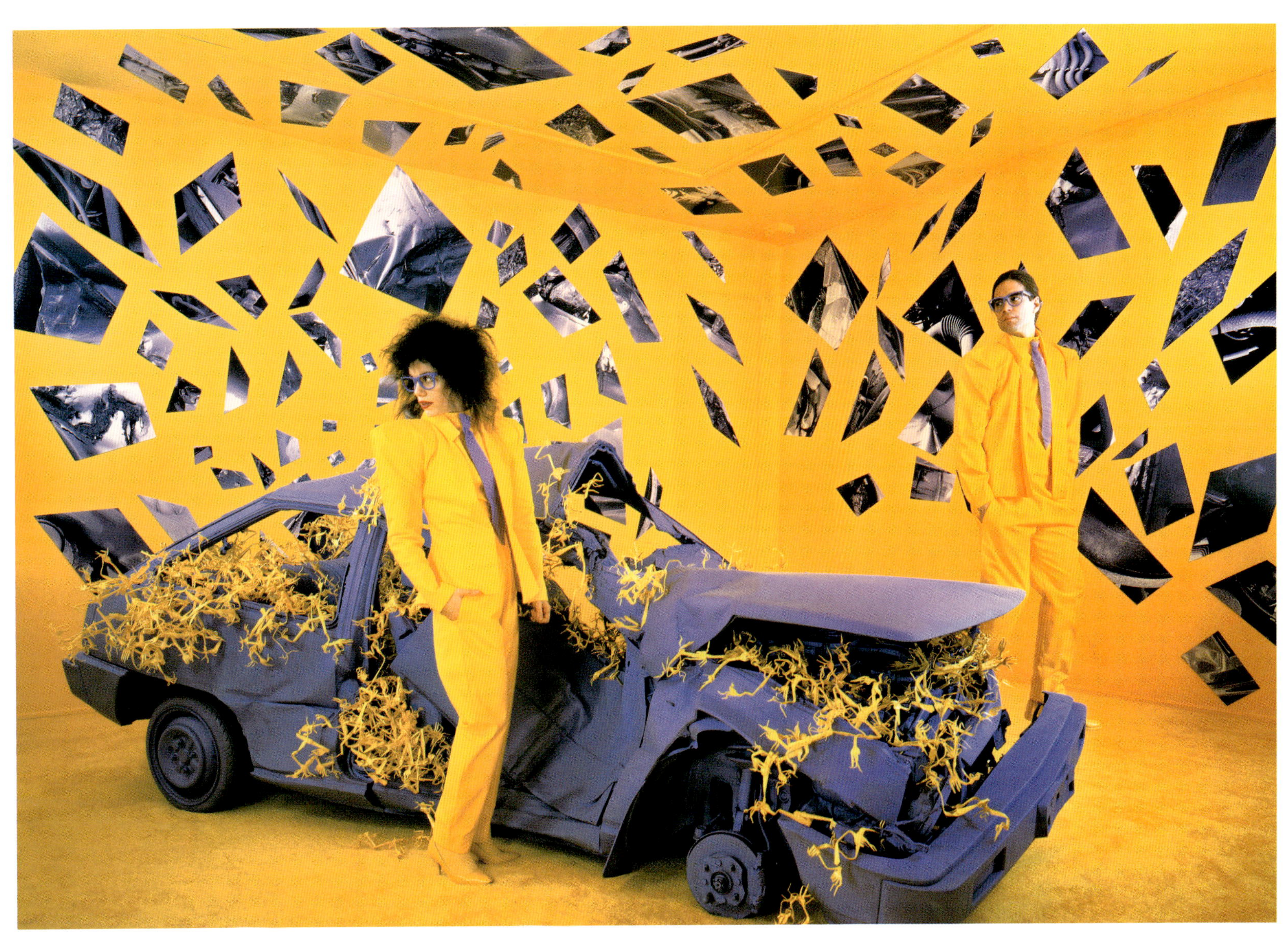

The Lost and Found, 1986 (cat. 33)

E N T E R T A I N M E N T

The Photographs of Sandy Skoglund by Carol Squiers

In her installation works and photographs, Sandy Skoglund creates antic dream worlds of ordinary life gone seriously awry. Her green cats prowl a corpse-gray kitchen emitting a poisoned glow; her blue leaves invade the dull brown stupor of an office. Large pastel babies struggle weightlessly in a barren moonscape. Chewed wads of gum infest a placid scene of relaxation. Her vision is at once playful and lacerating, an entertaining theme park of phobic theatricality and pop-cultural distress.

It is not only her subject matter that confounds the viewer, especially the one who starts out with the much maligned preconception that seeing is believing. As if to doubly refute that questionable precept, Skoglund often exhibits the installation pieces that are the subject of the photographs along with the images themselves. The photo and the installation are nominally the same and yet they are different in both obvious and maddeningly subtle ways. Shifting back and forth between the installation and the photograph, the viewer can never reconcile either the similarities or the differences.

Roland Barthes wrote that the essence of photography is the quality of showing what-has-been, what he called the *noeme* of the medium.[1] Skoglund brings that quality to the fore and then folds it back on itself, calling into question our perception of what has been and what exists in the present. The installations she exhibits in concert with the photographs have about them an unreal air of being at once both present and past, in front of the viewer and yet not exactly what is portrayed in the photographs, especially because the "real" people in the photographs are always already gone from the exhibited tableaux.

Skoglund sets up a series of tensions that the viewer must struggle to bridge. Most obviously, her work plays out the tension between two-dimensionality and three-dimensionality, between photography and sculpture. The photograph is a record of something that no longer exists in precisely the way in which the photograph delineates it. Throughout her work Skoglund sets up a series of disquieting oppositions, among them visuality versus content, celebration versus critique, whimsy versus horror, the banal versus the extraordinary, the dream versus the nightmare. It is this complex web of contending forces that gives her images their compelling power, even while their fanciful subjects amuse and enthrall.

Skoglund began making room-sized installations and photographing them in 1979. They were conceived at a time when ideas about artmaking were undergoing radical changes. The notion that a monolithic major style could define an entire period—color field painting, for instance—had been under attack for more than a decade. Disenchanted with the narrow definitions of high art, and nurtured by the low-art subjects and attitudes of pop, artists began deploying a variety of disparate styles, theories, and techniques in the late 1960s and throughout the 1970s. Among them were process, systems, and other types of conceptual art, body art, feminist art, earthworks, performance, site, installation, and large-scale sculpture, pattern painting and decorative art, photography, filmmaking, and video. Continental theory was also influential, in the writings of figures such as Roland Barthes, Claude Lévi-Strauss, Jean Baudrillard, and Michel Foucault. Skoglund confronted this dizzying array of options and created an intensely unique figuration.

When Skoglund graduated from the University of Iowa in 1972 with a Master of Fine Arts, she was a painter and filmmaker; she had not studied photography, nor had she any regard for it.[2] But she was intrigued by conceptual art, which was being made by her fellow students at Iowa and written about in the national art magazines. Arriving in New York in 1972, she found that many artists were making art that fell under the conceptual rubric. So were the teachers in the art-foundation program at The Hartford Art School, where she began teaching the following year. She read all that she could on this diffuse and varied practice and felt a kinship especially with the repetitive forms and activities of what was called systems art. After throwing all of her student artwork away, in 1973 Skoglund began to make systems pieces such as *The Holes in a Saltine Cracker* (page 30), using a Xerox copier; it was her earliest encounter with making mechanically reproduced images and the influence of it can be seen in much of her later photographic work.

She began the first piece by making two Xerox copies of a crumpled sheet of paper. One she hung on the wall and the other she crumpled and Xeroxed again. Making two copies of that image, she crumpled it and Xeroxed it again. That process of crumpling and copying was repeated until she had more than 100 pieces of Xeroxed paper and realized that the piece, entitled *Crumpled and Copied* of 1973 (page 30), was theoretically endless. "I initially found this work rewarding—it was very cerebral," says Skoglund. "Obsession and repetition in the process of making things is one constant element in my work." During much of the 1970s Skoglund did what she calls "pseudoscientific, analyti-

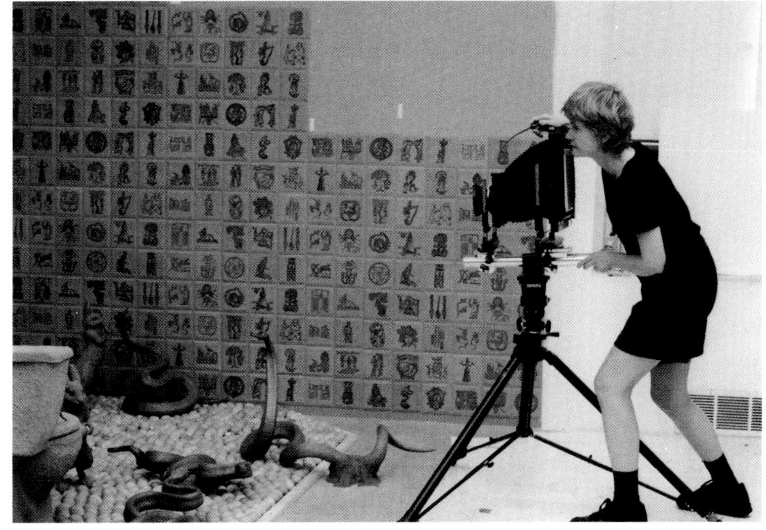

Sandy Skoglund photographing her studio installation of *Walking on Eggshells*.

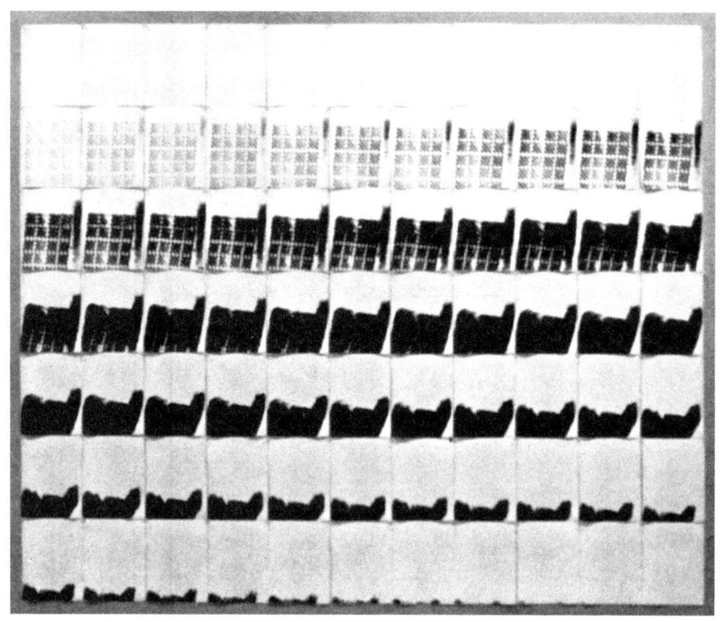

The Holes in a Saltine Cracker, 1973

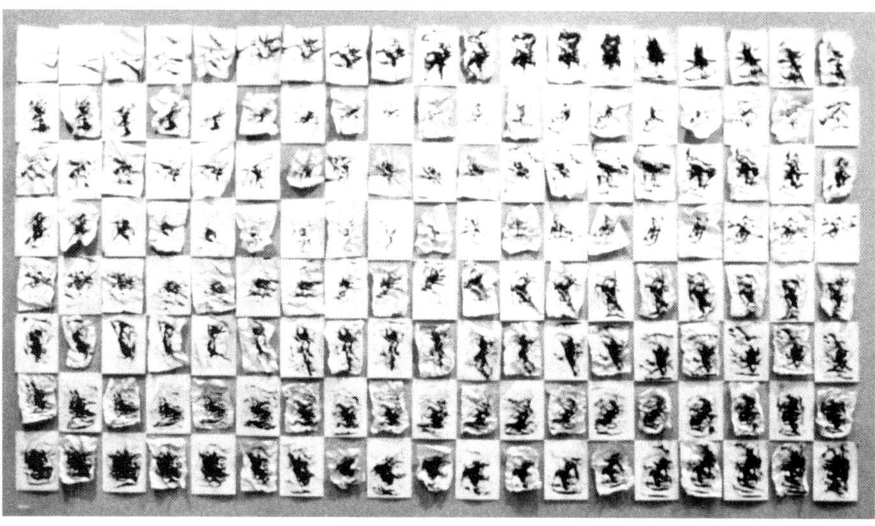

Crumpled and Copied, 1973 (cat. 1)

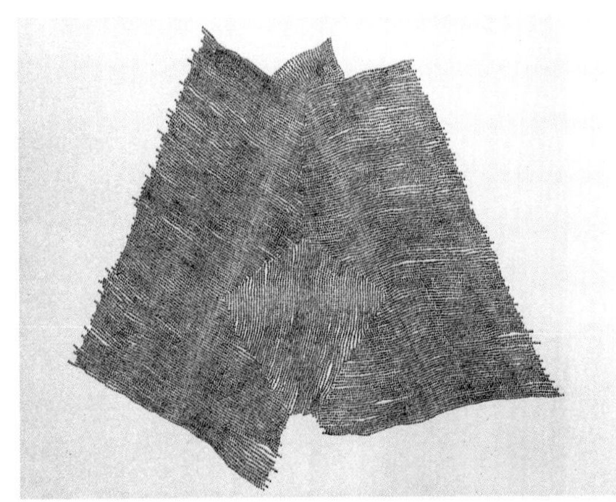

Starting with the Letter A., 1975 (cat. 7)

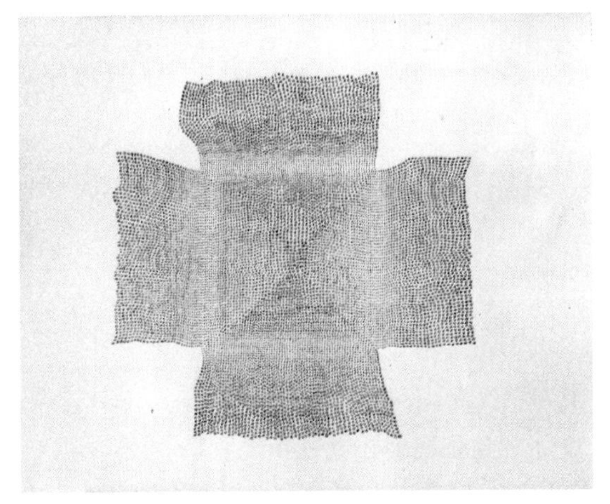

Starting with a Square, 1975 (cat. 8)

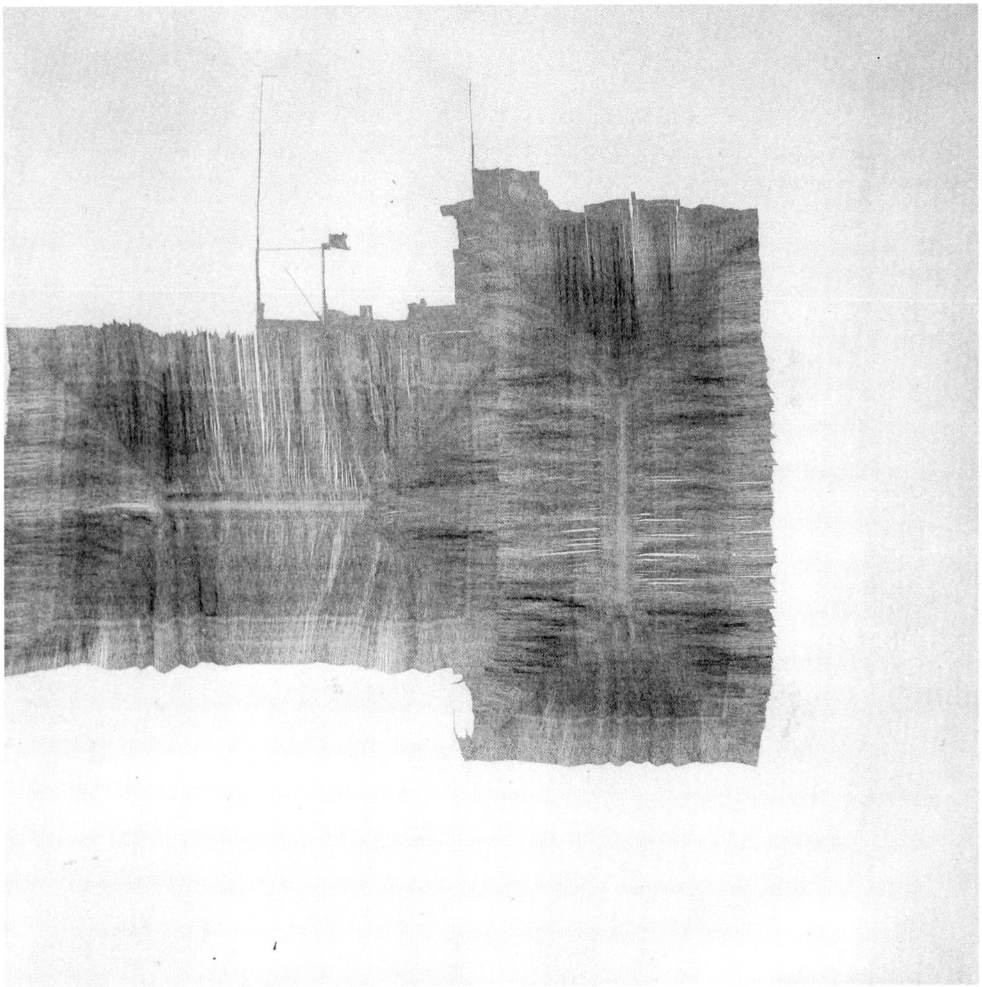

Starting with Two Lines, 1975 (cat. 5)

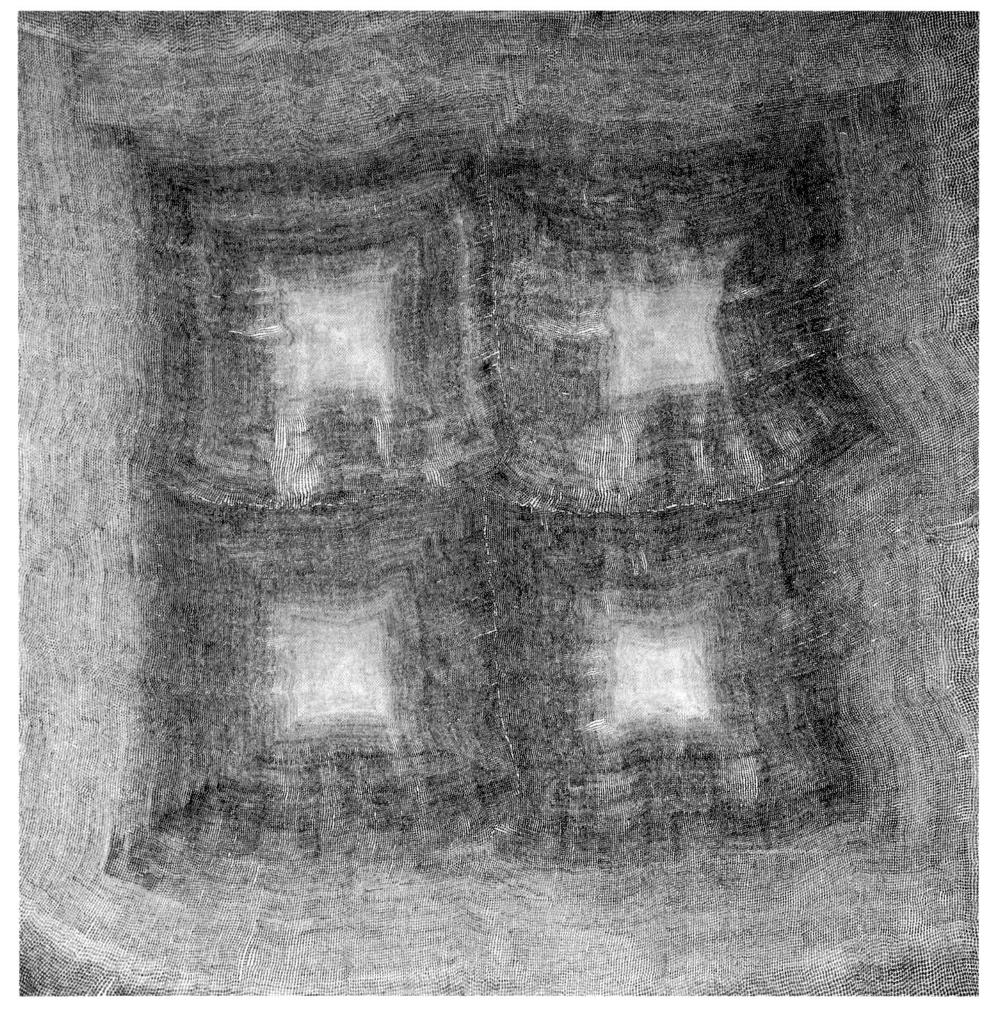

Starting with a Pencil Sharpened Once, 1975 (cat. 4)

cal works" that were influenced by conceptualism and performance art.

But the purely mechanical repetitions involved in making analytical art were ultimately unsatisfying for Skoglund. "It was an incredibly painful period," she says. "I was looking for a transcendental feeling; instead, I found boredom." Of greater interest to her were her performance pieces, some of which prefigure her later photographic practice. One, called *Percussion for Jelly Beans and Gumdrops with Solo Broom* (page 34), involved kicking twenty-five pounds of gumdrops and twenty-five pounds of jelly beans across a room and then sweeping the colored candies across the floor "in a parody of abstract expressionism." It was one of her first experiments in what she calls "the inappropriate use of food," a strategy that became important again more than a decade later.

But there was another strand of conceptualism that Skoglund was looking at: the photographically based work of William Wegman, John Baldessari, and Ed Ruscha. "Ed Ruscha's little

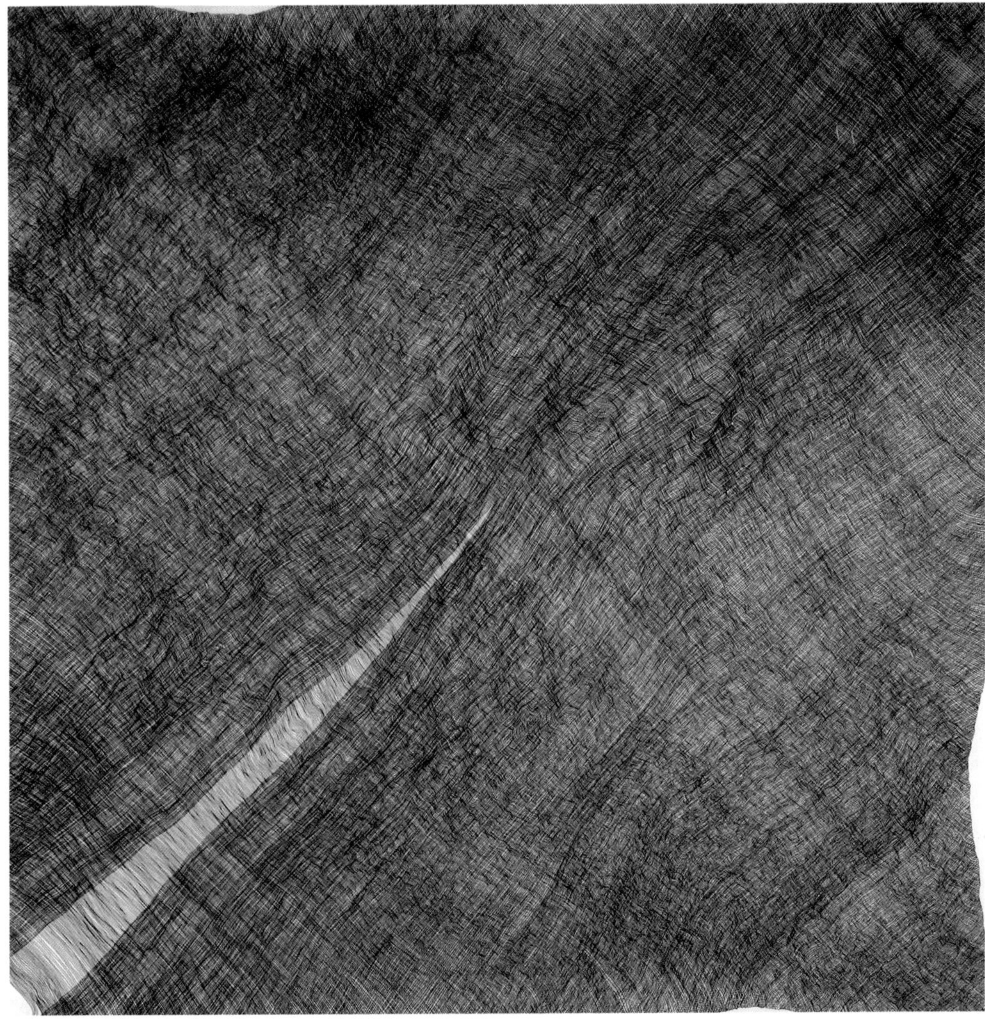

One Line Crossing Itself, 1975 (cat. 6)

books were totally brilliant," she says. "That was the first photography I saw that I really related to. I loved the anti-aesthetic—the dust, the scratches, the stupidity of the repetition in something like *Real Estate Opportunities* (1970) especially. There was the austere systems work by people like Mel Bochner and Dorothea Rockburne and then there was what some critics called joke art—Wegman, Ruscha, Baldessari. They were using photography, but they obviously didn't care about the fine print or any of the standard issues I had seen when I looked at the history of photography."

As a result, in 1974 Skoglund made her first photographs. As an experiment in serial imagery, she photographed the look-alike motel cottages that lined Route 1 from Boston, Massachusetts, to Portland, Maine. Looking at them head-on, she recorded how deadeningly similar they were, with only minuscule changes in the small white cottages to distinguish them from one another.

But these images didn't quell her dissatisfaction with the limitations of conceptualism and a concurrent growing disillusionment with the elitist construction of the art world. She had been

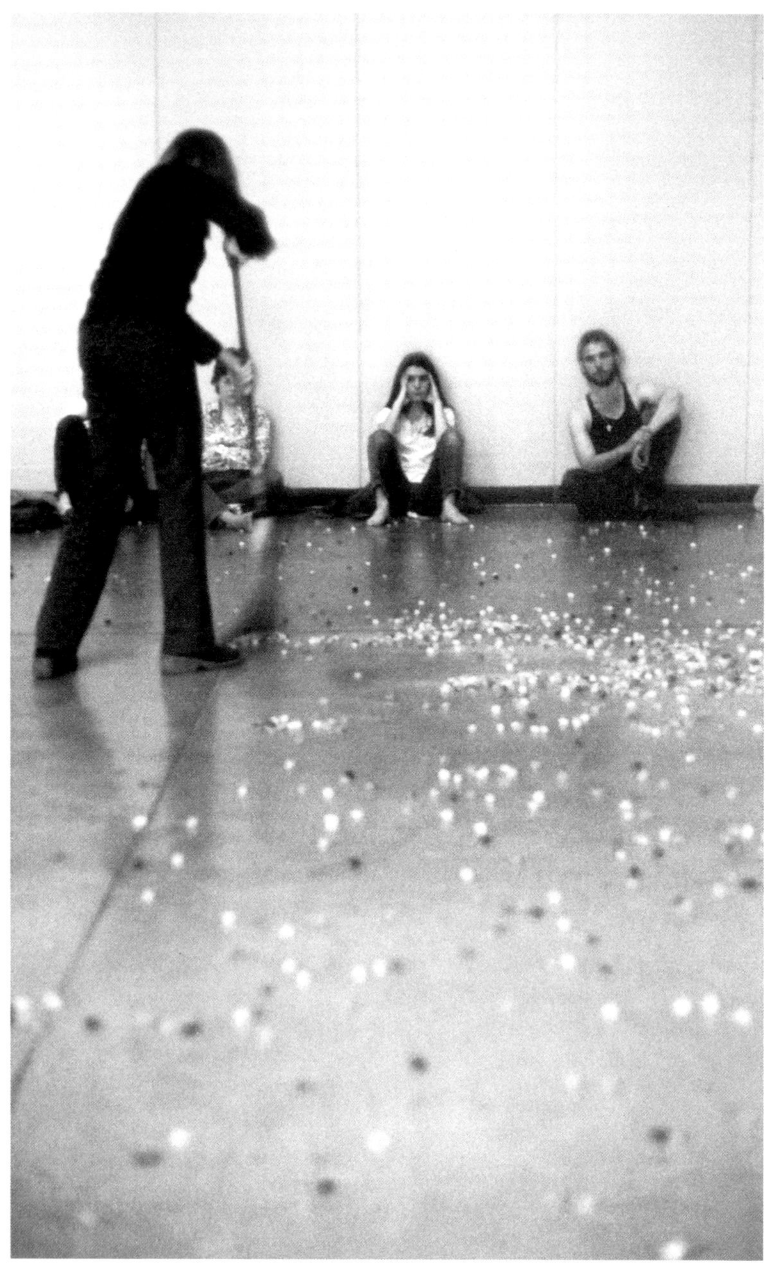

Percussion for Jelly Beans and Gumdrops with Solo Broom, 1975

making films off and on since her undergraduate years at Smith College, and now she turned to filmmaking once again. With her husband, Al Baccili, she made a film on commission from Newark, New Jersey, to document the state of the city's health-care system since the riots of the 1960s. Given $500 for the project, Skoglund ended up spending $10,000 of her own money to complete it. "I realized so much about truth and photography and people," she says of the experience. "It was ostensibly a documentary, but there is no such thing; everything is relative. Truthfulness is problematic in everything, and the camera is no more guilty [of being untruthful] than anything else."

It was her last film. Feeling artistically depleted, Skoglund left New York City for the summer, and moved into a house trailer in upstate New York. Its tacky luxury appealed to her, and she began photographing the inside of the trailer with a 2 1/4 camera. She also began making still-life drawings of the domestic objects that she bought especially for the purpose. "The photography started to make sense and I was having fun," she says. "I was laughing all the way to the mall."

Skoglund returned to New York in the fall of 1977 determined to learn photography, and began by looking at commercial food photography and liquor advertising. "I thought those photographs were amazing, mainly as examples of unbelievable, maniacal control," she says. "I felt I could milk them for myself as far as lighting and depth of field go—the overall, flat commercial lighting of the 1950s, the depth of field where everything is so sharp that it doesn't even look like a photograph anymore." She taught herself to print Cibachrome, a technique in which brilliantly colored azo dyes are embedded in plastic that has an almost mirror-like surface.

In 1978 she began doing food still lifes in bright colors, in which patterning was used to create spatial and visual ambiguity. Vegetables such as peas, carrots, and corn were arranged into geometric shapes that were juxtaposed with similar-looking paper

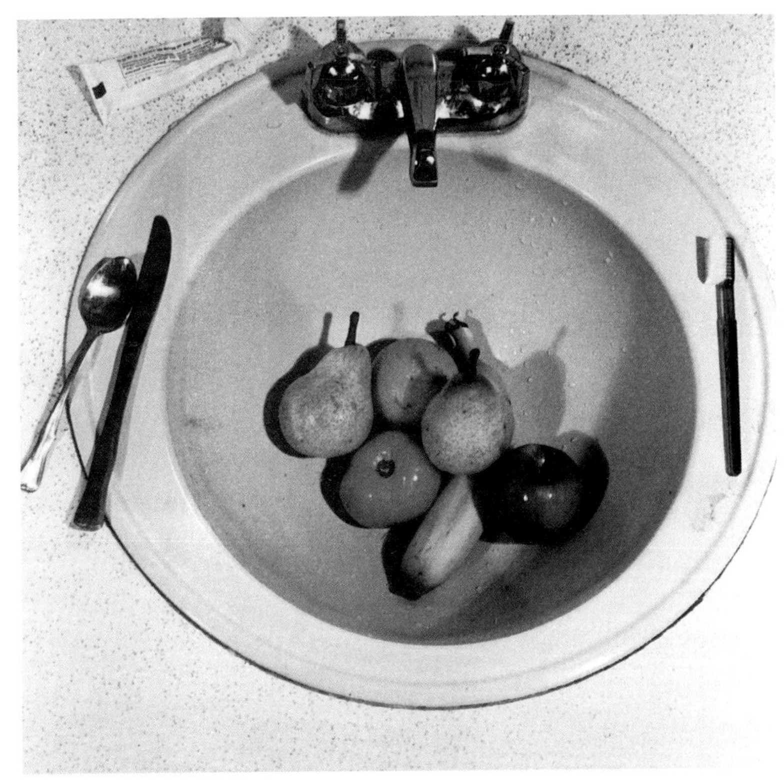

Pink Sink, 1977 (cat. 9)

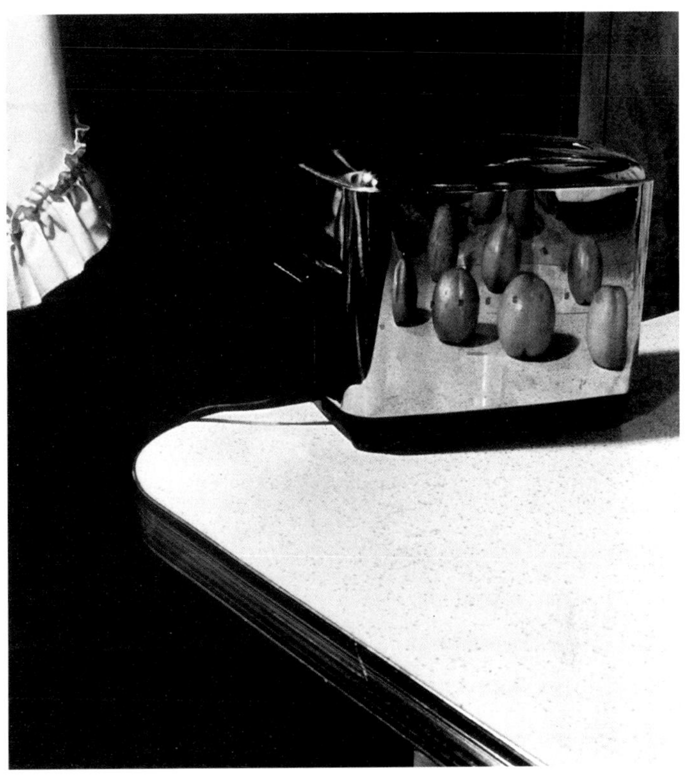

Peaches in a Toaster, 1977 (cat. 10)

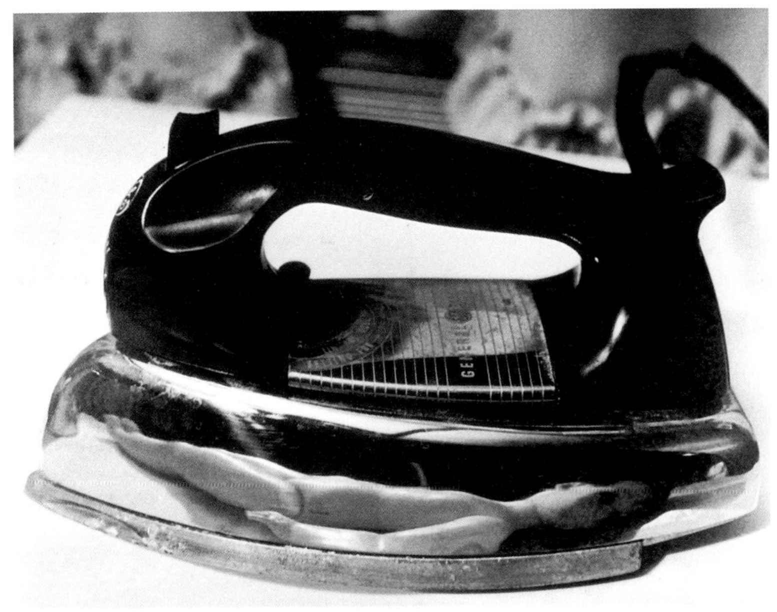

Iron, 1977 (cat. 11)

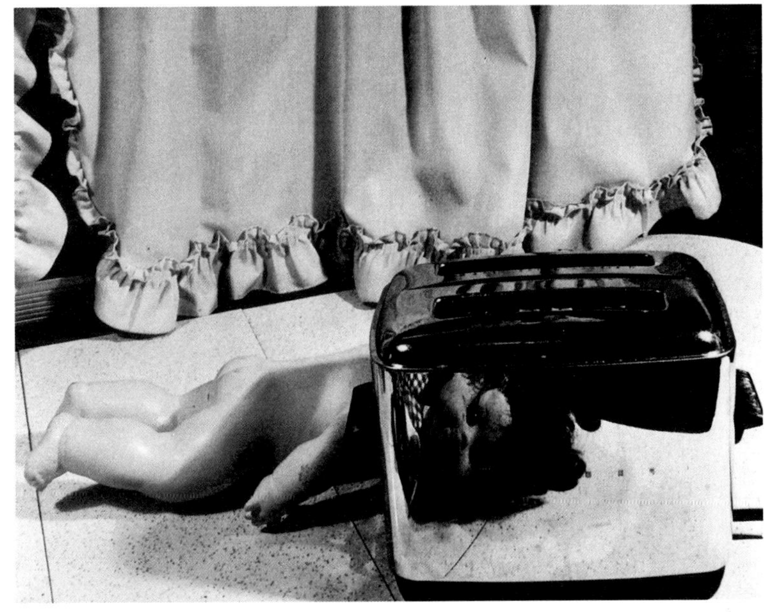

Toaster, 1977 (cat. 12)

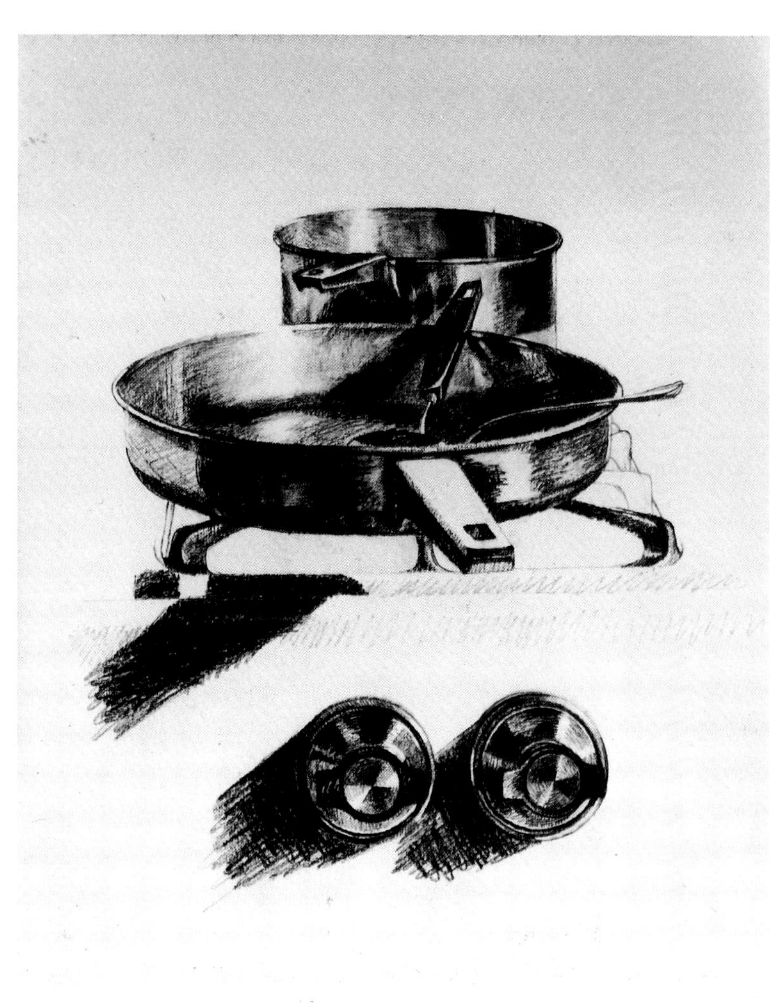

Pots and Knobs, 1978 (cat. 13)

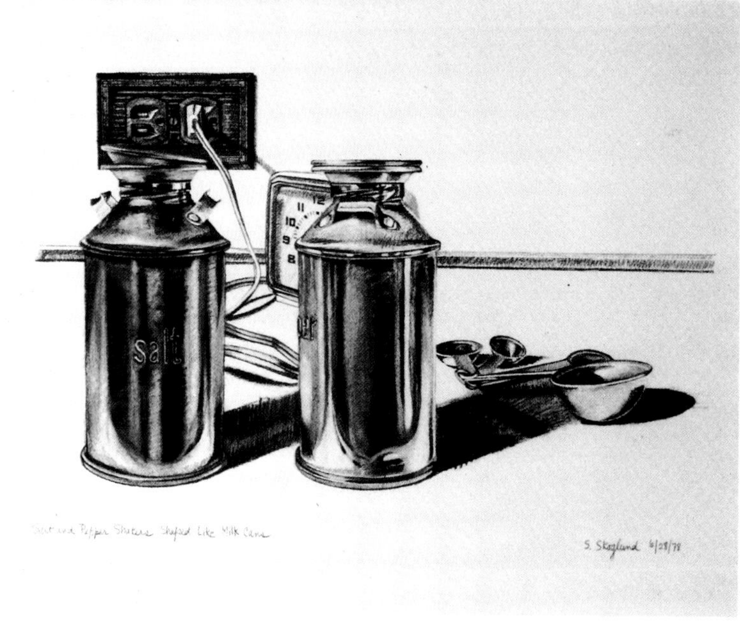

Salt and Pepper Shakers Shaped Like Milk Cans, 1978 (cat. 14)

plates and geometric-print tablecloths. "I was trying to control the world in order to photograph it; I thought that was very interesting in terms of our culture," she says. "I cranked this work out quickly because I was excited about how rational photography was as a medium." Pattern painting was getting a lot of attention in the art world then, and Skoglund used its influence in these pictures, but in a double-edged way, mining its artful geometry while sending it up.

In the photography world, critics and artists alike were just beginning to come to grips with the possibility of using color photography to make art; up until the mid-1970s, color was considered a primarily commercial medium. "The controversy over color photography being so commercial was a lot of fun for me," says Skoglund, who had looked at commercial color photography as her model. "As an outsider, the fact that color was not looked upon as art was just fine with me."[3] In the art world, photography was used mainly as a conceptual medium and any other kind of photographic work was generally scorned. At this point Skoglund felt herself neither as part of the art nor the photography world. "I realized that the idea of making art was not a good way to approach things," she says. "Instead, I saw myself as trying to make something that my relatives could understand."

About this time, Skoglund met Marvin Heiferman, director of photography at Castelli Graphics on Manhattan's Upper East Side. He had already started exhibiting color photography that had a humorous but critical edge to it, and he put one of her 22-by-28 inch still lifes in a summer group show. Buoyed by the artistic success of this work (despite the fact that it didn't sell), Skoglund decided to make even larger images.

"There was a lot of interest in making pictures bigger, brighter, competitive with painting, which is what I wanted to do," she says. She began to photograph a much larger space—the living room of a tenement apartment on Elizabeth Street in Manhattan—still using domestic objects and patterning to confuse the rational space that the photograph usually records. "I had this pictorial idea about a pattern and seeing through the pattern," she says. "The pattern almost denies the three-dimensionality of the thing that's being photographed; the pattern tends to lay on the surface while the viewer looks through this pattern at something else—an event or a real space that mingles with the pattern."

Skoglund painted the living room completely white and used disposable kitchen utensils arrayed on walls, floor, and furniture to create a patterned field of shape and color across the space. In the first construction (*Accessories*, 1979), a woman in a striped dress and coat stands in the white room, which is dotted with brightly striped paper napkins and plates (which were left over from her food still lifes). In another image, red and blue plastic spoons were hung vertically throughout the space so that they looked like drops—or sperm, she points out. In *Spoons*, 1979 (page 38), a man standing behind a chair looks like a catatonic mannequin; dressed in the red, white, and blue of the room's decor, he gazes sightlessly off to the side wearing eyeglasses whose frames and lenses are painted an opaque white.

Despite the similarities of this body of work to the previous still lifes, Skoglund here embarked on new, more psychologically freighted territory. The whiteness, overlaid with the patterning, produced a sense of claustrophobia and disorientation. The orderly repetitiveness of the domestic objects gave the scene a nightmarish quality, as did the ancillary role of the people, who were generally treated as affectless drones. Skoglund says she used them simply for scale. "At the time I had no idea what I was doing," she says. "It felt like I was making sculpture when there weren't people in the pieces. I wanted people to understand that this was a real space, not a dollhouse." But her use of human figures as secondary to the rest of the scene is one of her most disturbing devices.

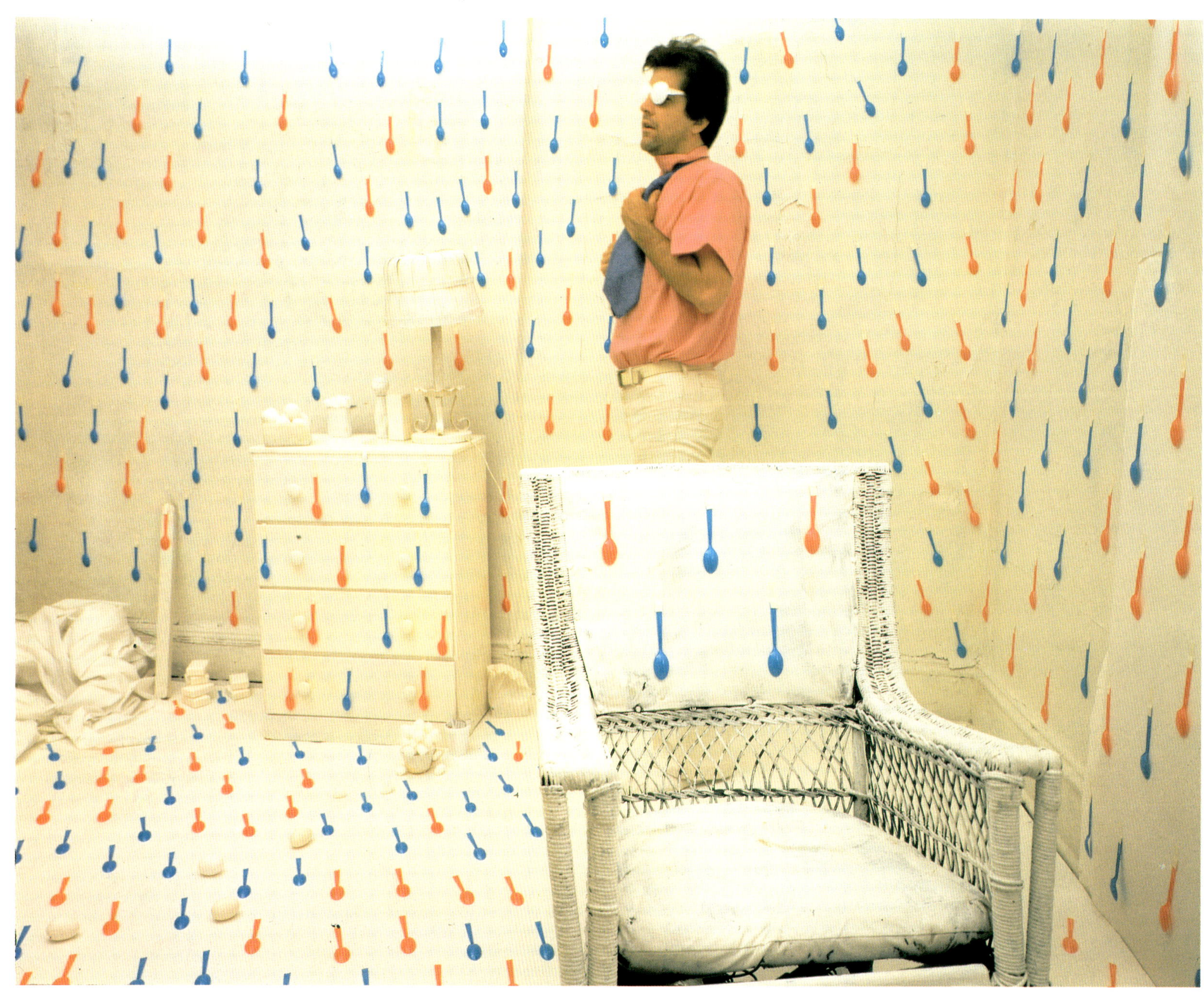

Spoons, 1979 (cat. 25)

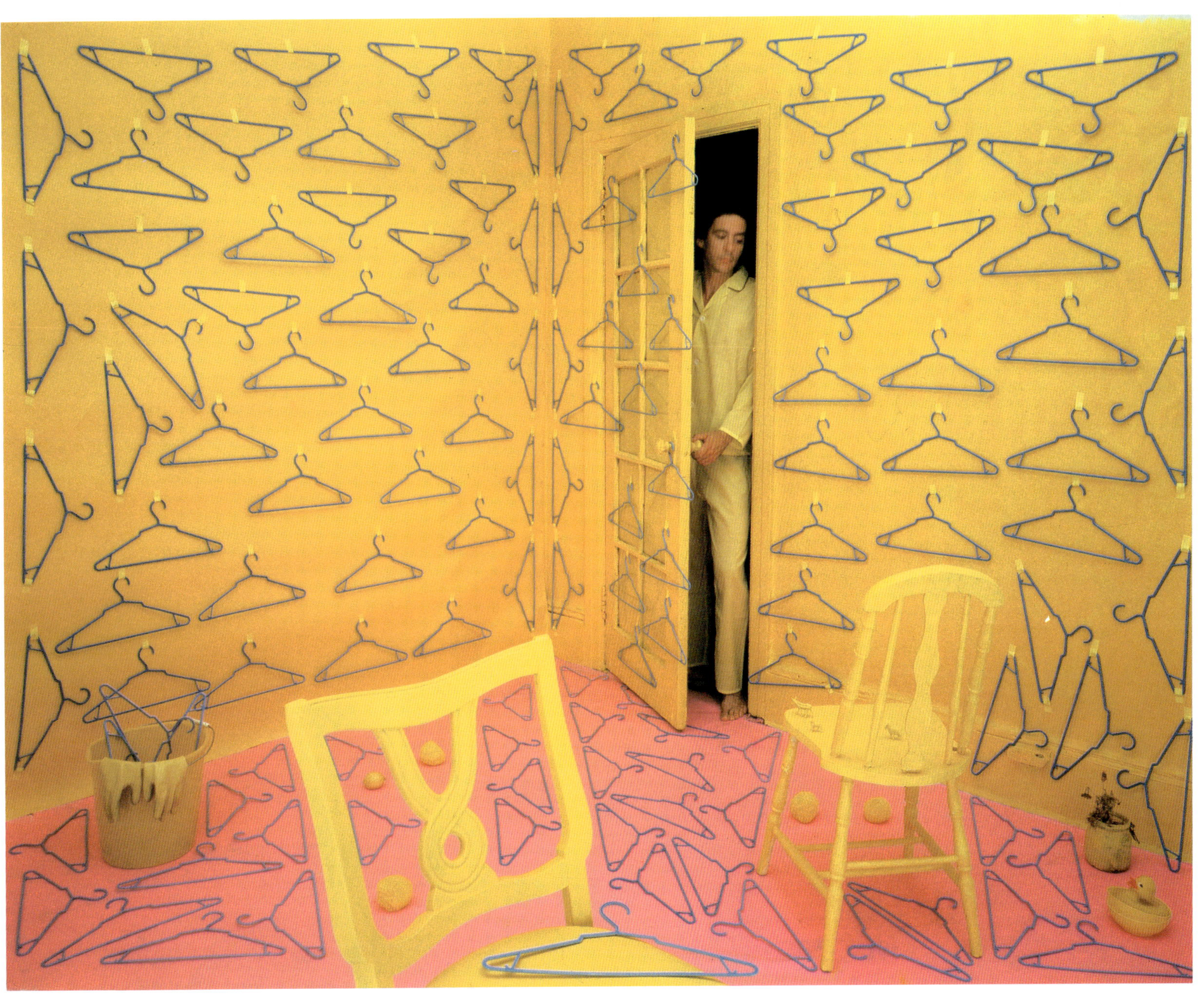

Hangers, 1979 (cat. 26)

In the third piece photographed in the apartment, entitled *Hangers*, 1979 (page 39), Skoglund added another new element: bright colors applied to the walls and floor that helped further flatten her already confounded spaces and add a garish, jarring note. The overall pattern of neatly arranged wire clothes hangers produced an interior space whose logic was ruled by compulsively rigid domestic imperatives; a hapless man entered it like a sleepwalker in room-matching yellow pajamas. Although she abandoned bright color in her next piece in favor of a deadening putty hue, color still added expressive weight to *Ferns* of 1980. Again, the confused space of a domestic environment seemed to overwhelm the withdrawn, putty-colored women. Here, the patterning of green fern fronds on the walls was less insistent than earlier patterns, but proved just as effective a flattening device.

Just as she had with the food still lifes, Skoglund was setting these images up solely to photograph them. In doing that she was following in a tradition in photography that began soon after the medium made its official debut. In 1976 this kind of photography was dubbed "the directorial mode" by A. D. Coleman, who sketched out its history.[4]

It began both as a form of popular entertainment and instruction and as a rather more rarefied form of art.[5] As entertainment and education, beginning about 1850, it flourished in stereographic imagery, which accommodated a wide range of scenarios, from "biblical episodes and classics of literature" to comic domestic and romantic scenes, sexually suggestive and overtly erotic tableaux, as well as novelties such as "ghost" photography.[6] During the same period, two artists, O. G. Rejlander and Henry Peach Robinson, also created directorial images, which were "mostly genre scenes and religious allegories" that often involved posed tableaux as well as the combination printing of more than one negative.[7]

Although there have been hiatuses in the making of directorial photography, particularly during the "purist" period of the f.64 movement, it is a major visual strategy. Its most influential arena has been that of commercial photography, which is wholly directorial. But artists have always made directorial images, although Coleman points out that until the late 1960s, certain such practitioners were often harshly criticized. In the 1960s, though, a range of artists, including Duane Michals, Ralph Gibson, Ed Ruscha, Les Krims, and Lucas Samaras, started making setup images that gave the genre visibility and a sometimes grudging respectability. By the early 1980s the directorial mode had become central to artistic practice for a diverse group of artists including Cindy Sherman, Laurie Simmons, David Levinthal, Eileen Cowin, David Haxton, and Barbara Kasten.

One thing that was fundamental to much directorial photography was the found object, whether used as surrogate figures, like the toys in Simmons's and Levinthal's work, or as props, in Sherman's pieces. But in 1980, when Skoglund was beginning a new piece that would include the figure of a cat, she decided to sculpt the animal herself rather than buying a readymade cat to photograph. "I needed a cat and I knew I wouldn't be able to control a real cat," she says. "I didn't want to critique 'catness' as seen by our culture, which is what would happen if I went out and got a found-object cat to photograph; using found objects is inevitably very tongue-in-cheek, coy, kitsch. So I decided to make a cat." It was a decision that would take her artmaking in an entirely new direction, involving her in hand-crafting elements of her photographs in a way that is, to her, more reminiscent of folk art than postmodern art.

It would also begin the series of installation works and photographs for which she is best known. The first group of three, *Radioactive Cats* (page 10), *Revenge of the Goldfish* (page 42–43), and *Maybe Babies* (page 83), was made between 1980 and 1983. The second group, including *A Breeze at Work* (page 60), *Fox*

Games (page 14–15), *The Green House* (page 23), and *Gathering Paradise* (page 67), was made between 1987 and 1991. The majority of works are set within mundane spaces, often of a domestic nature: kitchen, bedroom, living room, patio, office. One, *Maybe Babies*, is set in outer space (it has often been wrongly identified as a postnuclear holocaust landscape, with Skoglund's acquiescence), although the black-painted shingled house backdrop gives the scene a domestic effect. All of them are colored in extremely limited palettes of two or three colors, and shades or tints of them. All are populated by multiple figurative sculptures of Skoglund's making—cats, goldfish, babies, leaves, foxes, dogs, squirrels. In them she refined and complicated the original pictorial idea that she had begun in the food still lifes—overlaying space with a pattern that the viewer looks through into an ambiguous picture space. These pieces, however, would be much more labor-intensive than anything she had done before, especially in the manufacture of the figurative elements and the depth of meaning created because of them.

Until she began *Radioactive Cats* in1980, Skoglund had learned only the most rudimentary sculpture-making technique when she was at Smith. Using this technique—what she calls "scrunching up chicken wire" and covering it with plaster bandages—she began trying to make a cat. Only after three or four tries did she make an animal that was identifiable as a cat, rather than "a small dog or a large rat or any other animal with four legs." After she had five of them, she began to like the way they looked together and decided to continue making them, creating a group of cats for the photograph rather than the single cat of her original idea. "By cats number 12 and 14, they really started to come to life," she says.

The problem was that the cats looked almost too good. "I was afraid that in the photograph they would look like real cats," she says. "I wanted it to be clear that they were sculptures." She was also concerned about animating the still photograph. "I wanted to make it sort of explode in front of the viewer," she says. Making the cats an unnatural color was her solution, hence the resulting "radioactive cats" painted a screechingly bright green. "The political climate was very paranoid about nuclear war at that time and I wanted to tie my work in with the popular consciousness," she explains. "Radioactive was a word that was quite commonly used." The resulting image, shot in the kitchen of the Elizabeth Street apartment, is a spooky tableau of two elderly people, their backs to the camera, seemingly going about their daily life in a bleak gray environment surrounded by twenty-five glowing cats, a kind of "postnuclear holocaust" vision.

But as significant as the subject matter was, Skoglund was perhaps even more concerned with the transformation of the subject into a photographic object. "I began to use the camera because I was doing things that no one would see unless I took a picture of them," she says. "I was really trying to make a photograph that didn't look like a photograph; I had a desire to make painterly visual statements." One way she achieved that was by limiting the color to varying shades of gray and green, which went against the prevailing idea of a color photograph being inherently full of different colors. The overall use of two colors across the visual field flattened the space out, while the identifiable objects were used almost as abstract visual elements, much as she had done previously with spoons and hangers. What was different here was that Skoglund decided to exhibit *Radioactive Cats* both as an installation and as a photograph, the first time she had done that. And although they are nominally the same in terms of subject matter and constituent elements, for Skoglund, setting up the installation for the photograph is a much different process from putting it up as a piece for public viewing.

"People tend to see the photograph as a documentation of the installation," says Skoglund. "It never occurs to them that the

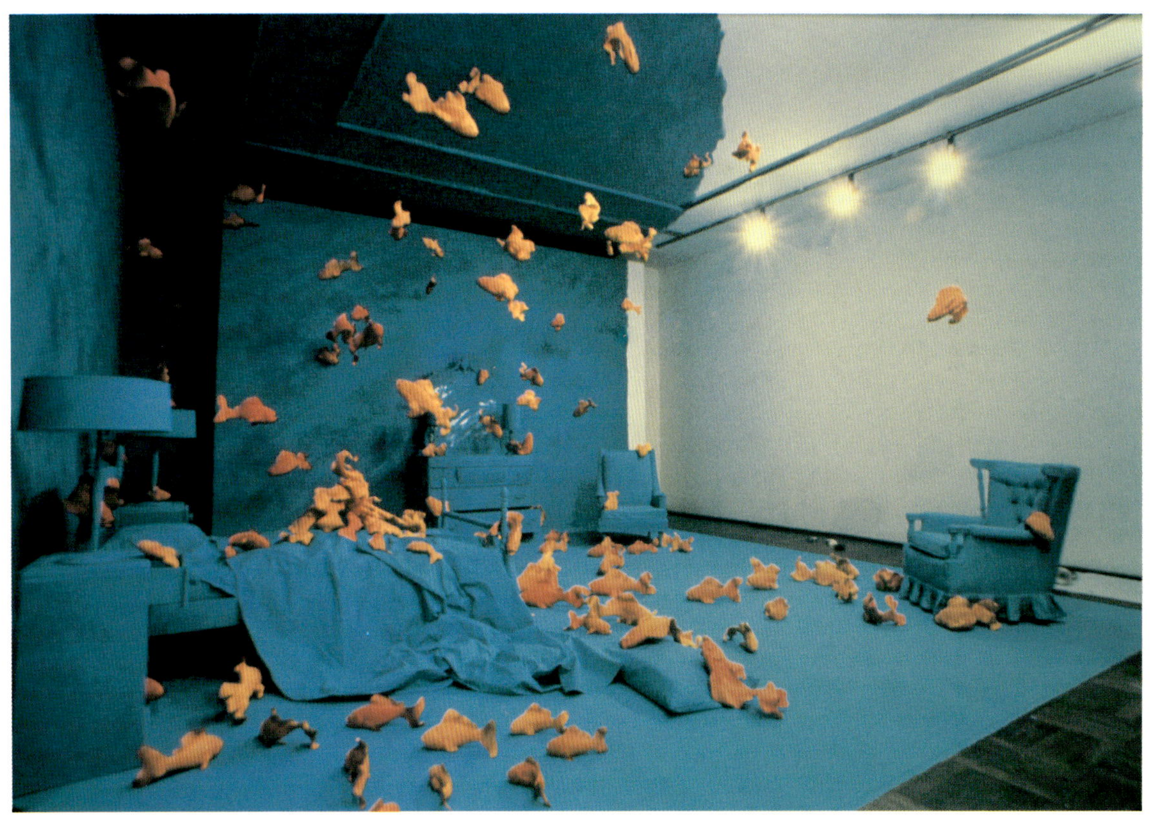

Revenge of the Goldfish (installation at Castelli Gallery), 1981 (cat. 28)

camera goes down first, and everything is brought in and organized for the camera and with the camera."

After making all the handmade sculpture and gathering all the other furniture, props, and actors she will need, Skoglund starts by placing the camera. The picture is built by constantly referencing what it looks like to the camera. In the early days, that meant running back and forth between the camera and the installation to check how things looked. Later on she acquired Polaroid backs for her 4 by 5 and 8 by 10 Toya view cameras and was able to check the progress of an installation by taking Polaroids of it. Especially important to Skoglund is the arrangement of the handmade sculptures in the photographs; they are not allowed to overlap to any degree, nor to obscure one another (there was some minor overlapping in *Cats*), which is one device that produces the hyperreal, dreamlike quality of the pieces.

By exhibiting the photograph with the installation, Skoglund raises a question about the identity of the work of art. "It's about duality—where is the work of art, which one is the work of art—neither one is really it," she says. "This is difficult for people in the art world who are concerned about definitions of the work of

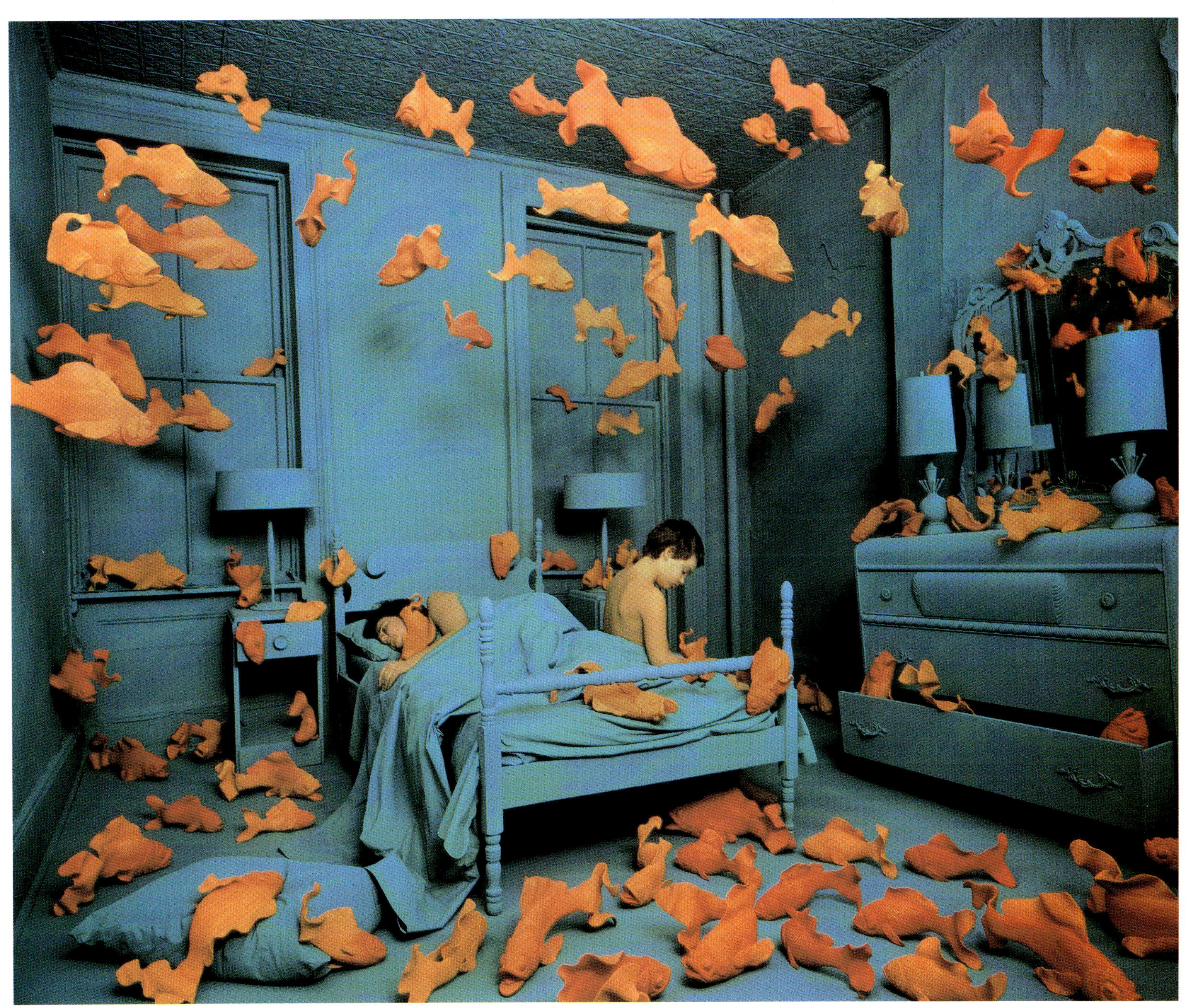

Revenge of the Goldfish, 1981 (cat. 29)

art. Dealing with both things equally is problematic; people either focus on the installation or the photograph." As Skoglund sees it, she starts out by making individual works of art (the sculpture) to go into other works of art (the installation), which then becomes another work of art (the photograph), a processs she sees as "collapsible."

Radioactive Cats brought Skoglund a lot of attention, although most people saw only the photograph. The installation was shown in 1980 at Real Art Ways in Hartford, Connecticut, and at 626 Gallery, an alternative space in New York City, and once in 1981, at the Addison Gallery of American Art in Andover, Massachusetts; it wouldn't be shown again until 1990. But it caused enough of a furor that Castelli Graphics finally gave her a show in 1981, in which she displayed *Revenge of the Goldfish* as both an installation and a photograph.

For *Revenge,* Skoglund spent the entire summer of 1980 sculpting from clay the oversize goldfish in the piece. "It was a strange recapitulation of working in a factory, an experience I had over and over as a teenager working part-time and summers in these American industrial-wasteland environments," she says of the repetitive quality of making the goldfish that populate what is perhaps her most magical piece. In it, the oversize, brilliant red fish seem to swim through the dreamlike atmosphere of a bright turquoise bedroom. There, one person—an adult woman—is sleeping, and a second—a boy—is sitting in a daze on the edge of the bed, seemingly oblivious to the fishy apparitions. The iconography managed to be at once playful and disturbing. The oversize fish were cute in a frightening way, like some freaks of nature that had overrun a human habitation. Goldfish are, in fact, freaks. They were bred in ancient China from the carp, and engineered for aesthetic traits that are often grotesque. With this piece, Skoglund embarked on a continuing exploration of the relationship between the human and the animal worlds, culture versus nature.

In *Revenge of the Goldfish,* the relationship between the woman and the nude boy was seen as problematic. "I wanted it to be sexually charged," says Skoglund, who remembers that incestuousness and homosexuality were both cited in responses to the piece. Certainly, the nature of the sexuality involved was ambiguous, the piece sketching out a rather bleak picture of human relations. Fittingly, the title, *Revenge of the Goldfish,* is derived from science fiction, an art form notoriously cynical about humanity and its ability to manage its future.

After *Revenge* Skoglund embarked on her third large installation, *Maybe Babies* (1983). For viewers who had been fascinated by the antic dreaminess of the previous two pieces, this one was a frightening counterpoint. It placed in the foreground the anxiety and fear that had been more tempered in its predecessors. In it, twenty oversize babies in mottled shades of pink and blue seem to float weightlessly in a threatening black environment, while a man looks on from a window. When it was exhibited at the Leo Castelli Gallery, many viewers saw it as another nuclear holocaust scenario, a reading Skoglund herself tacitly encouraged by allowing it to be exhibited as such. Others read the mottled pinks and blues of the babies' skins as bruises, invoking a child-abuse scenario, or a comment on the politics of abortion, meanings that were not part of Skoglund's thinking, but that she doesn't completely reject. "That's one of the great things about working figuratively," she says. "If the politics are open rather than closed, the piece adapts to the environment rather than the other way around."

In fact, the setting was supposed to be outer space, while the title suggested that maybe these creatures weren't babies. "Maybe they are children of the damned," says Skoglund. "I felt skeptical about the human race when I made this—it's a really hostile piece, questioning whether the human being as an animal would turn out to be a mistake, because humans are animals that have choices, but they often make bad choices rather than good ones." Her thinking on this was informed by her readings in the history of religion, on the rise of the Judeo-Christian system and religions such as Buddhism that supplant paganism. "What you get is a questioning of good and evil and the ability to make choices," she says, "a problem that didn't express itself in paganism, which was mainly about death and asking why we're going to die."

After doing these three large, time-consuming pieces, Skoglund scaled down her artmaking to a more manageable level. For *Patients and Nurses* of 1983, she used a minimal number of props, none of them handmade, and four models, to create a witty but frightening view of puny humanity at the mercy of the medical establishment. She also embarked on a series of paintings based on photographs, as well as a series of dye-transfer photographs. For these works she took a number of different images and collaged them together in the darkroom, using real settings and props rather than ones she created herself. This series, *True Fiction* (pages 76–79), spans the years 1984 to 1987.

In installation works made between 1984 and 1992, Skoglund introduced a new element: what she calls "the inappropriate, uncanny flirtation with abnormal forms of behavior." This included the use of chewed gum, raw meat, snack foods, and other food substances as artmaking material. The first was *Germs Are Everywhere* (page 6), followed by *Spirituality in the Flesh* (page 47), *Body Limits* (page 46), *The Cocktail Party* (pages 62–63), and *Atomic Love* (page19) all of 1992, and *The Wedding* of 1994 (page 2). For these food-related pieces, Skoglund did extensive research and development.

Germs Are Everywhere is a small, relatively simple installation with one model and few props. It exists only as a photograph. For it, Skoglund and an assistant had to chew an undetermined but extremely large amount of gum, enough to cover the walls and props of the installation with the masticated wads that serve as the "germs." Her research involved sampling different types of gum, testing for color and consistency in the chewed gum, and even experimenting with casting the wads in bronze and then painting them pink to see if they would closely resemble the real thing—which they didn't. "Ultimately the photograph is still the thing that matters," she says. "It has to translate—you have to be able to see something that has the visual characteristics of gum with teethmarks in it in the photo." Real gum mounted with epoxy was used, and it had to be scraped off the surfaces and thrown away after the image was taken.

In contrast to the yucky whimsy of *Germs Are Everywhere*, Skoglund's next food piece, *Spirituality in the Flesh*, is almost horrifyingly macabre. It is the simplest photo she has done: a female mannequin wearing a blue dress seated on a stool. What is disconcerting about it is that the mannequin, stool, floor, and background wall are all covered with raw hamburger in all its bloody glory. The piece existed only to be photographed—and only for a short period of time. "After an hour, the hamburger does not look like that," says Skoglund. "It's constantly changing, as the blood, which is making it red, oxidizes and turns brown."

The very process of making the piece ranged from the distasteful to the repellent. "Every aspect of this involved extreme alienation from what's considered normal behavior in society," says Skoglund. This ranged from doing color tests with raw meat, to lying to the butcher about why she wanted eighty pounds of hamburger—an excessive amount for her to consume all at once—to pressing the meat into place. "It was an experiment in horror," she says. "It's the only piece I've done where I've really physically touched death. I felt like I was digging around in my mother's grave. This is the ultimate reduction—what you're going to become—the ultimate reality."

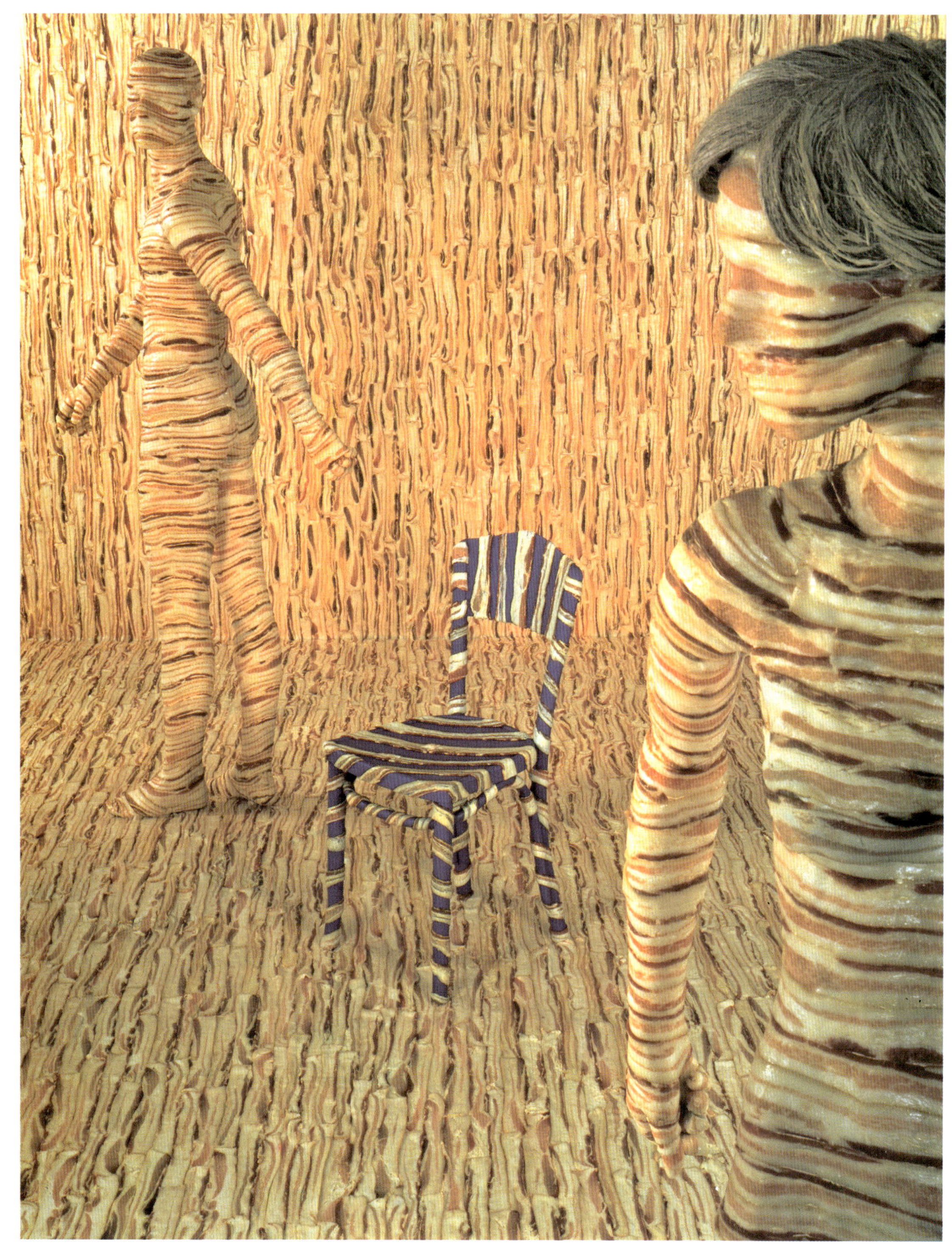

Body Limits, 1992 (cat. 40)

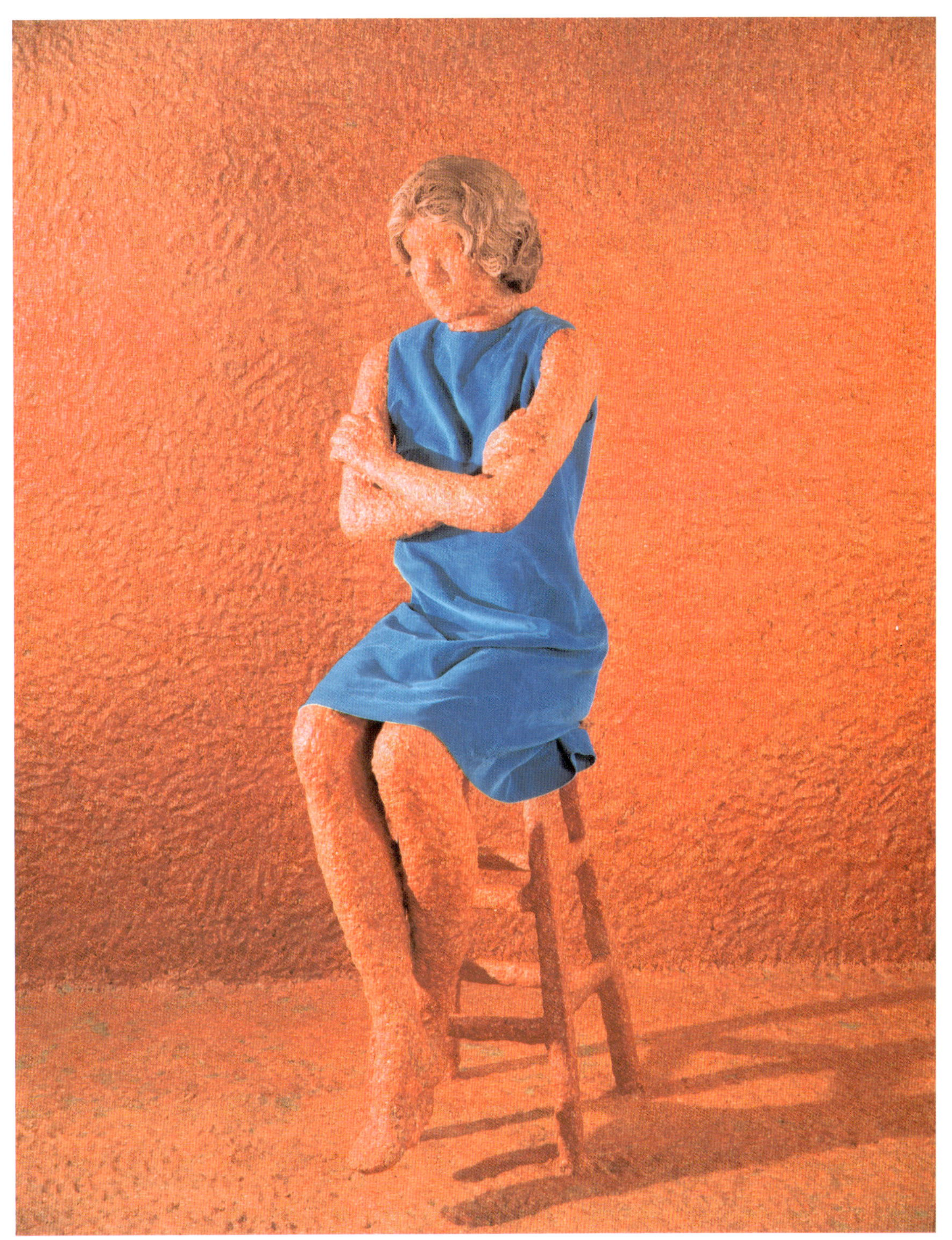

Spirituality in the Flesh, 1992 (cat. 39)

Far from being put off by the objectionable aspects of the piece, Skoglund followed it up with one made of raw bacon, entitled *Body Limits*. "These two pieces break the mold for me, in that the handmade object is absent and the material is really important," she says. In *Body Limits*, two mannequins, a chair, and the wall and floor are covered with fatty strips of bacon. For Skoglund, this meant sorting through a thirty-pound box of bacon to find usable strips, which were then matched according to the stripes of fat and meat. The whole thing had to be assembled and photographed in one session, although it took three tries until it worked. This performance aspect to the work, what Skoglund calls the "destruction of or interaction with the materials for the camera," is what she began to emphasize in her subsequent work.

Talking about her use of raw meat in *Spirituality in the Flesh*, Skoglund says, "It's perhaps the first time that I've started to put myself into my pieces. There's a benign quality to most of the work up to this point. The way that I've worked with the animals is pretty benign—you have ways out. The only way out of this picture is not understanding that it's red meat."

Indeed, there are many aspects of her work that are diverting, that offer a "way out," from the cute animals to the bold colors to the odd materials to the installation/photograph dichotomies. But Skoglund uses those diversions to keep the viewer inescapably reined in, bouncing from one kind of visual delectation to another, one perceptual conundrum to another.

Skoglund has always created scenarios in which the only way out is through the dark recesses of the contemporary soul. That passage progresses in her fantastical tableaux from common alienation to nuclear poisoning to bleeding meat. Death is one subtext of her artmaking, which is at the heart of all photography, according to Barthes. "Photography is a kind of primitive theater," he writes, "a kind of *Tableau Vivant*, a figuration of the motionless and made-up face beneath which we see the dead."[8]

Skoglund recognized the theatricality of photography and chose to make its effects primary and deliberate rather than secondary and accidental. Then she doubled the effect, in two and three dimensions, creating further complications by structuring vignettes in which the living are as affectless as the dead, and where animation proceeds from the inanimate. Here, daily life is a series of miraculous exhilarations that are at once humorous and sad, terrifying and mundane. Repetition is used to express singularity, while orderliness intimates chaos. Her materials and subject matter can border on the kitsch, but her storytelling goes to fearsome depths.

In a 1997 installation work, *Walking on Eggshells* (page 59), Skoglund's imagery includes snakes and rabbits. Her research for it extended from current texts on sociobiology, such as *The Origins of Right and Wrong in Animals*, to studies of animal iconography in the history of art, as well as the popular imagery of the Easter bunny. The slimy snake versus the cuddly bunny, the stigmatized versus the lovable, the sinuous versus the rotund. Skoglund continues to broaden her construction of visual, topical, and psychological oppositions. Although she has produced other works in addition to the installation/photographic projects, those large pieces most effectively give visual form to the depth, complexity, and levity of her concerns.

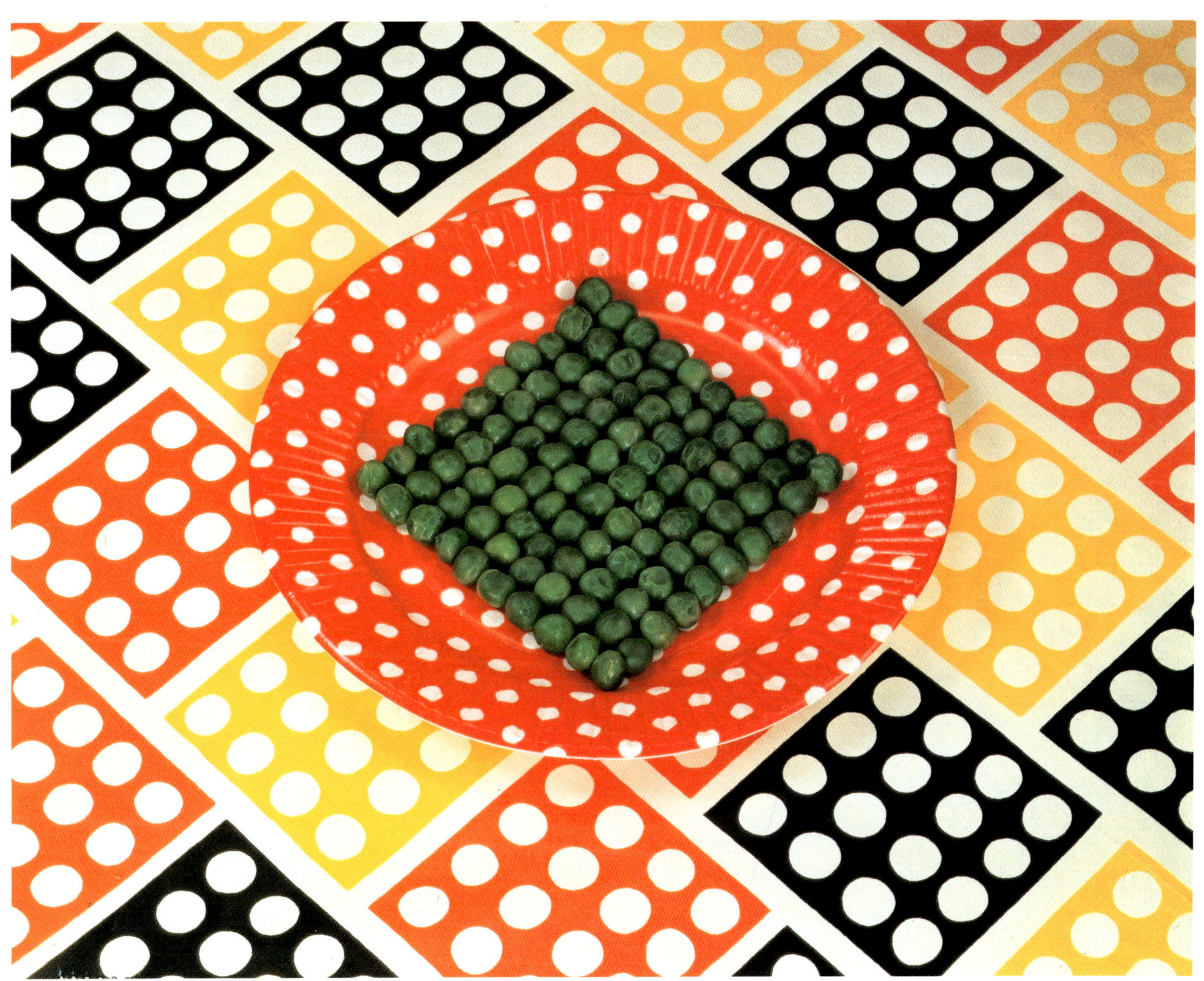

Peas on a Plate, 1978 (cat. 17)

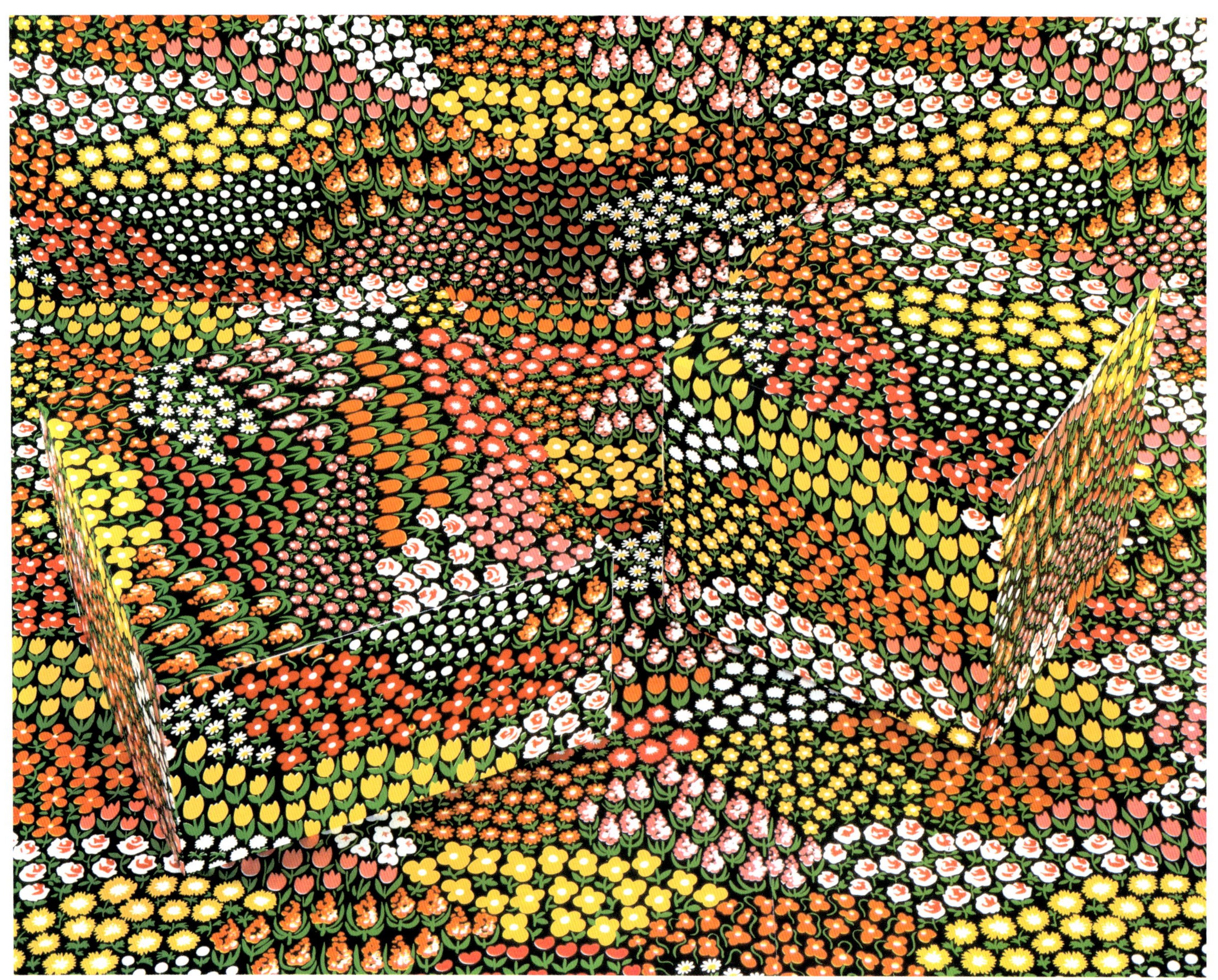

Two Boxes, 1978 (cat. 19)

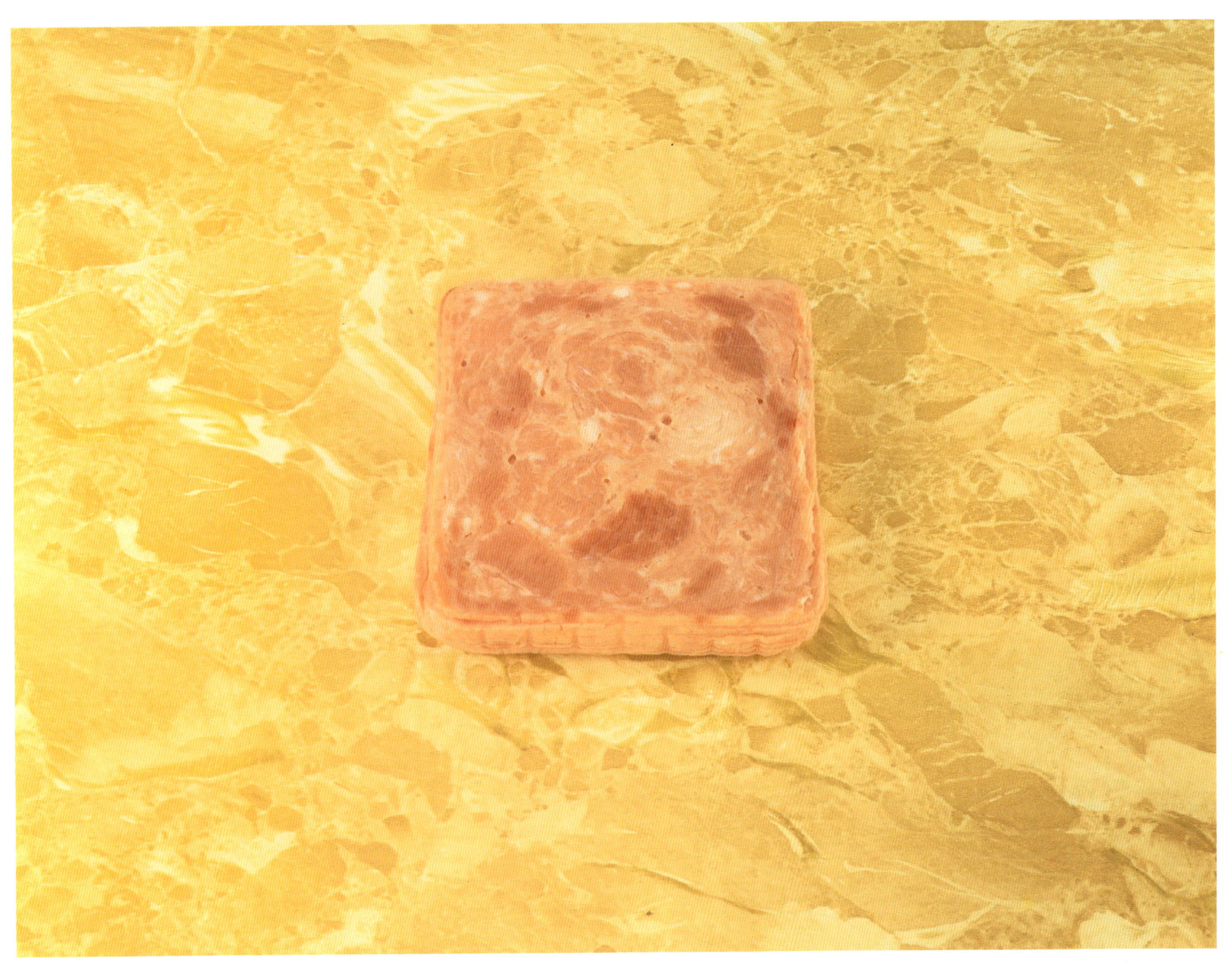

Luncheon Meat on a Counter, 1978 (cat. 15)

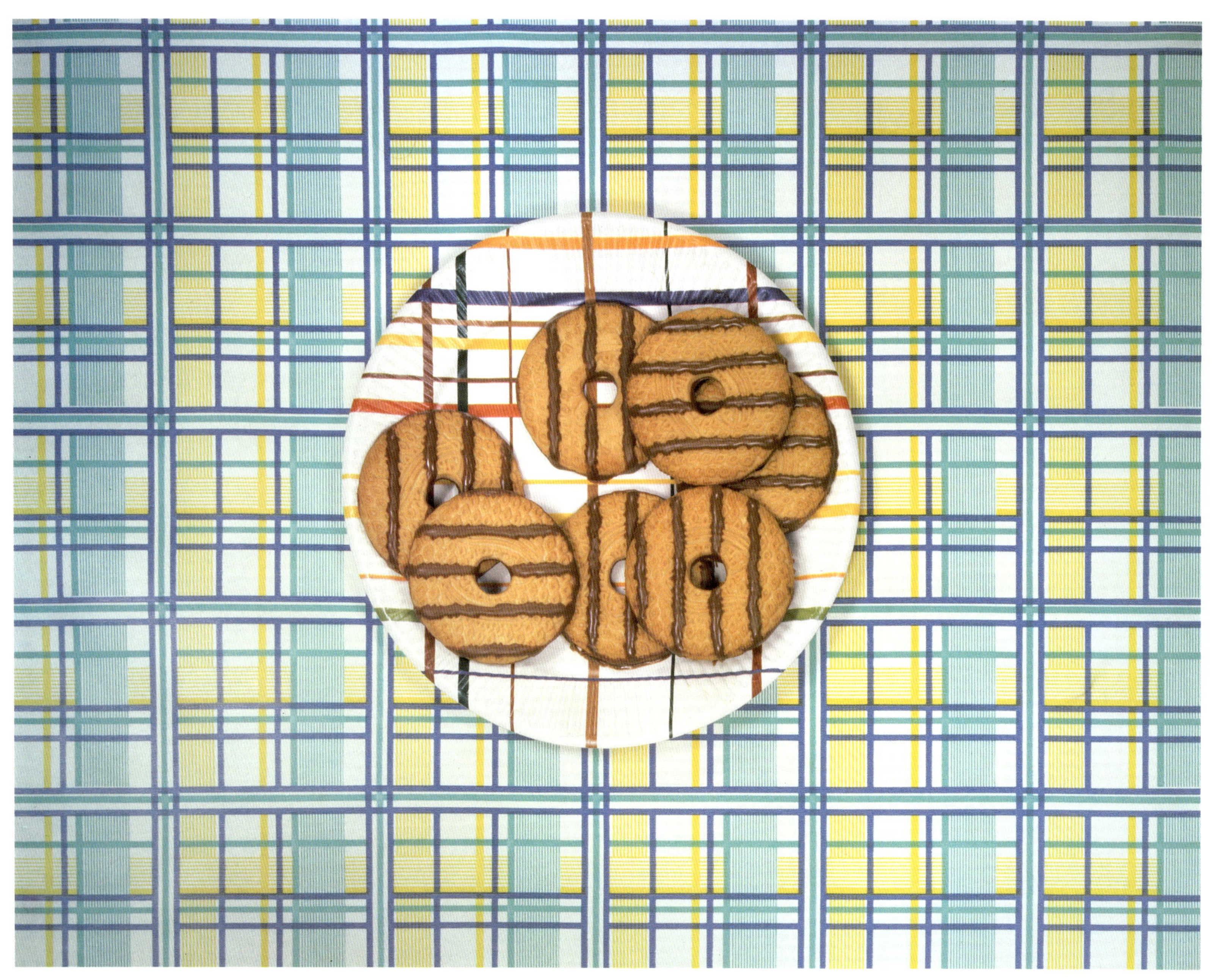

Cookies on a Plate, 1978 (cat. 16)

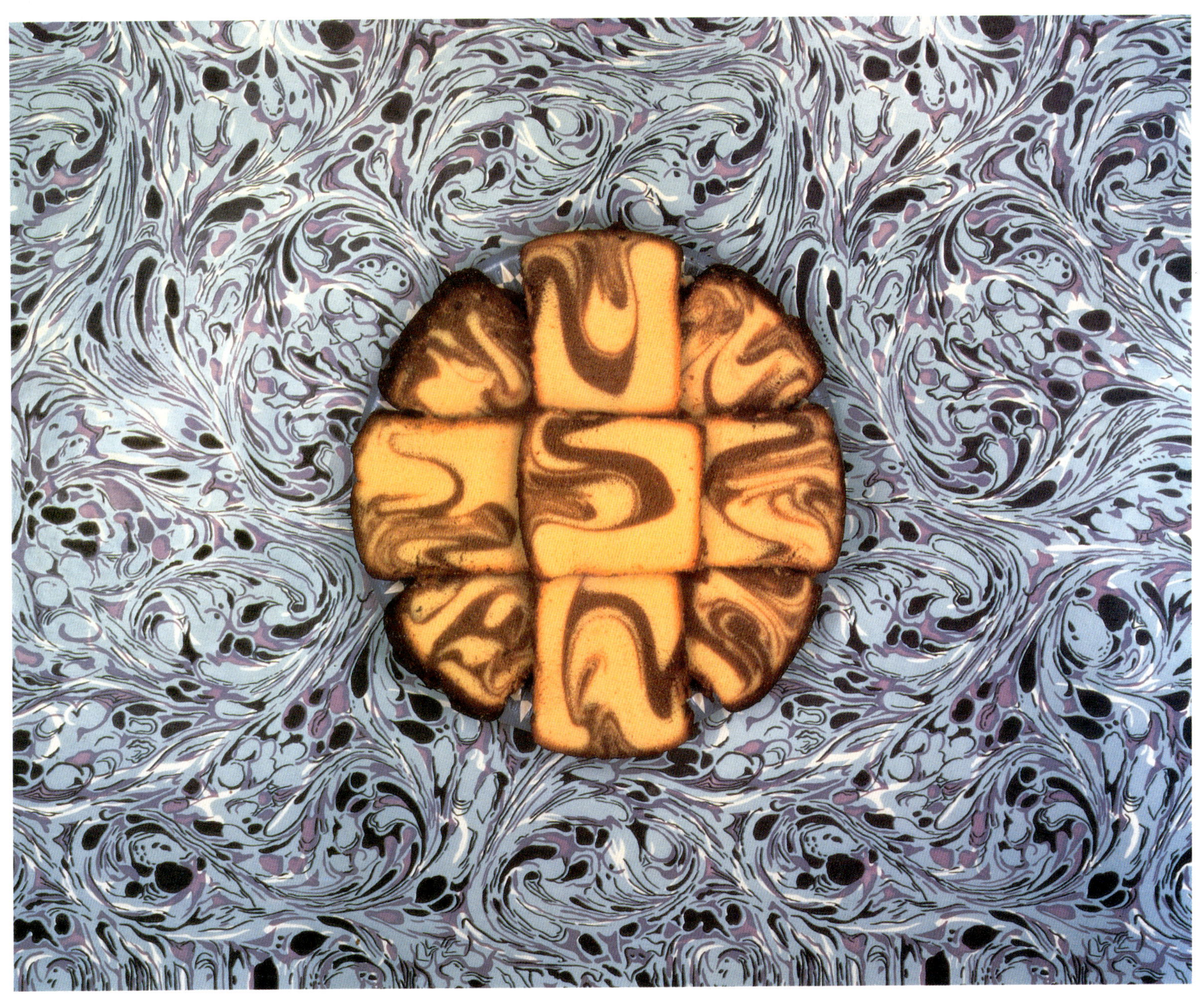

Nine Slices of Marblecake, 1978 (cat. 18)

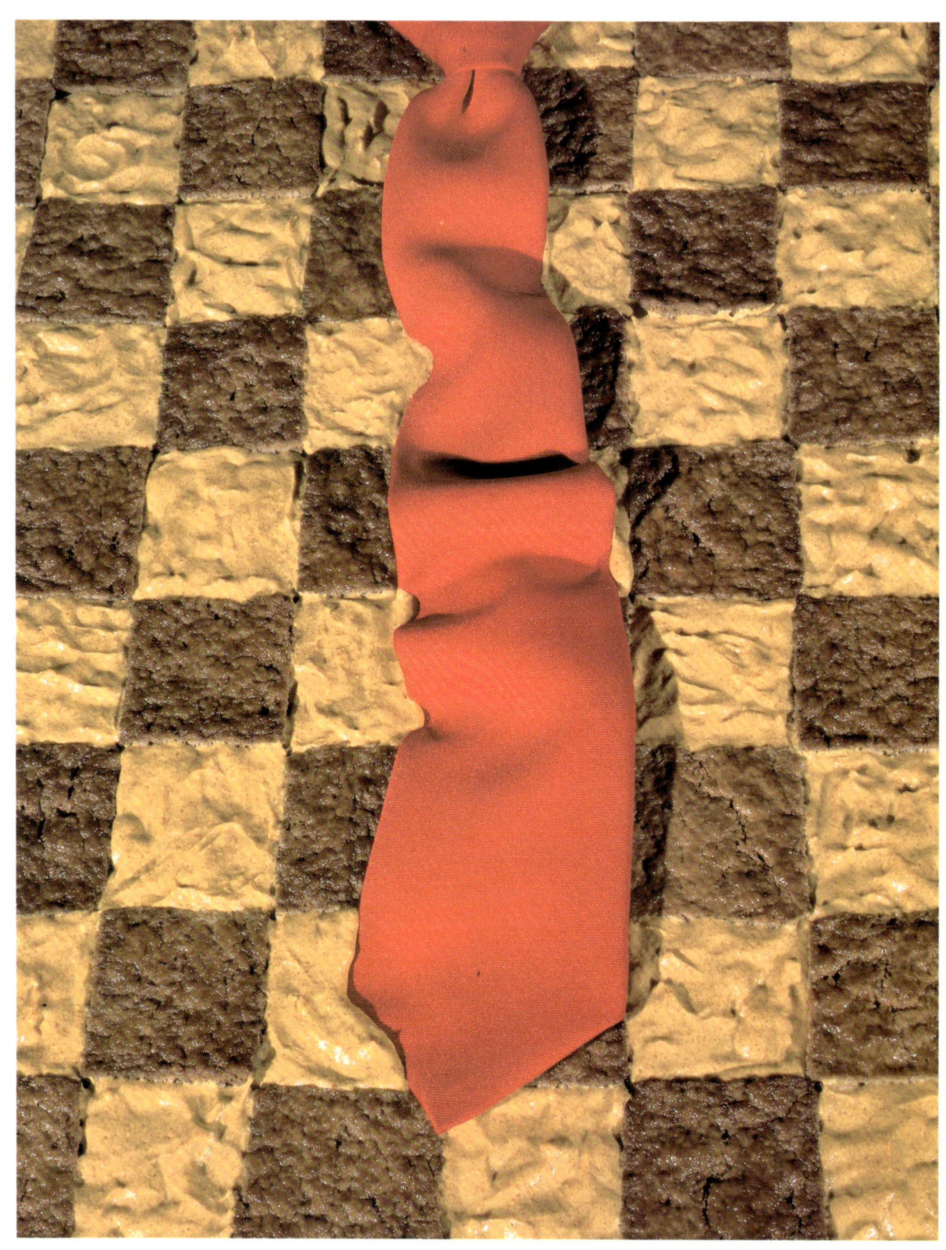

Thirty Burgers with Mustard, 1995 (cat. 48)

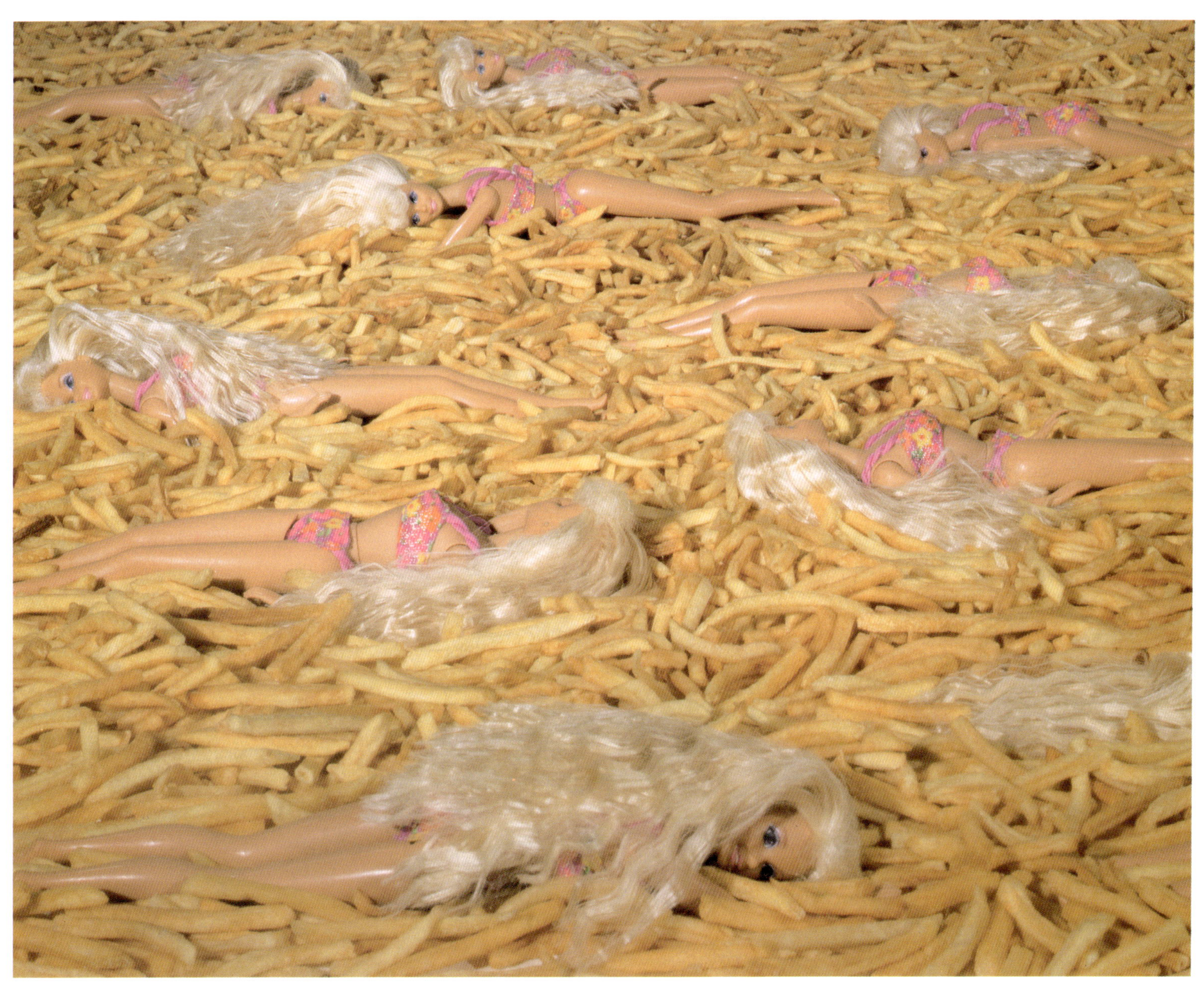

At the Shore, 1994 (cat. 47)

WALKING ON EGGSHELLS

by Linda Muehlig

Sandy Skoglund's newest installation *Walking on Eggshells* and the photograph based on it (page59) are the most recent additions to this important body of work, the sculptural tableaux and their photographic counterparts created by the artist over the last two decades. Like her other installations, in which art becomes the stage where expectations are undermined and the familiar is altered, skewed, or even upended, *Eggshells* is a magical precinct in which the mundane is made extraordinary.

Fiercely labor-intensive, researched, crafted, controlled, and even obsessive in their creation, Skoglund's installations are conceived and carried out with greater attention to organization and execution than most military or building campaigns. *Walking on Eggshells* is a bravura work combining large-scale cast paper appliances, a floor made of thousands of empty eggshells, sculptures of snakes and rabbits, as well as a hieroglyphic wall of cast paper tiles with printed images of animal icons, all arranged in a setting based on the most private of domestic spaces. It is easily the most complex of Skoglund's installations, a dazzling display whose visual wealth is paralleled by its thematic concerns with daily ritual, popular culture, paganism and ancient religions, and the history of art. Its complex evolution will be considered first in the context of Skoglund's installations and their evolution, then in a discussion of its creative process.

In keeping with *Reality Under Siege*, the title chosen by Skoglund for her mid-career retrospective, the title of *Walking on Eggshells* (a commission for the exhibition) is both literal and open-ended in meaning. After the tableau was assembled, a path was walked through the thousands of empty eggshells that make up its floor, thereby enacting the title of this work and ironically completing its creation with a destructive act. Performance, or at least the imprint of its aftermath, is a continuing aspect of Skoglund's work, dating from *Percussion for Jelly Beans and Gumdrops* of 1975 (page 34). In that performance piece, Skoglund used a broom for a paintbrush, sweeping spilled candies into different patterns and color combinations on the floor. Performance, with the artist as active agent or directing others, appears in a variety of ways throughout Skoglund's work, ranging from the endlessly repeated actions of the mechanized figures in the installations *Cocktail Party* (page 62) and *Atomic Love* (page 19), to the careful placing of Smith College students who volunteered to participate as models in the photoshoot for *Babies at Paradise Pond* (page 85). The path of broken eggshells more specifically recalls another trail left by the figures of a bride and groom in the installation *The Wedding* (page 2), whose sticky trip through yellow marmalade was documented in the installation photograph. The actual act of walking on eggshells produces a predictable and inescapable result, and, as the artist has said, helps to identify the flooring as eggshells rather than another, less fragile material. Walking on eggshells, however, is also an aphorism suggesting anxiety and careful attention in making one's way with conscious reference to the opportunities and threats presented by the environment.

As Carol Squiers observes in this catalogue, Skoglund's installations developed from early room environments such as *Spoons* (page 38) and *Hangers* (page 39), which were an outgrowth of the playful patterning evident in the artist's *Food Still Life* series of photographs (pages 49–53), to more sculptural and increasingly complex configurations. Although Skoglund's installations are developed for the camera eye—that is, for the vantage point of a stationary lens—they maintain their presence as separate and distinct works of art as well as being corollaries to the installation photographs based on them. Therefore, while they are the mise-en-scène for the photograph, the installations are not simply an artifact of the photographic process. In fact, the installation photographs often differ in subtle or marked ways from the installations themselves, reinforcing their separate but related identities.

The most obvious changes are the live figures often used for the photographs, which are replaced by mannequins in the installations as in *The Wedding* and *The Cocktail Party*, or are simply withdrawn. The installations can be enlarged or reconfigured when they are exhibited, creating variants on the compositions of their related photographs. There are sometimes dramatic reversals of palette between the installation and photograph: gray foxes cavort in a red restaurant interior in the *Fox Games* installation (page 14), but in the photograph, the foxes are red and the restaurant and all its furnishings are gray. In *The Wedding* installation photograph, the walls are strawberry red and the floors are yellow marmalade, as they were originally in the installation. Skoglund, however, decided to reverse the colors of the installation, after the photograph was completed, and the tableau now has floors made of strawberry jam and walls of marmalade dried into a kind of pliant cement on sectioned panels.

Skoglund's preservation of her sculptural tableaux as distinct works equal in artistic status with the photographs based on them is an unusual, if not unique, practice compared to the methods of other contemporary tableau artists. It differs from the photographic tableaux of an artist such as Jeff Wall, whose dramatic panoramas are ephemeral set pieces produced and shown as back-illuminated, gigantic color transparencies that approach the scale and grandeur of epic painting. In the work of other contemporary "directorial mode" photographers in this country and Europe, such as Laurie Simmons, Boyd Webb, Bernard Faucon, and David Levinthal, the tableaux of assembled and manipulated objects exist primarily for the production of the photographs.[1]

In some cases, Skoglund's installations have experienced a kind of organic death. In two installations from 1992, the finite existence of the tableaux was inevitable: *Spirituality in the Flesh* (page 47) incorporated uncooked, ground meat used for the background and the "flesh" of the seated mannequin; *Body Limits* (page 46) was made with strips of bacon wrapping the figures, furniture, wall, and floor. Attempts to save *Body Limits* with a protective coating proved impossible, and Skoglund's initial hope of refrigerating (and thereby saving) *Spirituality in the Flesh* was given up as impractical. Threats to other installations,

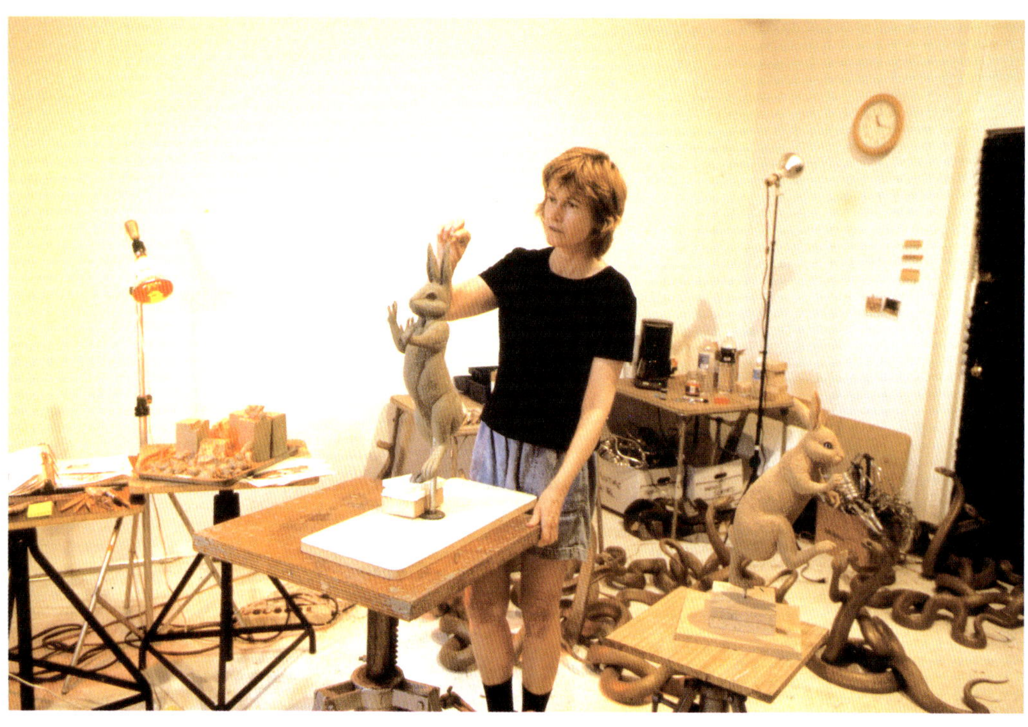

The artist sculpts a rabbit for *Walking on Eggshells.*

such as the moth hatch that burst the raisins covering the floor, walls, and mechanized mannequins in *Atomic Love* (page 19) were unanticipated. Not surprisingly, the insect plague altered the appearance of this tour de force, almost pointillistic rendering of surface patterning that shifted and reconfigured as the mechanical figures moved. While this installation is no longer completely preserved, Skoglund's assistants have painstakingly revived some of the objects from the tableau by replacing the raisins and coating them with sealant. Other preservation attempts have been more successful: the floors and walls of *The Wedding* were saved by drying, and the cheese puffs covering the surfaces and sculpture of the *Cocktail Party* installation, while not subject to decay, were frangible and were reinforced to prevent crushing.

As Skoglund has said, the confrontation with mortality in *Spirituality in the Flesh* was forestalled or arrested in the photograph, but played out in the actual encounter with the materials, which quickly decomposed as she worked.[2] Food, ranging from its most basic form as flesh or vegetable matter to the highly processed, Day-Glo artificiality of a popular brand of cheese-flavored snack, is a recurring motif in Skoglund's work, both as subject and medium. She is among a number of contemporary

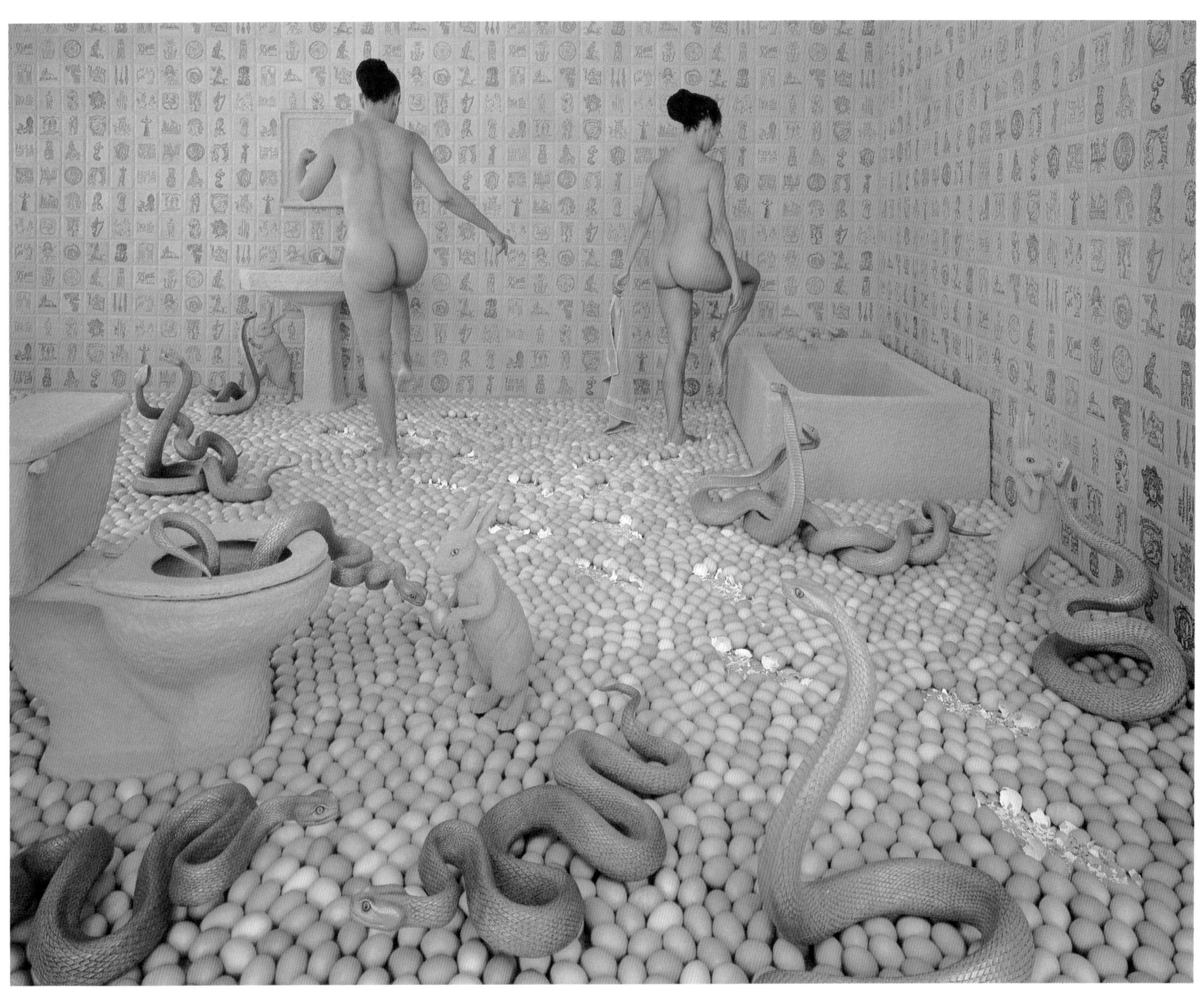

Walking on Eggshells (photograph), 1997 (cat. 46)

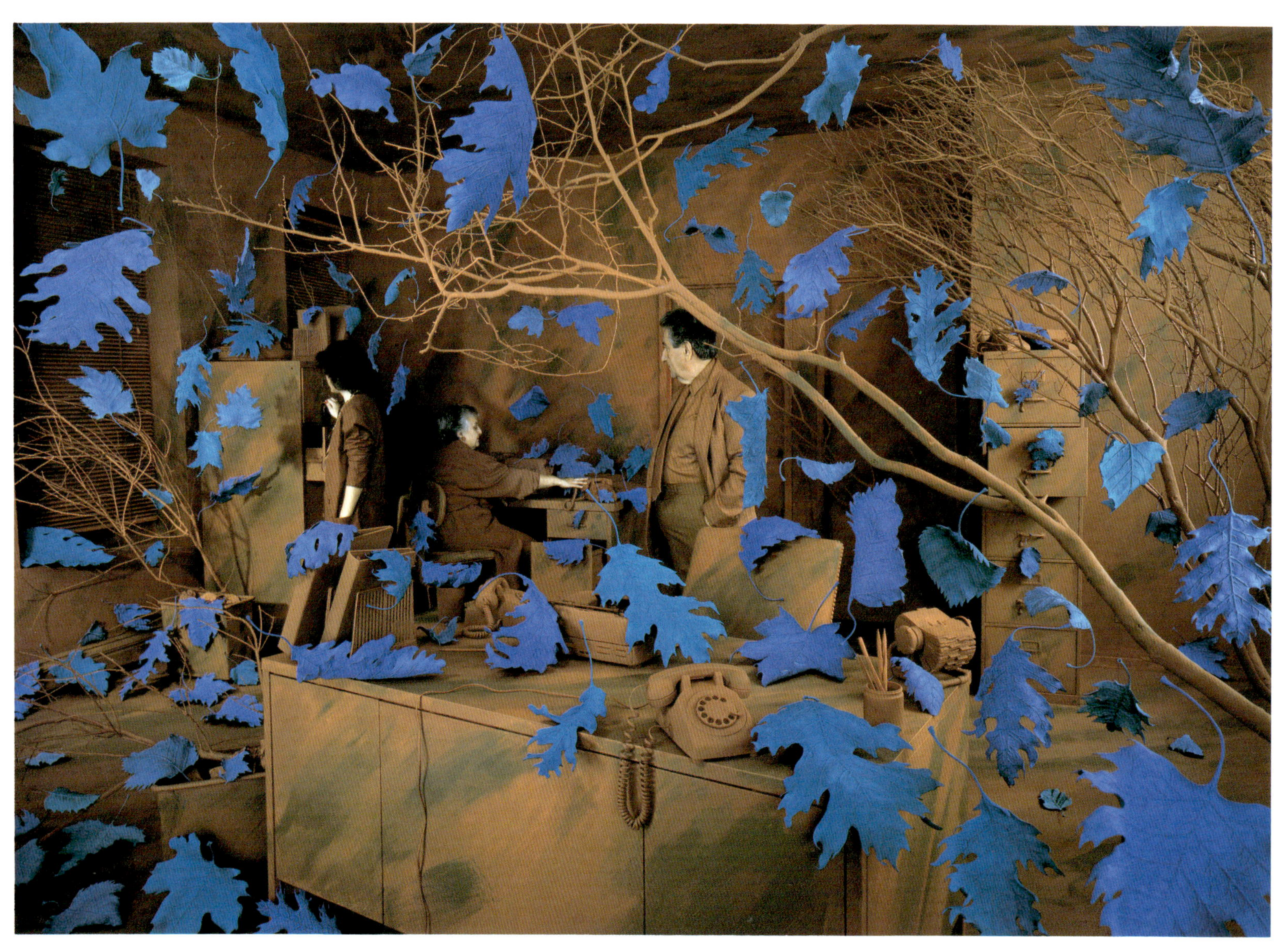

A Breeze at Work, 1987 (cat. 34)

artists who have used food as an art material, among them Janine Antoni, whose *Chocolate Gnaw* of 1992 is a weighty monolith of chocolate and lard shaped by biting. Others, like Skoglund, have converted frosting, jam, and raisins into the stuff of art.[3] Skoglund's use of food, however, plays out grander themes of apotheosis and apocalypse. Food attains a kind of immortality in her 1978 photographic *Food Still Life* series, which parodies commercial advertising's false promises of the impossible perfection of its wares, and becomes an active and sometimes self-destructive agent when used as an artist's material in the installations.

Skoglund's efforts to preserve the organic or food-based installations, and her sometimes heroic salvage efforts, serve two ends: the continued existence of the sculptural installation as a work of art and the artist's existential grappling with the forces of entropy and decay. This confrontation, an effort to prevent "disappearance," which Skoglund equates with death,[4] takes place on a physical level during the creative and production process, but it is also mirrored in thematic concerns with consuming—whether of food, popular culture, or life itself. In *Walking on Eggshells*, the eggs have the dual association as "absent food" (in the form of the natural but empty containers left behind) and, as a symbol of fecundity, potential life. Her inclusion of snake and rabbit sculptures in the installation also carries connotations of food and death in the sometimes predator/prey relationship of these animals in nature. As well as being egg layers themselves, some species of snakes prey on birds' nests for eggs.

Skoglund invests time and labor in coming to terms with, if not overcoming, the properties of her materials, many of which are deliberately chosen for what she terms their "inappropriateness." The artist cast the leaves in *A Breeze at Work* (opposite) in bronze and fashioned the roses studding the surfaces of *The Wedding* from silver-glazed high-fired clay, reversing their identity as fragile ephemera by endowing them with inorganic permanence. To emphasize the contradiction, Skoglund suspended the bronze leaves in the air, as though they had been casually lofted by a breeze and scattered through the interior of an office space. Likewise, fragile, biodegradable materials are put to antithetical use as durable goods: foodstuffs become architectural materials or clothing fabrics in various installations. The hard is made to look soft, the soft is made hard. Extending beyond trompe l'oeil, the installations reverse and confound expectations on many different levels, including the basic way we come to know the world by touch, experience, and association. The tableaux draw us in by constructing an environment that is both familiar and disturbingly out of sync: a living room, albeit one carpeted in artificial grass and inhabited by purple dogs (*The Green House*, page 23); a bedroom, which becomes a bowl of giant goldfish (*Revenge of the Goldfish*, page 42); a bathroom, but one made of paper and eggs, where blue-eyed snakes slither and rabbits boldly challenge them (*Walking on Eggshells*).

Skoglund's brand of hybridization situates her work not only in relation to a relatively brief tradition of artists who stage scenes for the camera, with roots in Victorian photographic *tableaux vivants*,[5] but also within a much longer art-historical and pancultural tradition of placing sculptural objects in narrative contexts or associative relationships. In its broadest interpretation this includes a variety of expressions: from multifigured mythological scenes on Greek pediments to Chinese temple Buddhas surrounded by bodhisattvas and lohans; from the saints, angels, and apostles arrayed on the portals and façades of French Gothic cathedrals to the gods, chacmools, and skulls of Aztec temples. The ability of sculpture to concretize ideas has allowed it to become the "objective correlative" or physical expression of verbal or literary narratives in a uniquely different way than painting or drawing. Because it is three-dimensional, it occupies and shares human space; it has presence and location. Whether symbolic or an actualization of a concept, entity, or religious formulation, it enters our world and our plane of existence.

Ancestral to Skoglund's sculptural installations are European *presepios* or *crèche* tableaux, which grouped highly realistic figural sculptures, sometimes dressed in actual clothing, in a Nativity scene. These tableaux, especially those of seventeenth-century

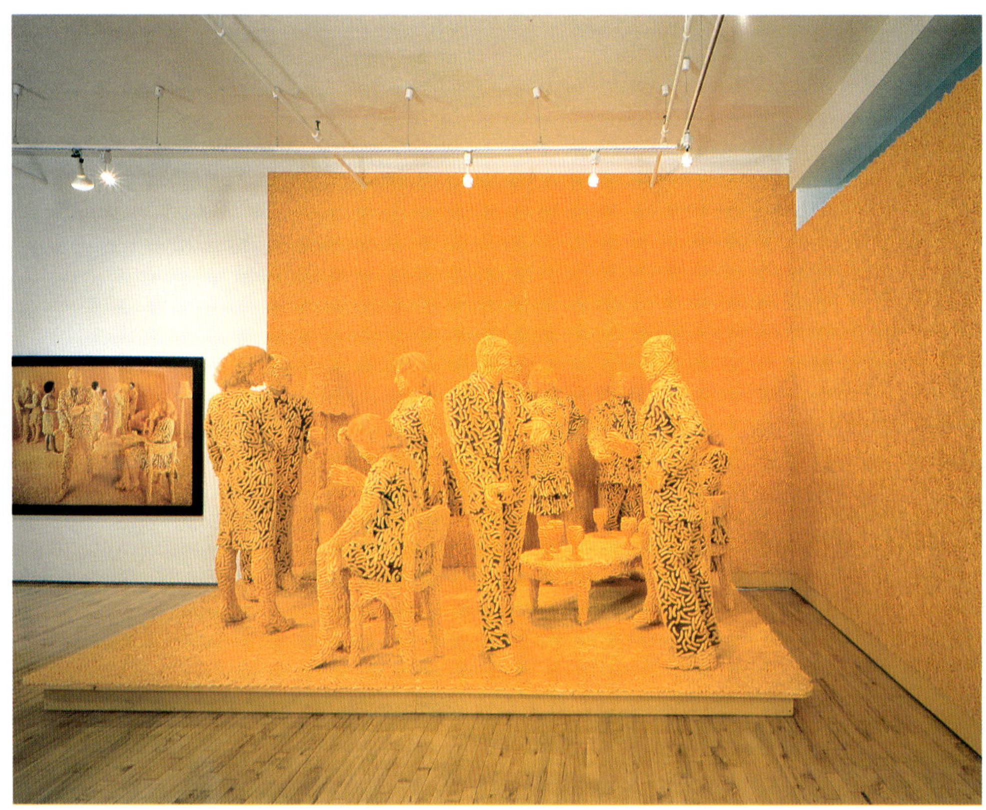

The Cocktail Party (installation at Janet Borden Gallery), 1992 (cat. 42)

Naples, portrayed the otherworldly in convincingly concrete terms for an audience with a shared belief system, a didactic strategy common to much religious art. This is fundamentally different from the postmodern tactics of Skoglund's installations, in which meaning is assembled by the viewer rather than prescribed by authority. In place of a church or temple in which sculpture is displayed and understood as a system of religious signs or symbols, Skoglund's domain is the middle-class home and its various rooms, where household objects, people, and especially animals are sometimes portrayed with exacting but off-kilter verisimilitude in baffling, or at least unexplained, relationships. In her installations, popular culture and fast food are the common glue replacing religion or any other kind of commonly held philosophy. As will be discussed later, *Walking on Eggshells* underscores this rupture by including a lexicon of forty-five images drawn from art history, icons changing in a chronological development from a past rich with meaning to a present in which meaning is diffused.

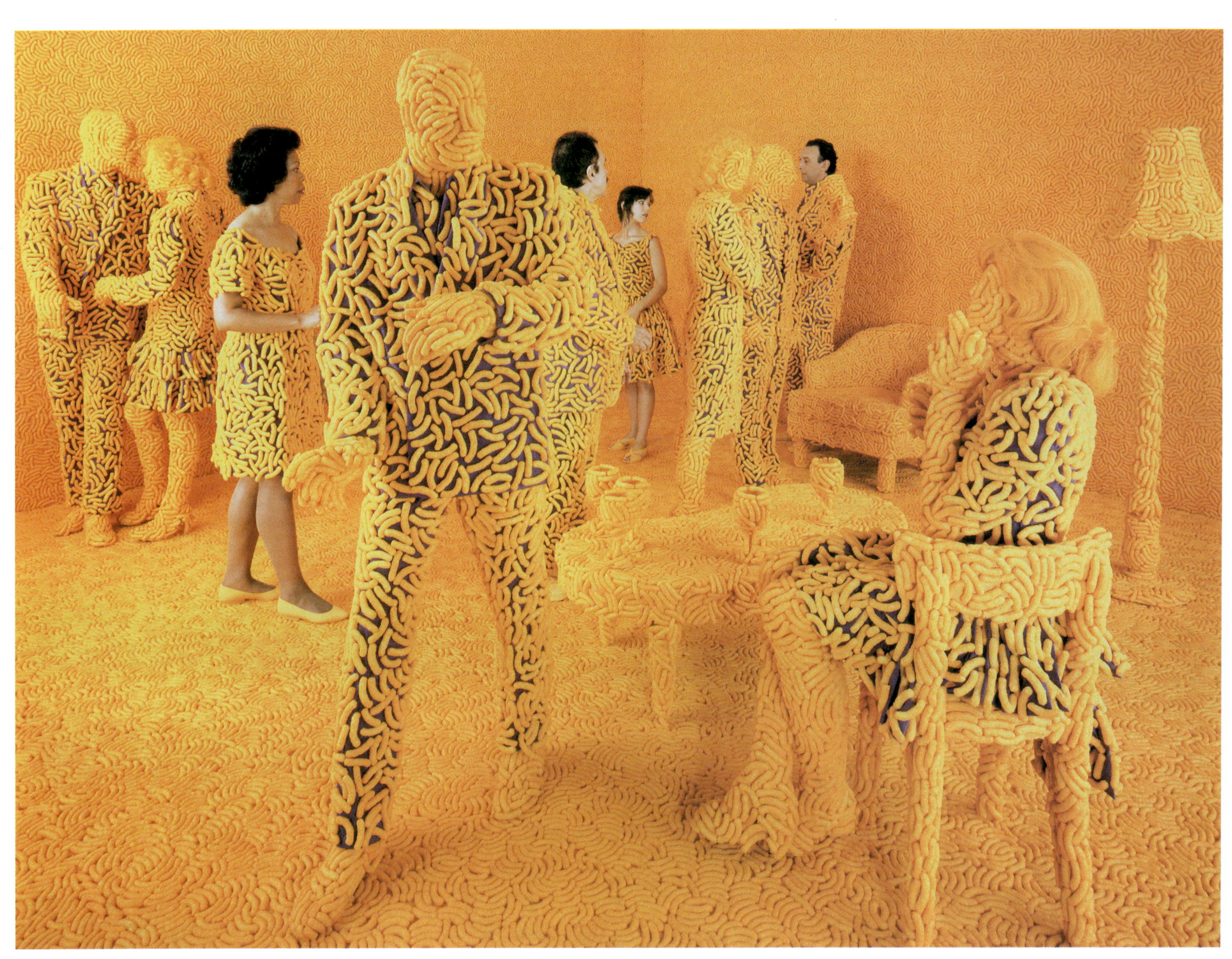

The Cocktail Party (photograph), 1992 (cat. 43)

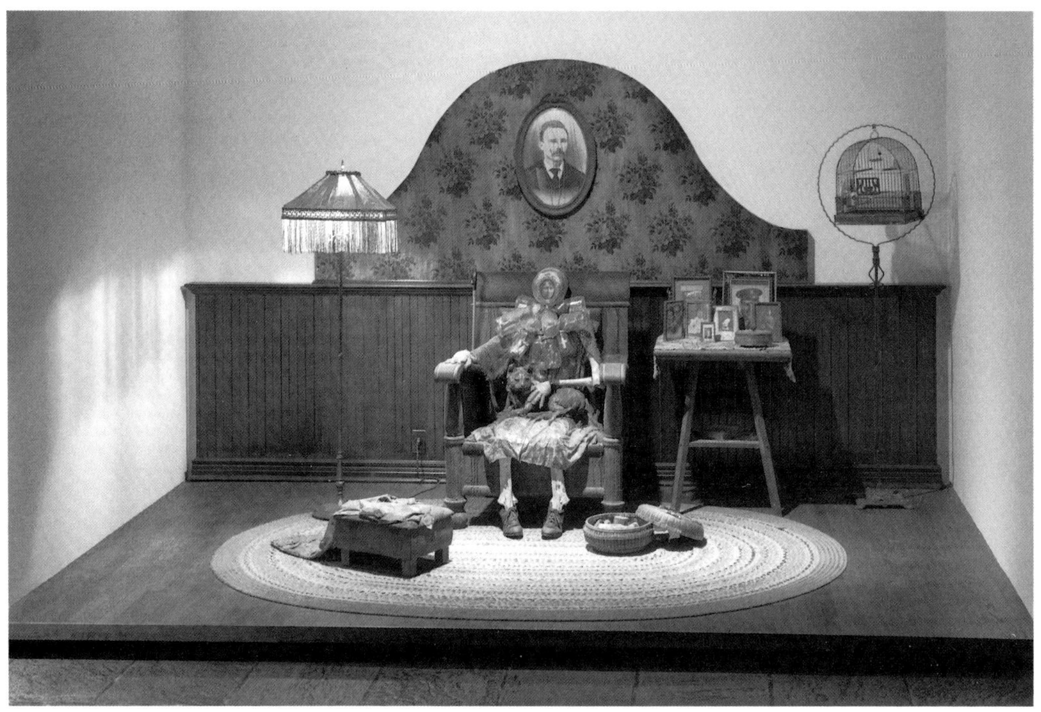

Edward Kienholz. *The Wait*, 1964–65. Courtesy Whitney Museum of American Art, New York, Gift of Howard and Jean Lipman Foundation, Inc.

Antecedents for Skoglund's installations can be seen in the environments created by the Surrealists in the first half of the twentieth century, for example, in the corridor of mannequins and "grotto" with beds, brazier, and leaf-covered carpet assembled by various artists for the International Surrealist Exhibition of 1938 in Paris.[6] The Surrealists' ventures into popular culture and commerce, particularly fashion, have resonance with Skoglund's work as well. *Narcissus White*, the quickly dismantled window display created by Dalí for Bonwit Teller's in 1939, included a wool-lined bathtub, mannequins, and bedroom furniture,[7] elements later echoed in *Revenge of the Goldfish* and *Walking on Eggshells*. Skoglund herself has mounted a store window display. Commissioned with a number of other artists to create Christmas windows for Barneys in New York, Skoglund conceived her *Sock Situation* installation (page 26) with a holiday-appropriate palette: red socks festooned a green kitchen in which three tuxedoed department-store mannequins posed, one of them tidying the space with a vacuum cleaner.[8]

Because Skoglund's installations have often been described as dreamscapes or explorations of the unconscious, the adjective "surrealist" has sometimes been applied to her work. Although Skoglund herself is uncomfortable with this characterization, she acknowledges a historical debt to surrealism and dadaism. Marcel Duchamp's notorious *Fountain*, the urinal that caused a furor when it was submitted to the American Society of Independent Artists exhibition in 1917, is an inescapable reference for the bathroom fixtures of *Walking on Eggshells* (and like Skoglund's installation work, it had its own photographic corol-

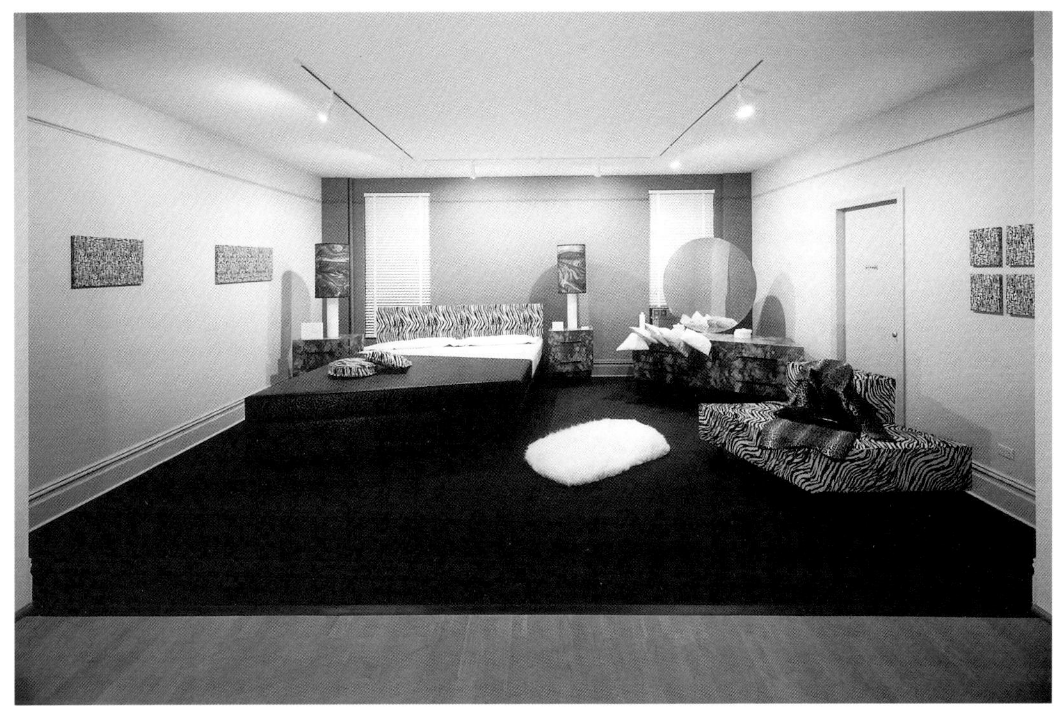

Claes Oldenburg. *Bedroom Ensemble, Replica 1*, 1969. Museum für Moderne Kunst, Frankfurt, courtesy Claes Oldenburg and Coosje van Bruggen

lary in a photograph by Alfred Stieglitz).[9] The influence of Duchamp's "readymades," objects from hardware stores and shops appropriated and displayed as art, can be seen in Skoglund's tableaux in the use of prefabricated items or found objects; in Skoglund's case, however, the early installations that consisted mainly of "readymades" such as hangers and spoons, were later succeeded by installations that combined her own sculptures—cats (*Radioactive Cats*), foxes (*Fox Games*), dogs (*The Green House*), babies (*Maybe Babies*, page 83) and squirrels (*Gathering Paradise*, page 67)—with prefabricated props and furniture.

Skoglund's combination of sculpture and objects was anticipated by the assemblage and tableau works of the 1960s, such as those of Edward Kienholz and Nancy Reddin Kienholz, artists whom Skoglund admires. Edward Kienholz's tableaux, such as *The Beanery*, a replication of a West Hollywood dive filled with its down-and-out clientele, and *The Wait* (page 64), a dust-encrusted figure of an elderly woman in her living room, have been described as "soiled arenas," characterized by claustrophobia and despair.[10] These grittily authentic environments often include life-cast figures, adding to their disturbing sense of hyperbolic reality. Skoglund's tableaux also make use of mimesis, but to different effect. Her sculptures (usually animals, but also human babies) are handmade and then cast from molds, rather than cast from life. Studied minutely in photographs and articles, her sculptural versions of animals reconfigure aspects from different breeds or types to create convincingly realistic creatures, which are then dissociated from nature by their color, by their unnatural multiplication (a herd of chihuahuas, basset hounds, and other dogs, a flock of squirrels), or by their invasion of human space (foxes prowling in a restaurant, snakes and rabbits populating a bathroom).

While many of Kienholz's interiors permit the anxious identification of the viewer with the depressing circumstances of the figures that inhabit them (and some, like *The Beanery*, allow the viewer to enter and become part of the claustrophobic space), Skoglund's environments are placed at a remove from everyday experience by their heightened, limited palette and use of inappropriate materials.[11] The projection of the viewer into the space of a Skoglund installation is therefore less direct and at the same time more complex, because the familiar is confirmed and contradicted at the same time. The installations evoke antithetical responses—humor and anxiety, recognition and disorientation—and viewers impose their own meanings on the work. These interpretations may be entirely unintended by the artist but she considers them no less valid than her own thoughts and ideas. (*Maybe Babies*, for example, has been interpreted as a statement on abortion.)[12]

It is Kienholz's use of domestic interiors, and those of George Segal, Claes Oldenburg, and other pop artists of the 1960s, however, that present a more immediate precedent for Skoglund's rooms. Kienholz's *In the Eleventh Hour Final* (1968) exactly reconstructs a living room, with the addition of the Vietnam casualty count on its television screen and a *TV Guide* on the coffee table (updated with a new issue for each showing).[13] Lucas Samaras and Claes Oldenburg both re-created bedrooms, in Samaras's case his own bedroom in New Jersey. Oldenburg's *Bedroom Ensemble, Replica I*, of 1969, (page 65) was based on a motel called Las Tunas Isles near Malibu, whose suites were decorated with animal skins.[14] Oldenburg's stated desire to "make the house" led him to create his *Bathroom* objects (1965–66), consisting of hard and soft sculptures of a tub, washstand, toilet, and scale.[15] The bathroom as subject was also treated by George Segal, in his *Woman Shaving Her Leg* of 1963, which places a plaster life-cast figure inside a real tub surrounded by real tiles, and by other pop artists including Roy Lichtenstein, Tom Wesselmann, and Jim Dine.[16] Although pop strategies differ from those of postmodernism, pop's elevation of the mundane, represented by the most intimate of living spaces in the American domestic landscape, looks forward to *Walking on Eggshells*.

While precedents for Skoglund's most recent installation can be traced within the grand arc of twentieth-century art, the particular history of *Walking on Eggshells* represents new departures and innovations, as well as revisitations, of her own work. From its inception as a collection of word associations and visual ideas, jotted as sketches in the artist's notebook, *Walking on Eggshells* took a circuitous path, beginning with an idea to combine a birthday party theme and a pink palette with the viscous, indefinable green of Vaseline. In service of this idea, many small, plastic babies (sold in stores as party favors) were purchased and sewn onto bright blue fabric. This early formulation was superseded by an entirely different thought, to create an installation with sculptures of monkeys disporting themselves in a laundromat setting. This was set aside when eggs and eggshells came to mind, as she said, "in a flash," along with the phrase "walking on eggshells," which became the installation's title.[17] She envisioned the eggs as thousands of "units" arranged on the floor, which might deceptively resemble cobblestones in their numbers and uniformity. They would be identifiable to the viewer as eggshells by their breakage; their various shades of brown would determine the palette of the installation and, she hoped, would impart a sepia tonality to the installation photograph.

Next came the idea to use snakes and rabbits in the installation. At first, Skoglund experimented with copper- and gold-leafing actual, freeze-dried rattlesnakes, ordered through a catalogue company. Subsequently, however, she decided to sculpt and cold-cast her own snake sculptures, not only for aesthetic reasons but also because of her concern that using real reptiles presented animal-cruelty issues. Many photographs of snakes and rabbits were pinned to her studio wall during this research period. The snake sculptures, with their triangular, rattlesnake heads, became a

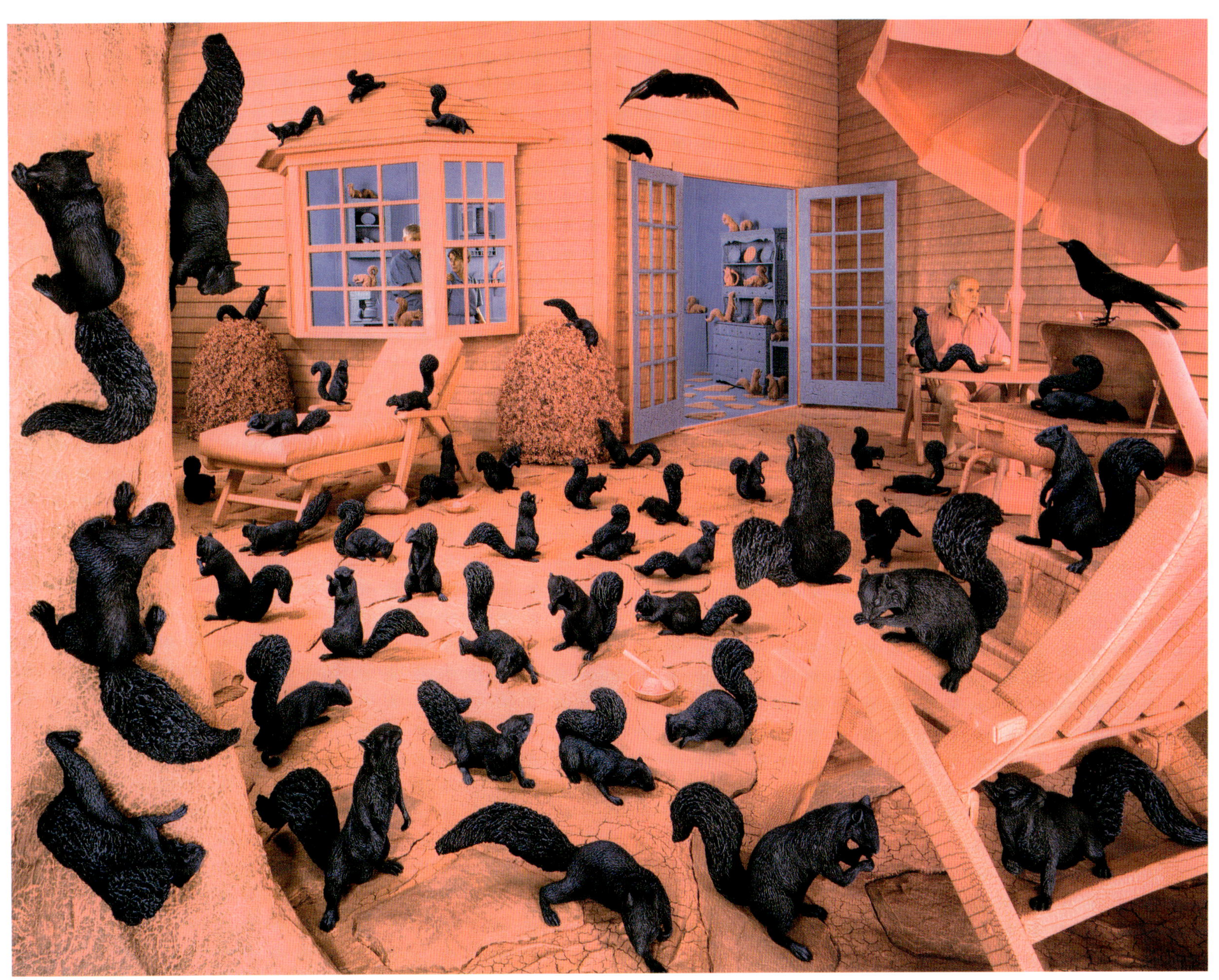

Gathering Paradise, 1991 (cat. 38)

cross between different species, and the rabbits became a hybrid of hares and bunnies.

In developing the new installation, Skoglund wanted her snakes to relate to each other in a naturalistic way—hence the pairing of male snakes "sparring," a behavior associated with competition for mating rights. She also planned that the snakes would interact with the rabbits in some way.[18] Skoglund had earlier made rabbit sculptures, which she animated and covered with the same cheese-puff snacks that would be used in the *Cocktail Party*, for her contribution to the group exhibition called *Putt Modernism* in 1992.[19] Those cartoon bunnies, with their big, balloonlike heads were the forerunners of the more realistic, feisty rabbits with human hands in *Walking on Eggshells*.

For the animal sculptures in *Eggshells*, Skoglund consulted taxidermy catalogues to order a variety of glass eyes, which were spread in an unsettling mix on a table in her studio while she made her final color selection. She chose blue irises, which were identified in the catalogue as "Siamese cat" eyes, for both the reptiles and rabbits. The eyes would provide startling pinpoints of color contrast in the installation. Curiously, the blue eyes rendered the handsome, calligraphically sinuous snakes less dangerous in aspect, while the first rabbit sculptures developed a somewhat baleful blue stare.

According to Skoglund, the bathroom was chosen as a setting for this tableau because this was a domestic interior she had not previously treated as a subject; it was also a "specific" room, in terms of function and objects, and was associated with a ritual activity.[20] The privacy issues related to this particular household space—reinforced by the usual inclusion of a locking door—are equaled only by the bedroom. The most banal physical aspects of plumbing, tiles, and porcelain still connote intimate bodily functions: the act of seeing another in this setting—of viewing a bathing ritual—is charged with elements of voyeurism and taboo. While some cultures have embraced public bathing, there is an opposed tradition in mythology, literature, and the visual arts in which the bath becomes a gendered space, an erotic theater where women in various states of undress are observed by men. Of the many examples that could be cited are the stories and images associated with Artemis and Actaeon, David and Bathsheba, and Susanna and the Elders. There is a nearly endless list of images by male artists depicting the female form exposed by the act of bathing, in which the artist and the viewer of the artwork become the unobserved observers outside the frame: in western European art, these include Boucher's Rococo pink bacchantes, the voluptuous harem nudes of the nineteenth century, and the intimate bathing scenes of Degas and Bonnard.

Skoglund had originally thought that she would include two life-cast figures in her tableau in order to explore ideals of beauty; however, a paired male and female in combination with snakes coiling at their feet would inevitably evoke Edenic associations of Temptation and Original Sin. In staging the installation photograph, she planned to use only one figure, a female model whose skin tones matched well with the overall palette of the installation, and who would be shown nude and seen from behind as she crushed a path through the eggshells. Always pragmatic, Skoglund had also employed an understudy for the first model, but then realized that the two women were very similar in appearance and could both be used for the installation photograph. This doubling not only adds another visual element but raises questions about the paired relationship of the women: are they twins or possibly sisters, and why do they share this private space together? As one figure approaches the sink and the other the bathtub, they seem oblivious to the animal life roiling near their feet. The implicit vulnerability of their exposed bodies, in combination with the twining, rearing snakes creates an erotic subtext that is charged with a volatile but ambiguous mix of sensuality and danger.

If Skoglund's use of perishables in *Spirituality in the Flesh* and *Body Limits* pushed the boundaries of inappropriate materials, her decision to create the bathroom appliances from cast paper in *Walking on Eggshells* represents a different, but equally intractable, extreme. Created from plaster and rubber molds taken from actual fixtures and then reworked, Skoglund's cast-paper sculptures required extensive labor and the technical expertise of Dieu Donné Papermill (New York City) to achieve two intact versions of each fixture (one for the installation, the second as insurance). Replacing porcelain in an environment normally associated with water, the cast paper drains, faucets, bathtub, sink, and toilet belie their relative fragility (as well as their vulnerability to water) by being made to resemble a kind of rough, heavily textured terracotta. Skoglund originally intended to use ceramic wall tiles in the background, but rejected them as "too appropriate." She then toyed with the idea of casting soap for the walls, but went forward instead with making cast paper tiles of the same texture and color as the other fixtures. Finding that she was dissatisfied with their appearance, Skoglund determined that the tiles should be made individually, taking this opportunity to give the work another dimension and direction that was entirely new in her career. Amplifying the possibilities already presented by her sculptures, she eventually created a series of forty-five cast-paper, relief-printed tiles with images of snakes and rabbits drawn from the history of art and popular culture. These are arranged chronologically, from the earliest, a snake motif after an Egyptian gold pectoral from the twelfth dynasty, to the latest, an Easter bunny seated on an egg throne from a contemporary mail-order catalogue. The series repeats on the walls of the installation in blocks of five vertical columns of nine tiles. The first block begins at the upper left corner and is read down each column. The next block of forty-five images begins at the bottom of the column and is read upward (page 73).

The inclusion of the tiles, printed with Skoglund's line drawings after well-known and obscure historical images of snakes and rabbits, resituates the installation in time. The walls, dense with images, become a visual text of icons related to a variety of narratives and cosmologies of meaning. In researching a vast pictorial store, Skoglund made selections from Minoan, Egyptian, Mesoamerican, western European, African, Asian, Near Eastern, American, and Native American sources. Her search was an outgrowth of her study of the natural behavior and appearance of snakes and rabbits for her sculptures, but it expanded to include a timeline of the changing ways in which animals have been represented in relation to human culture. Skoglund has long believed that contemporary life is divorced from the "original essence" and that religion and the social sciences were created, in part, to repair a separation from the natural world.[21] While her concept for the tiles was being developed, Skoglund was reading Mircea Eliade's *A History of Religious Ideas*.[22] Although she said it was a coincidental choice at the time, the book surely had an effect on the artist's process of assimilating not only images but ideas for the tiles, especially in terms of the syncretic nature of early religions and their incorporation of animals as deities, intercessors, and powerful symbols.

A guiding principle during this time was Skoglund's hypothesis that the spiritual power of paganism and early religions had been diluted over time, going underground to resurface in enervated forms in contemporary popular culture. Animals, anciently invoked as deities and revered in religious rites, have become cartoons in the denatured zoo of television and the media, prized as pets for their very helplessness. Skoglund's succession of tile images reveals a progression in the ways in which two particular animals, the snake and the rabbit, have been reconceptualized over time from signs, symbols, and other powerful agents affecting human lives. In the case of the snake, the vestiges of its demonization as evil remain (for example, from Christian embodiments of Satan as a serpent), as well as a generalized fear or repugnance for its imagined texture and slippery feel. Rabbits have undergone an equally ignominious transformation by "cutefication" (a term coined by the artist) as the Easter bunny. Both characterizations can be seen as inversions of roles originally ascribed to these animals, or at least as the reduction of a potent image through commercialization (the bunny as the purveyor of Easter holiday products) or by a gradual slide into irrelevance (the sideshow of annual rattlesnake roundups and trophy trading in Texas).

Serpents have a symbolic tradition associated with fertility, both phallic and feminine, with regeneration, and, as signs of earthly and divine kingship, with power. Skoglund's tile images of snakes include a number of pictorial quotations from the Egyptian *Book of the Dead*, the generic name given to papyrus sheets with vignettes and magical texts or spells that were intended to facilitate the passage of the dead through the underworld to attain afterlife in the Field of Reeds (tiles 4–6, 9–11).[23] Tile 9 represents a vignette from Spell 182, in which protective deities hold snakes, symbols of regeneration, in a pictorial register below the mummy of the deceased. Spell 87 (tile 5) shows the *Sa-Ta* snake walking on human legs, a vignette accompanying the text for a spell for becoming transformed into a snake: "I am a long-lived snake. . . . I pass the night and am reborn, renewed and rejuvenated every day."[24] In addition to their regenerative properities, serpents were associated with a number of deities in the Egyptian pantheon, including Apophis, the cosmic evil serpent who seeks to prevent the progress of the sun-boat (tile 11).[25] The rearing cobra is a manifestation of Hathor, a fiery female solar deity and serpent goddess, who also has the ability to alter her shape to become a cow (tile 1, in which Hathor is shown suckling Amenemhet III, with serpents coiling downward from a sun disc and another surmounting the cartouche on the cow's back). Hathor-Sekhmet is also associated with royal power in the guise of the cobra rearing with hood flared above the brow of Egypt's rulers (tile 3, limestone-relief profiles of Pharoah Akhenaten and Queen Nefertiti). This association of the feminine principle with serpent power is also reflected in other early cultures: by the Minoan Snake Priestess (tile 2), who brandishes snakes in each hand, and the Gorgon Medusa, who turned to stone all those who dared to look upon her face, crowned by coiling serpents (tile 13, from a detail from the west pediment of the Temple of Artemis at Corfu, and tile 34, a seventeenth-century marble by Bernini).

The ability of some snakes to climb is reflected in various mythologies or religions and in imagery pairing snakes with trees. This is exemplified in Skoglund's wall by tile 8, based on an Egyptian tomb painting of a long-eared tomcat attacking the serpent Apophis at the base of the sacred *ished* tree of Heliopolis (an allegory of light overcoming darkness),[26] and by Christian imagery associated with the Fall of Adam and Eve (tiles 21, 26, and 28). However, it is the chthonic association of snakes with the earth and the underworld that created elemental symbolic links of the serpent with agriculture and fertility. The Etruscan deity Tages (tile 14), with his snaking, phallic legs and childlike appearance, was said to have appeared in a newly plowed furrow outside Tarquinia, where he emerged to make prophecies.[27] The Aztec emblem of Quetzalcoatl (tile 24), the feathered serpent, signifies the fruitful earth and agricultural fertility as well as recalling the Toltec ruler Quetzalcoatl, represented in tile 31 seated on a litter or throne with serpent ornaments, from an early colonial manuscript from Mexico.[28] In Indian mythology, serpent kings and queens (Nāgas) were associated with water and the moon and were portrayed as a combination of human form and the body of a snake (tile 19). Symbolic of birth, death, and the cyclical nature of the universe, they also signified the act of sexual union.[29] An image from a medieval English manuscript (tile 22) warned of the danger of unbridled sexual desire in the form of mating adders and their young.[30] This appears to be a version of the *Uroboros*, the snake coiled and feeding upon its own tail, a symbol in a number of early cultures for the birth/death cycle and infinity.

Christian formulations of the serpent reinterpreted the relation of snakes to humankind, and especially in relation to the concept of Original Sin, which now became linked with female frailty and sexual depravity (tiles 21, 26, and 28). In the temptation of Adam and Eve depicted in Masolino's Brancacci Chapel fresco of about 1425 in Santa Maria del Carmine (tile 26), as well as in Michelangelo's Sistine Chapel ceiling fresco (tile 28), the serpent that offers the forbidden fruit coils up the Tree of Wisdom, but is personified as a woman with a distinctly human face. William Blake's Eve (tile 36), entwined in an almost sexual embrace by the serpent's coils, takes the apple directly from its mouth in his watercolor *The Temptation and Fall of Eve* of about 1800–1803, one of twelve illustrations for Milton's *Paradise Lost.* This formulation foreshadows later nineteenth-century images of women as sexual temptresses. Associated with Lamia, the serpent goddess, and Lilith, Adam's first mate, women in lubricious fin-de-siècle paintings and sculpture were portrayed in almost bestial relation with snakes and other animals.[31]

Tellingly, Skoglund's wall has no modern images of snakes from any cultures other than those on the African continent (tiles 40–43). In various African nations, pythons and adders are often used as architectural elements (as in tile 43, a palace door with snake carvings) and are also represented in masks. Tile 42 combines images made after the Bwa masks of Burkina Faso, which are fourteen- to sixteen-foot-long constructions worn by young men and danced during dry-season ceremonies, funerals, and for rites of passage.[32] These images are still-potent survivals of ancient cults and snake deities, which have no real parallel or compelling presence in modern western European and American cultures.

On the other hand, Skoglund's contemporary images of rabbits tell a different story. Following the artist's chronology, but this time in reverse order, the most recent images of rabbits she has included are the Easter bunny (tiles 44 and 45). This personification of the rabbit as a cuddly creature that delivers colored eggs to human children each year has its faraway origins in the ancient (and persistent) symbolism associated with abundant fertility and with pagan and Christian celebrations of spring. Pairing the rabbit with an egg, however, seems to be a conflation of two different kinds of fecundity (or at least two different kinds of procreation). This otherwise illogical union becomes routine, transformed by popular culture, which casts the bunny as the symbol and salesman of a yearly celebration welcoming warm weather.

The rabbit family is also made familiar as a kind of tamed and ordered animal analogy to the human family, illustrated on Skoglund's wall by the happy bunny parents and children in tile 44. The same kind of equation is reflected in popular stories and moral tales such as Beatrix Potter's *Adventures of Peter Rabbit,* in which naughty Peter disobeys his mother by entering the forbidden garden of Mr. McGregor (a latter-day retelling of the biblical story of Temptation and Original Sin). Other fables anthropomorphize the rabbit, but this time as a wily trickster outwitting other larger animals. Brer Rabbit from the African-American *Tales of Uncle Remus* always successfully outfoxes Brer Fox in the end, and Bugs Bunny is the modern cartoon equivalent of the legendary trickster. In the Native American tradition, the rabbit is a clever hero that takes on and overcomes animals as large as a bear. In *The Flint Bear and Rabbit* (tile 39), from Marie L. McLaughlin's *Myths and Legends of the Sioux,*[33] the Rabbit approaches the Flint Bear, a creature half animal and half stone, to replenish his store of flint for arrowheads. Invited to chip away ever larger pieces, the Rabbit splits the Flint Bear in half and flees, chased by angry bears. The Rabbit calls for snow, and when a great storm blows up, his heavy pursuers are caught in the drifts. Because of his small size and quick feet, he is able to dispatch his enemies one by one with his club.

As a Christian symbol, the rabbit or white hare is associated with the Virgin's chaste fecundity. White hares are shown playing at the feet of the Madonna in Albrecht Dürer's woodcut *The Holy Family with Three Hares* of 1497–98 (tile 27). A ring of three chasing rabbits, with their ears conjoined to form a triangle, symbolizes the Holy Trinity in a window dating from the early sixteenth century from Paderborn Cathedral in Germany (tile 23).[34] In another unusual use as a Christian symbol, the rabbit is celebrated as a metaphor for unwavering faith: its speed and shorter forelegs allow the rabbit to outrun its pursuers more easily by taking the difficult uphill path(tile 35).[35] This appears in an engraving entitled *Ardua Facilius* from *Symbolographia,* an early eighteenth-century book of emblems by Jacobus Boschius.

In China, the rabbit or hare is the fourth sign of the ancient zodiac, a yin animal with lunar associations (tile 20). The rabbit also had lunar associations in Mesoamerica, where it was believed that the moon, personified as a female deity, was inhabited by a rabbit. An Aztec jadeite sculpture of a rabbit with a helmeted man's head emerging from its belly, of 1350–1521 (tile 25), may refer to birth and death cycles or a victim captured in battle. In addition, rabbits were also associated with the gods of drunkenness.[36] In Egyptian art, the rabbit was a standard phonetic sign and was also a valued food, depicted on tomb paintings being held by the ears as an offering for the funerary banquet. Rabbit or Cape hare amulets (tile 15) were worn in life to endow the wearer with fertility; in death, they were included in tombs as a symbol of rebirth and regeneration.[37] As a sacred animal, the rabbit was associated with the Goddess Wenut of Hermopolis in Middle Egypt (tile 12). Tile 12 unites the serpent and rabbit motif: the rabbit, symbolizing Wenut and the district of Hermopolis, is encircled by the Cosmic Serpent, anciently associated with the city before the appearance of light. During this time, the eight creation genies with heads of frogs and serpents swam together and formed the primeval egg, from which the bird of light emerged and set into motion the beginning of time.[38] With this pictogram, Skoglund brings the many meanings of the tiles and their images full circle, back to a primal myth of creation.

In keeping with Skoglund's own description of her work, *Walking on Eggshells* accomplishes a "deliberate proliferation and excess towards a dizzying, spectacular visual end."[39] With ties to the ancient and natural worlds and a foothold in the present, *Eggshells* enters the supratime of mythology and simultaneously occupies the fleeting contemporary moment, widely expanding the narrative scope of Skoglund's previous installations. For the artist, the installation has returned her to an early course of study, art history, and the exhibition *Reality Under Siege* has brought her back to the site of her beginnings as an artist at Smith College. Creation, both as primal fecundity and as artistic conception, are basic to this work and to Skoglund's longer and continuing endeavors: *Walking on Eggshells* represents Skoglund's valedictory and fertile ground for the rest of her career.

WALKING ON EGGSHELLS: TILE KEY

1. *Hathor Suckling 12th Dynasty Ruler Amenemhet III,* after a motif from an Egyptian gold pectoral, c. 1991–1783 B.C.E. (Beirut Museum)
2. *Minoan Snake Goddess or Priestess,* after a faience sculpture from Knossos, Crete, c. 1500 B.C.E. (Archaeological Museum, Heraklion, Crete)
3. *Pharaoh Akhenaten and Queen Nefertiti,* after an Egyptian limestone relief, latter part of the reign of Akhenaten, c. 1352–1336 B.C.E. (The Brooklyn Museum)
4. *Egyptian Book of the Dead, Spell 37:* Nakht warding off songstress-snakes, after a vignette from the funerary papyrus of the royal scribe and chief military officer, Nakht, 18th–19th dynasty, c. 1550–1307 B.C.E. (The British Museum, London)
5. *Egyptian Book of the Dead, Spells 87 and 88:* Sa-Ta snake and crocodile god Sobk, after a vignette from the funerary papyrus of Ani, royal scribe, 19th dynasty, c. 1307–1196 B.C.E. (The British Museum, London)
6. *Egyptian Book of the Dead, Spell 168,* after a vignette from the funerary papyrus made for a

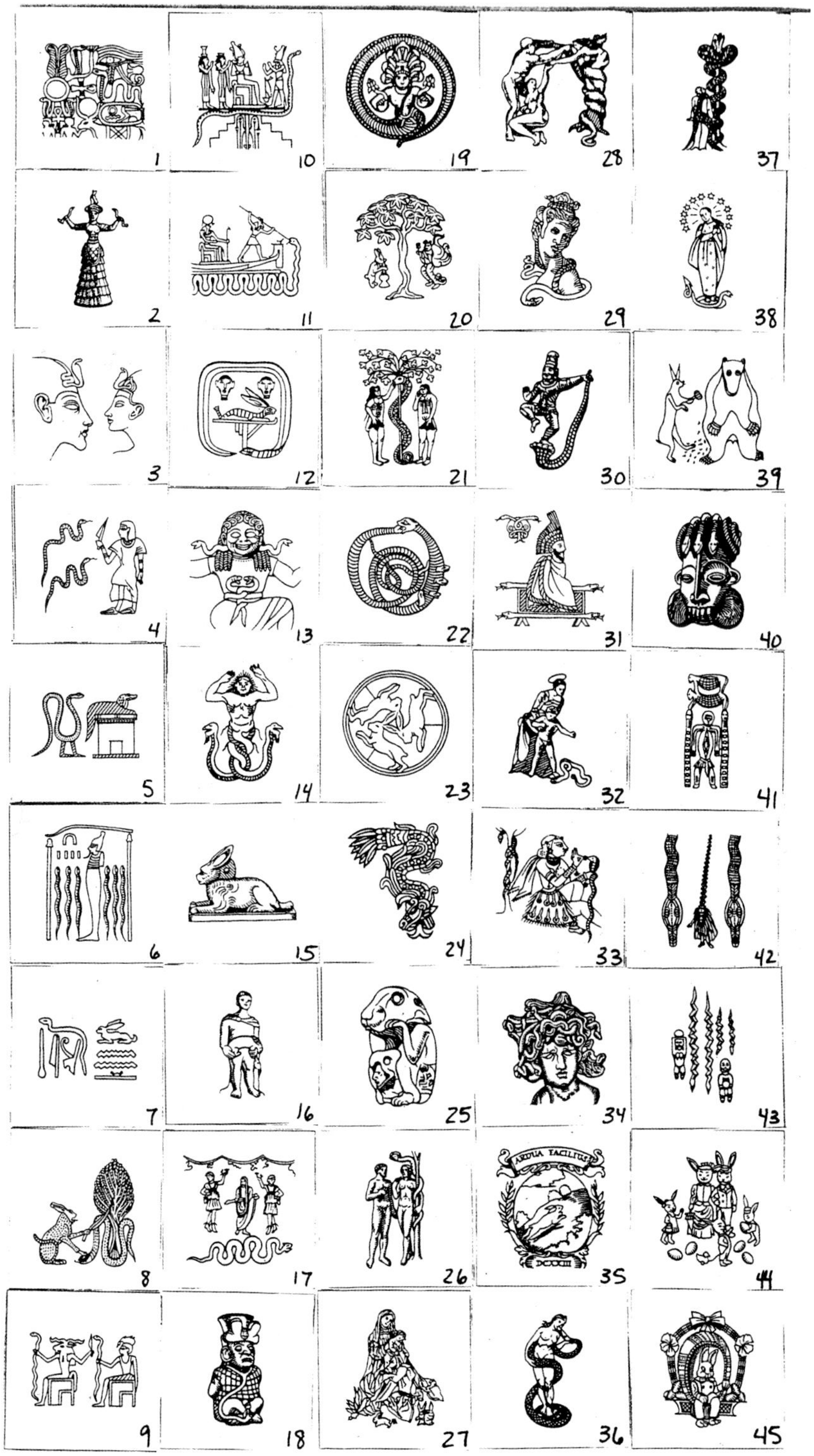

1 10 19 28 37
2 11 20 29 38
3 12 21 30 39
4 13 22 31 40
5 14 23 32 41
6 15 24 33 42
7 16 25 34 43
8 17 26 35 44
9 18 27 36 45

Line drawings by Sandy Skoglund for tiles in *Walking on Eggshells*

scribe/priest, 19th dynasty, c. 1307–1196 B.C.E. (The British Museum, London)

7. *Hieroglyphic*, after an Egyptian hieroglyphic, 19th dynasty, c. 1307–1196 B.C.E.
8. *Cat, Serpent, and Solar Tree*, after a detail from an Egyptian wall painting in the tomb of Inherkhau, Thebes, 20th dynasty, c. 1196–1070 B.C.E.
9. *Egyptian Book of the Dead, Spell 182*: protective deities brandishing snakes, after a vignette from the funerary papyrus of the chantress of Amun, Muthete Pti, 21st dynasty, c. 1070–945 B.C.E. (The British Museum, London)
10. *Egyptian Book of the Dead*, Osiris enthroned on staircase, after a vignette from the Egyptian papyrus of Padiamun, 21st dynasty, c. 1070–945 B.C.E.
11. *Egyptian Book of the Dead*, solar barque in the underworld, after a vignette from the funerary papyrus of Herytwebkhet B, 21st dynasty, c. 1070–945 B.C.E.
12. *The City of Hermopolis*, after an Egyptian symbol of the Cosmic Serpent encircling the city, 21st dynasty, c. 1070–945 B.C.E.
13. *Gorgon*, after the limestone-relief sculpture from the west pediment of the Temple of Artemis at Corfu, c. 600 B.C.E. (Corfu Museum)
14. *Tages*, after a carving of the Etruscan mythic figure, c. 500 B.C.E.
15. *Rabbit Amulet*, after an Egyptian green-composition amulet, Late Period, c. 712–332 B.C.E. (The British Museum, London)
16. *Romano-Celtic Hunter God Carrying Rabbit*, after a stone carving from Touget, Gers, France, c. 500 B.C.E.
17. *Wall Fresco in a Lararium*, after a detail from the Casa dei Vettii, Pompeii, 1st century B.C.E.
18. *Sacrificial Ceremonial Vessel*, after a Moche ceramic, North Coast, Peru, c. 200–800 (American Museum of Natural History, New York)
19. *Hindu Nāga Serpent*, after an Indian stone relief, 7th–8th century
20. *Lunar Rabbit Grinding Cinnamon Sticks into an Elixir of Immortality*, after a Chinese T'ang dynasty bronze relief, c. 700 C.E.
21. *Adam and Eve*, after a detail from the Spanish *Codex Vigiliano y Albeldense*, folio 17, 9th–10th century (Biblioteca del Monasterio de San Lorenzo, El Escorial, Spain)
22. *Adder and Mate*, after a detail from the *Harley 4751 Manuscript*, folio 60r, English, c. 1230–40 (British Library, London)
23. *The Holy Trinity*, after a window lunette, Paderborn Cathedral, Germany, early sixteenth century
24. *Quetzalcoatl, Feathered Serpent*, after a detail from a relief on the lid of an Aztec greenstone box, c. 1502–20 (Hamburgisches Museum für Volkerkunde und Vorgeschichte, Hamburg)
25. *Rabbit with Head of a Warrior in Eagle Helmet Emerging from Belly*, after an Aztec jadeite sculpture, Cempoala, Veracruz, 1350–1521 (Dumbarton Oaks Pre-Columbian Collection, Washington, D.C.)
26. *Adam and Eve*, after a detail from the fresco by Masolino in the Brancacci Chapel, Santa Maria del Carmine, Florence, Italy, c. 1425
27. *The Holy Family with Three Hares*, after a woodcut by Dürer, German, 1497–98
28. *The Fall of Adam and Eve*, after a detail from the fresco by Michelangelo, Sistine Chapel, the Vatican, Rome, Italy, c. 1510
29. *Cleopatra*, after a drawing by Michelangelo, Italian, 1534 (Casa Buonarotti, Florence)
30. *Lord Krishna Dancing with Seven-Headed Cobra*, after an Indian bronze sculpture, 16th century (Victoria and Albert Museum, London)
31. *Fair-Bearded Ruler Quetzalcoatl*, after a detail from Durán's

Historia de las Indias de Nueva España y Islas de la Tierra Firme, manuscript, early colonial Mexico, c. 1570 C.E. (Biblioteca Nacional, Madrid)

32. *The Madonna and Child with St. Anne*, after a detail from the oil on canvas by Caravaggio, Italian, c. 1605 (Borghese Gallery, Rome)
33. *Asavari Ragini*, after an ink and opaque watercolor on paper, Mewar, Rajasthan, India, c. 1600 (Victoria and Albert Museum, London)
34. *The Head of Medusa*, after the marble sculpture by Bernini, Italian, c. 1635 (Capitoline Museum, Rome).
35. *Ardua Facilius*, after an engraving from Jacobus Boschius, *Symbolographia, sive, De arte symbolica sermones septem* (Augsburg; J. C. Bencard, 1701) 3:623, pl. 3:33.
36. *The Temptation and Fall of Eve*, after a watercolor by William Blake from twelve illustrations to Milton's *Paradise Lost*, English, c. 1808 (Museum of Fine Arts, Boston)
37. *Moses Erecting the Brazen Serpent*, after a watercolor by William Blake, English, 1800–03 (Museum of Fine Arts, Boston)
38. *The Virgin "Tota Pulchra,"* after a Mexican painted tin shrine, mid-19th century (The Girard Foundation Collection, Museum of International Folk Art, Santa Fe)
39. *The Flint Bear and the Rabbit*, after an illustration for Marie L. McLaughlin's *Myths and Legends of the Sioux*, Bismarck, N.D.: Bismarck Tribune Co., 1916. (1990 reprint edition, courtesy the University of Nebraska Press).
40. *Helmet Mask*, after a Bamileke wood mask, Cameroon, 19th–20th century (The Metropolitan Museum of Art, New York)
41. *Snake Shrine Sculpture*, after a wood carving, Ishan, Nigeria, 19th–20th century (UCLA Fowler Museum of Cultural History)
42. *Snake Masks*, after Bwa masks from Burkina Faso, 20th century
43. *African Door with Snake Carvings*, after a palace door, 20th century (Honme Palace Museum, Porto-Novo, Benin)
44. *Easter Bunny Family*, after a catalogue for seasonal display products, American, 1995
45. *The Easter Bunny* seated on an Easter basket with a decorated egg throne, after a catalogue for seasonal display products, American, c. 1995

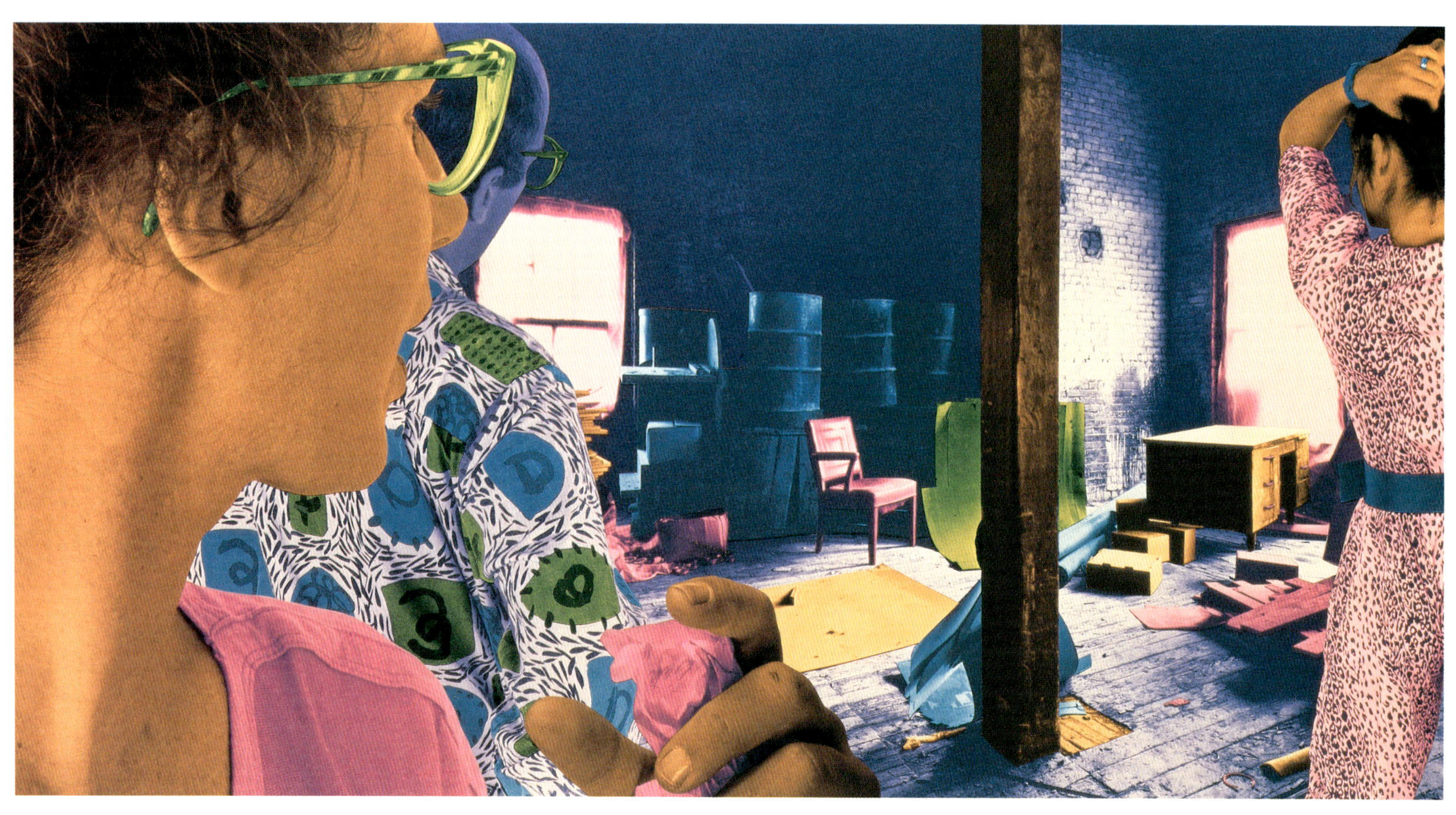

Possibilities of Trash, 1986 (cat. 22)

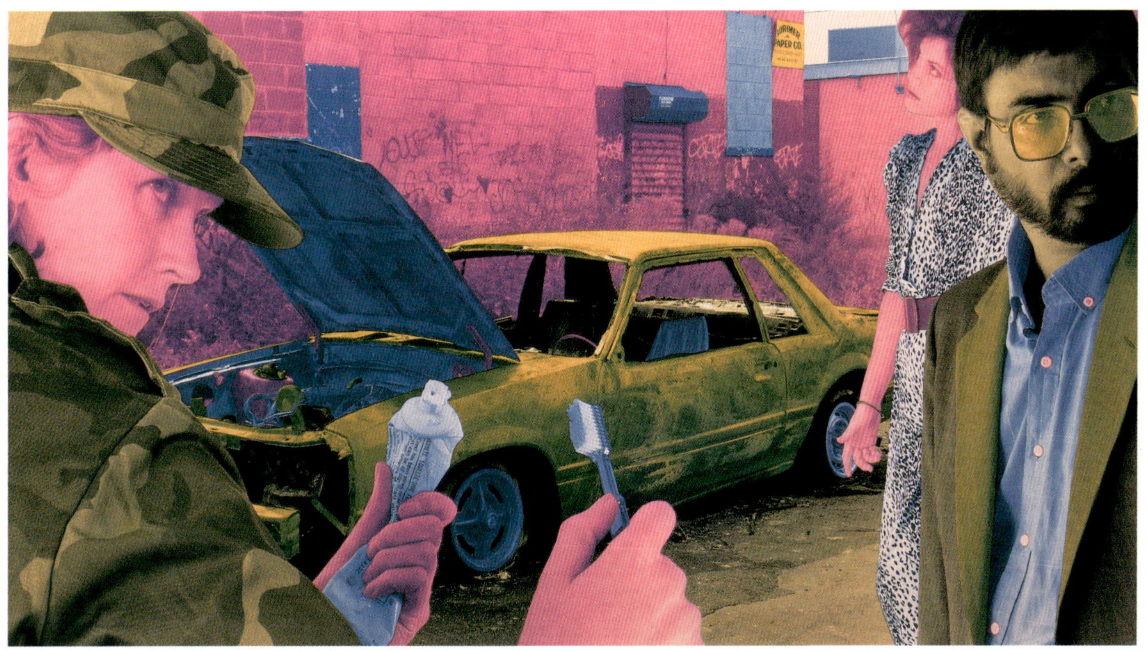

Laws of Interior Design, 1986 (cat. 24)

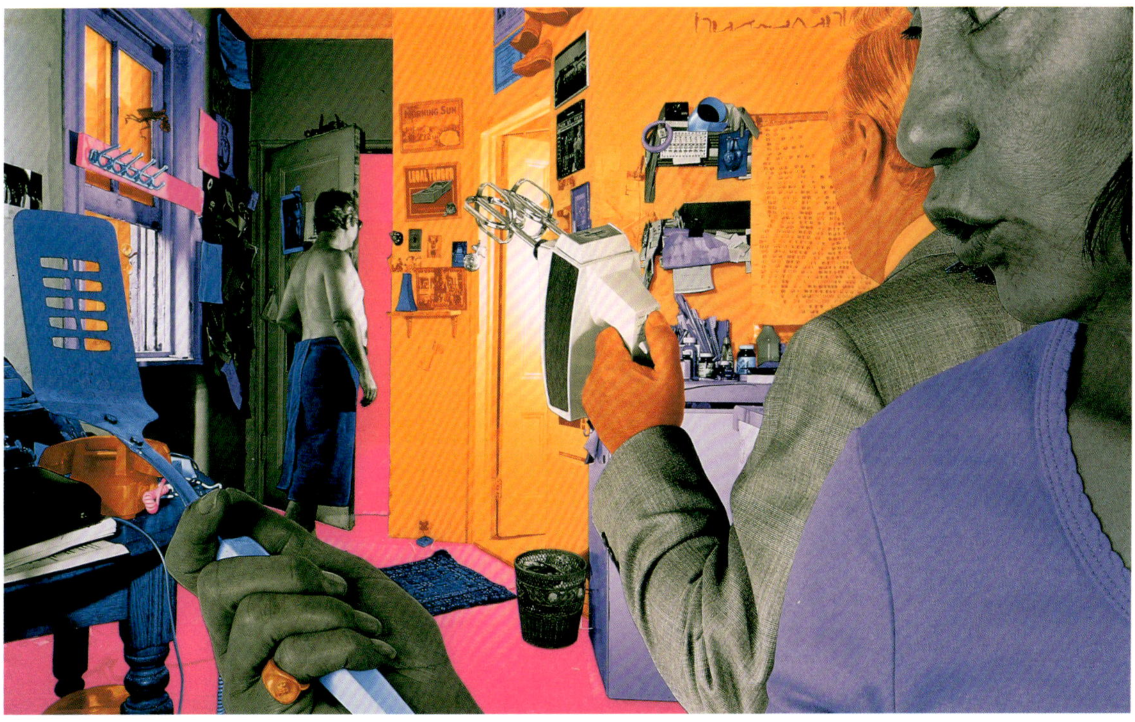

Parallel Thinking, 1986 (cat. 23)

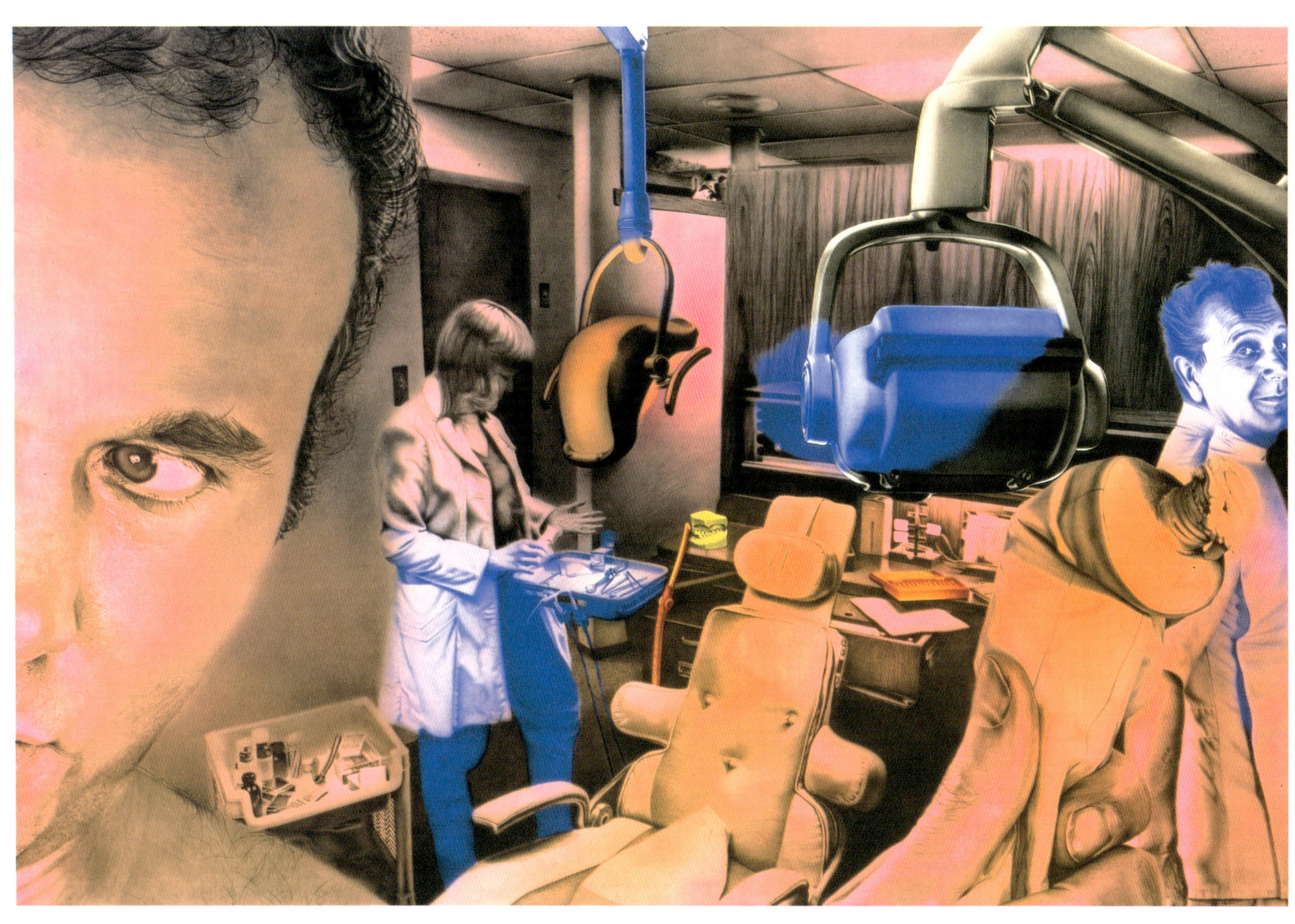

Tools of Expression, 1986 (cat. 20)

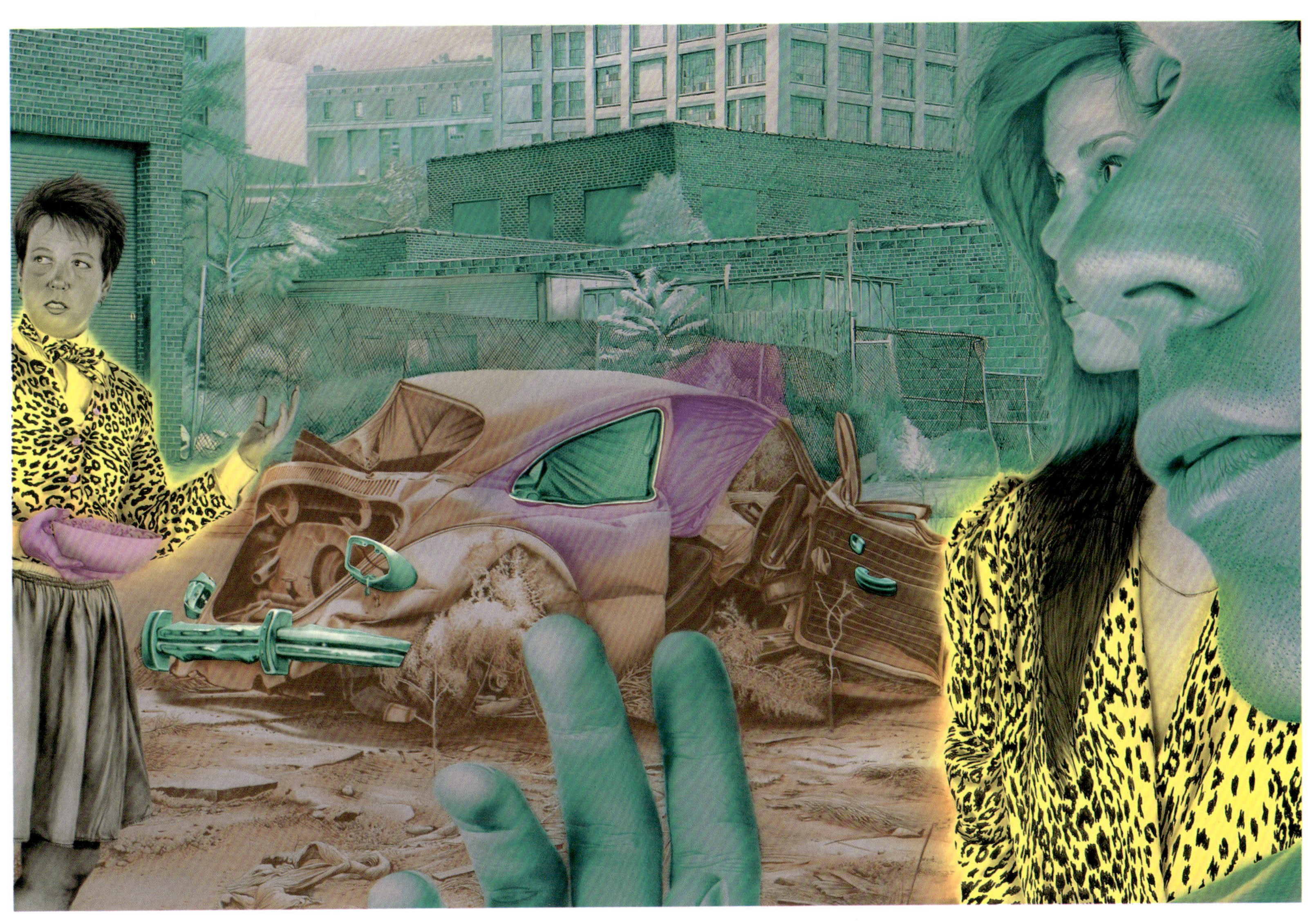

Life After Death, 1986 (cat. 21)

ON LOCATION IN PARADISE

The Lithographs of Sandy Skoglund by Ann H. Sievers

In 1991 Sandy Skoglund returned to printmaking after a hiatus of more than twenty years. Although she had entered graduate school at the University of Iowa with the intention of studying printmaking, she shifted her focus to painting after a single semester, and the path of her subsequent career ran from conceptual art to installations and photographs without ever circling back to prints. By the time she was ready to embark on a lithographic project, however, she had already been thinking about it for some time.

The impetus came from two sources, the first of which was Skoglund's desire for a new medium in which to render her photographic images, one that would give them "the physical presence of paper and ink."[1] The second was her wish to "resurrect" the sculptures she had created for her installation/photograph projects—to give the sculptures a new life.

Skoglund's idea was to take her sculptures, which had been created to be photographed in the highly controlled setting of an installation, and photograph them outside her studio—on location, as it were. Not for the first time, she felt drawn to leave the studio for a photographic project that incorporated found subjects. In the mid-1980s, for her *True Fiction* series (pages 76–79), she had spent a year photographing in the streets of New York and in the houses of friends and family to accumulate an image bank of settings for works that were later assembled as collages in the studio.[2] Wanting to work with certain specific backgrounds from contemporary American life—from archetypal domestic interiors to the burned-out cars abandoned on urban streets—Skoglund decided to photograph "the real thing". As she points out, "the found subject is really taken for granted in photography, but once you start making everything it becomes something you take less for granted, something that is an alternative strategy." Skoglund had already experimented with placing her sculptures in an outdoor setting in the course of developing *Maybe Babies* (page 83), in the summer of 1982, when she deployed sculptures for this installation in Brooklyn's Prospect Park. With her first lithograph, she returned to this strategy to produce a new variation on her hybrid art of sculpture, installation, and photography.

Her choice of lithography as the medium for her new photographic images resulted from a long consideration of various printmaking options. Years earlier, when she began to make color photographs, Skoglund had explored the idea of doing four-color etchings (photogravures) but had abandoned it when she saw that the process introduced so many variables that the artist was "more at the mercy of it than in control of it."[3] Over the years, the consideration of alternate techniques became "a kind of ongoing dialogue" for Skoglund, who eventually concluded that lithography could offer "the kind of refinement and photographic acuity" that she was unwilling to sacrifice.

Skoglund's first print, *Dogs on the Beach* (page 89) was based on a photograph taken shortly after the New York showing of *The Green House* (page 23) at Janet Borden's gallery in the autumn of 1990. Having decided to use the sculptures of dogs from this, her

(AND ELSEWHERE):

most recent installation, Skoglund determined that the location for the photograph should be an archetypal ocean beach scene. Janet Borden suggested the Jersey shore—specifically, a section of beach near Asbury Park. Like Skoglund's on-location work for subsequent prints, the photoshoot for *Dogs on the Beach* was completed in a single day, although she remembers that getting the picture was "a scramble." Production of the lithograph took considerably longer, occupying the artist and master printer Maurice Sanchez for several months in the fall and winter of 1991–92. This first lithograph, like Skoglund's subsequent prints, was editioned on an offset press at Sanchez's Derrière L'Etoile Studios.

The print *Cats in Paris* (page 88) resulted from an invitation Skoglund received a short time later to participate in a project organized by Alain Sayag, curator of France's Musée national d'art moderne (Centre Georges Pompidou), which had premiered Skoglund's installation *Fox Games* in 1989. Sayag, who was familiar with *Dogs on the Beach*, invited Skoglund and eight other international artists who work in photography to execute new works to memorialize the abandoned and soon-to-be demolished viaduct and associated structures of the A14 highway in the Parisian suburb of La Défense.[4] Skoglund's proposal was to set her "radioactive cats" free on the viaduct.[5] Although she had in mind from the outset to make a print, there was insufficient time to complete a lithograph for the Paris exhibition, *Arrêt sur Viaduc*.[6] Instead, she exhibited two unique Cibachrome prints made expressly for the exhibition from the black-and-white negatives she shot on location. One shot had been set up and photographed under the viaduct in the morning, the other atop the structure in the afternoon, after a light rain had left puddles on the pavement. For the lithograph *Cats in Paris*, Skoglund used a variant of the photograph taken atop the viaduct, proofing and editioning the print between September 1992 and February of the following year.

The artist's third lithograph, *Babies at Paradise Pond* (page 85), was the project of the 1995 Smith College Print Workshop,[7] and was commissioned for the exhibition *Sandy Skoglund: Reality Under Siege*. In a trip to the Smith campus to scout possible sites, Skoglund selected Paradise Pond,[8] a landscape with particular resonance for the artist (a Smith alumna), and one she thought would present a satisfactory composition for the camera. Following the March photoshoot featuring the sculpture from her 1983 installation *Maybe Babies*, the artist returned to campus in October to color-proof the lithograph with Maurice Sanchez during the Smith College Print Workshop. Further proofing and the final editioning of the print took place in New York in January of 1996.

The photograph for Skoglund's fourth and most recent print, *Squirrels at the Drive-In* (page 84), had been taken several years earlier, almost immediately after that for *Cats in Paris*, during the semester she spent as a visiting professor in Connecticut at the Hartford Art School (University of Hartford).[9] Because she likes to make her students aware of her life outside the classroom as a working artist, Skoglund discussed the Paris project with her class, telling them she would like to do a shoot in Hartford and assigning them the task of proposing a site. Of those suggested, the Hartford Drive-In struck Skoglund as the most unusual, and appealed to her as a setting that might not survive much longer.[10] For this project, Skoglund chose to use the sculptures of squirrels from her 1991 installation *Gathering Paradise* (page 67). She did not execute the lithograph, however, until 1996.[11]

Skoglund's working process in the location shoots for her prints is similar in many respects to the one that she uses in photographing her installations. In both cases she is "thinking about the space as photographic space, a rectangle that gets filled up" by the shapes of her sculptures and human models.[12] Before the sculptural elements are arranged in the studio or set up in the landscape, the camera is positioned and the scene is framed. Everything is placed for the eye of the camera, and the artist exercises a directorial control over the scene and its actors.

The strict control that the artist can exercise in her studio is impossible on location, however. Constraints of time, budget, and travel generally dictate that the entire setup, photography, and dismantling of the scene be accomplished in a single day. And of course, on an exterior shoot one must either accept whatever weather occurs or be prepared to reschedule the shoot.[13]

For *Babies at Paradise Pond*, Skoglund was determined to proceed no matter what the conditions on the scheduled day. Her first task in the morning was to set up and anchor her tripod and 4- by 5- inch view camera at the top of the steep hill overlooking the pond, framing the scene in such a way that the entire island was visible and appeared to float in the water. Under Skoglund's direction, the sculptures were then set in place one or two at a time by her two assistants and an army of volunteers from Smith (pages 86 and 87). First establishing the positions and interrelationships of key foreground sculptures, Skoglund then placed the more distant figures, gradually adding models she had chosen from the day's volunteers.[14] Throughout this process small black-and-white Polaroids shot from the view camera's vantage point enabled her to assess progress and to note the locations for added sculptures and models; periodic checks at the camera confirmed her decisions. In the late afternoon, her composition complete, Skoglund took the final black-and-white photographs.

Back in New York, Skoglund chose a single image from the numerous Smith "takes" and had color separations made from which aluminum lithographic plates were produced under the supervision of Allan Gunderson, a specialist in offset printing. Whereas the separations for her first two prints had been made with the traditional copy (process) camera method, by the time she began work on *Babies at Paradise Pond*, this method had been superseded by computer scanning.[15] Faced with an unfamiliar process, Skoglund characteristically undertook a series of experiments to determine the best black and white photographic source for the computer to scan in order to render the high degree of detail she desired in the final print.[16]

From the beginning she had sought in her prints a very different effect from that of her color photographs. Because she wanted the finished image to look as though its original source had been a single black-and-white negative, she sought closer tonal relationships than in her Cibachromes, where color is often used to separate the individual elements in the picture from one another, creating an effect of overall patterning (as in *A Breeze at Work*, page 60) and controlling—or subverting—the viewer's attempt to read perspective (as in *True Fiction*).

By basing her lithographic plates on color separations derived from the commercial process of four-color printing, the artist could incorporate color in her print while also gaining the dimensionality and tonal subtlety that result when black is created by printing four superimposed colors of ink.[17] Choosing the specific colors for each print, however, was accomplished in her first two lithographs only through considerable experimentation and trial proofing, starting from the standard process-printing colors (yellow, cyan, magenta, and black). *Dogs on the Beach* underwent a particularly extensive proofing process. For *Cats in*

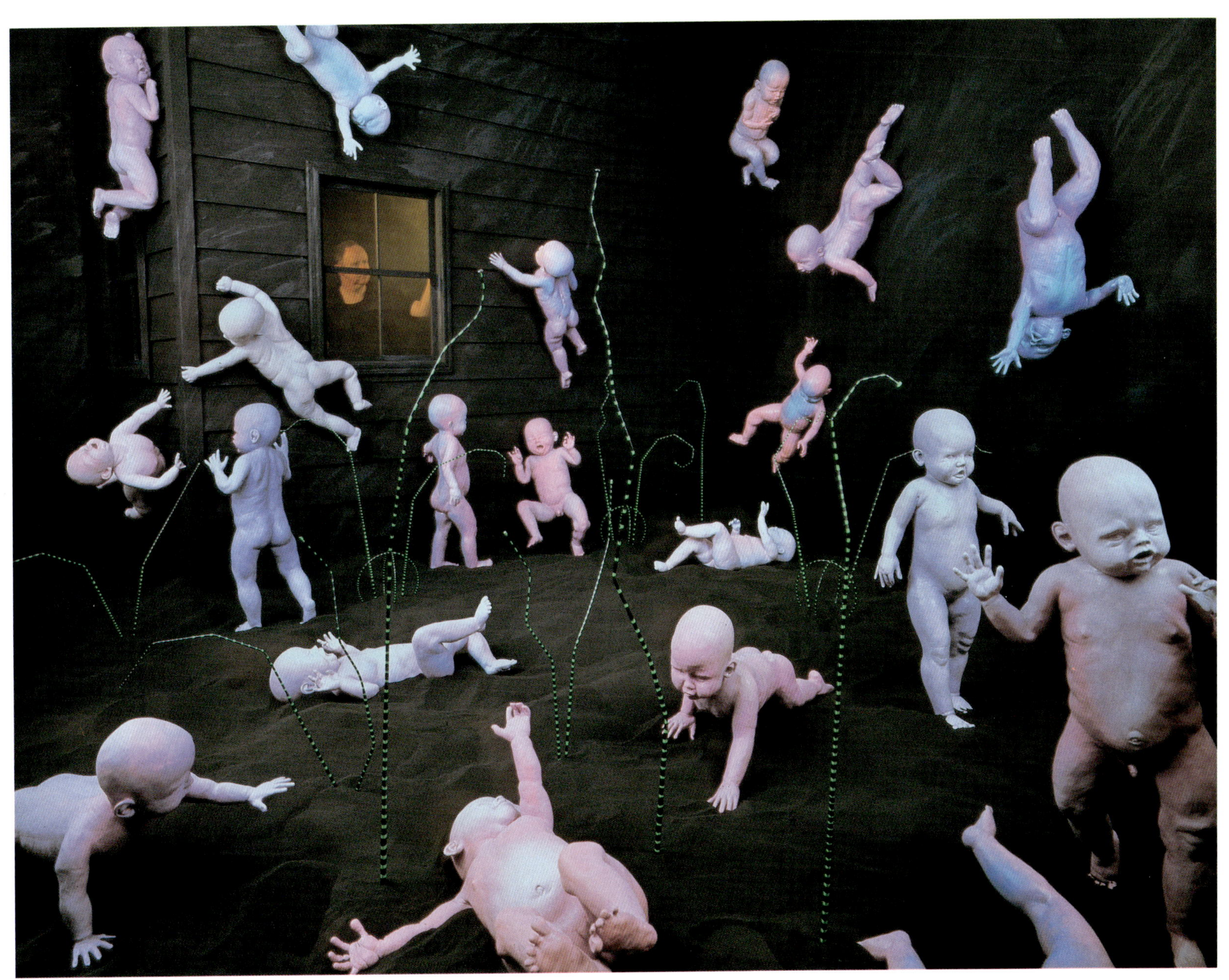

Maybe Babies, 1983 (cat. 30)

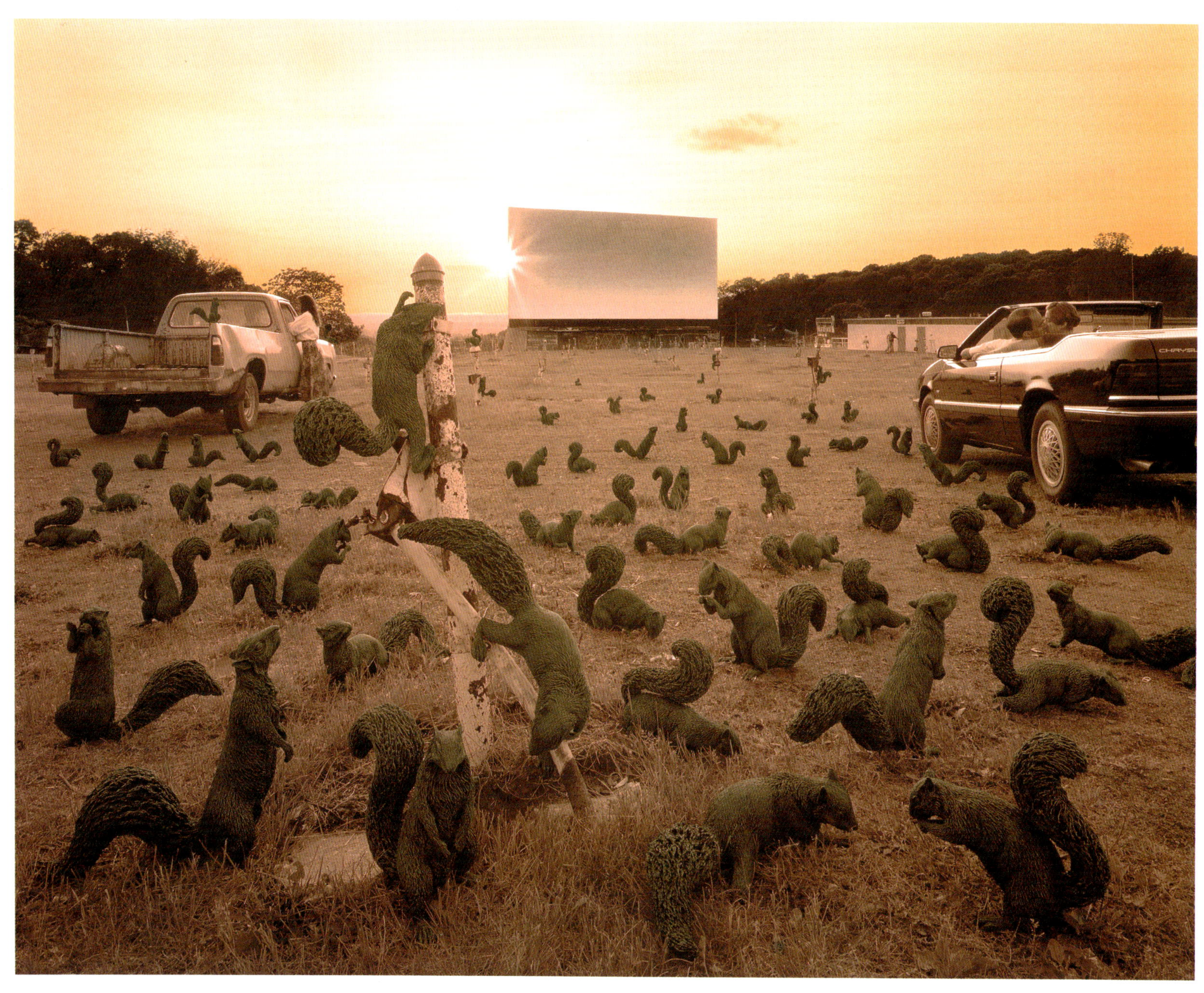

Squirrels at the Drive-In, 1996 (cat. 52)

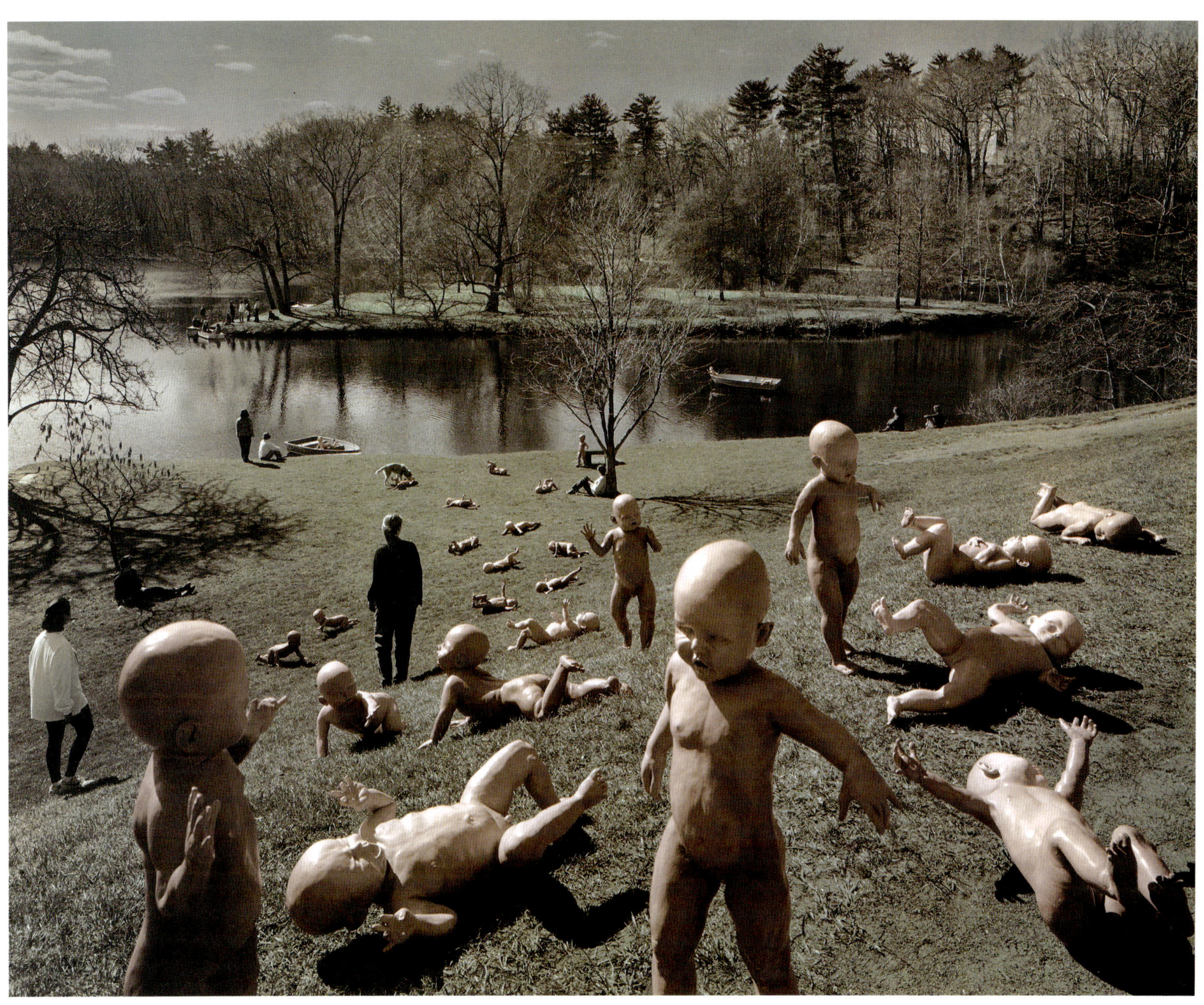

Babies at Paradise Pond, 1996 (cat. 51)

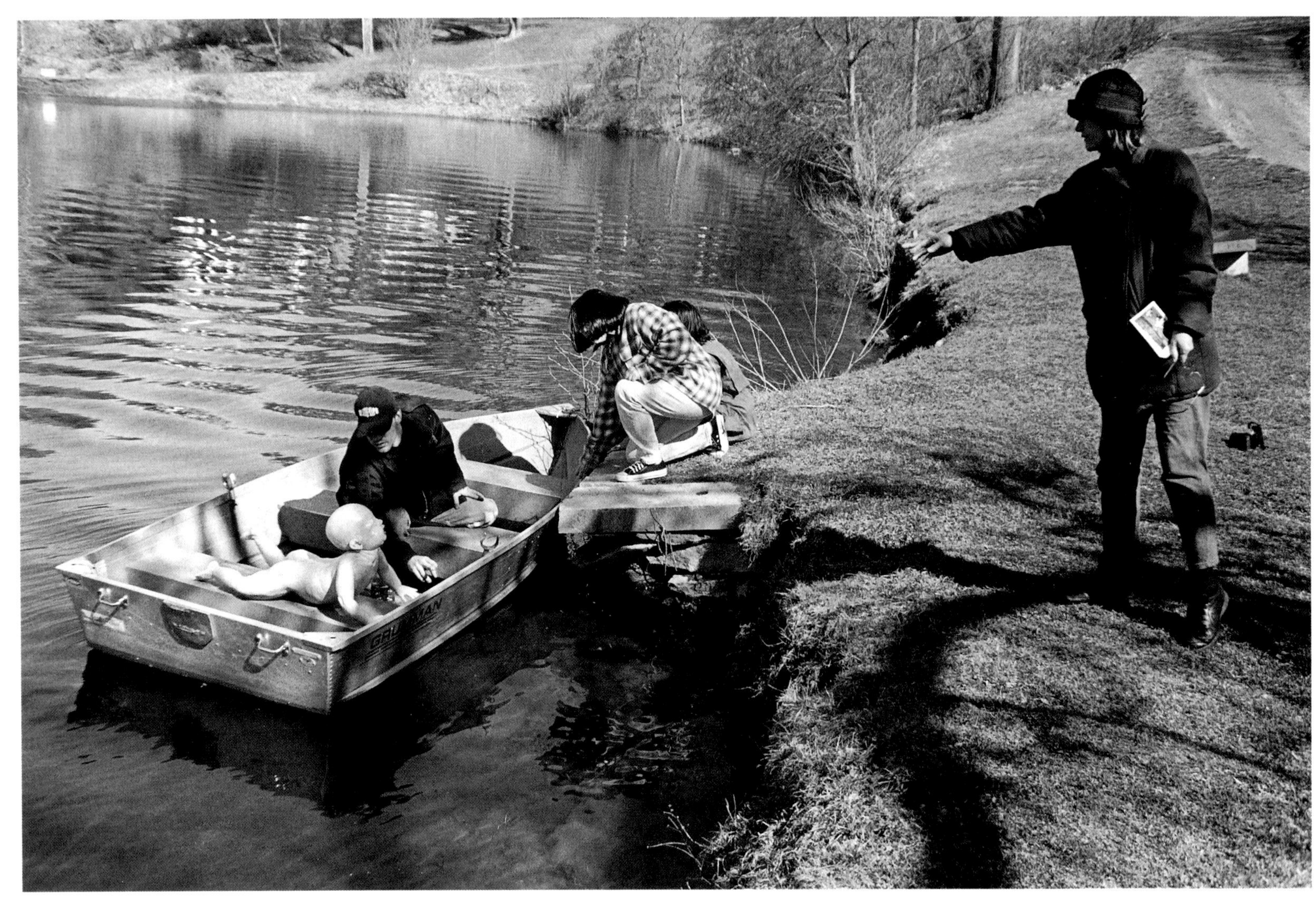

Preparations for the photograph of *Babies at Paradise Pond*, 1995

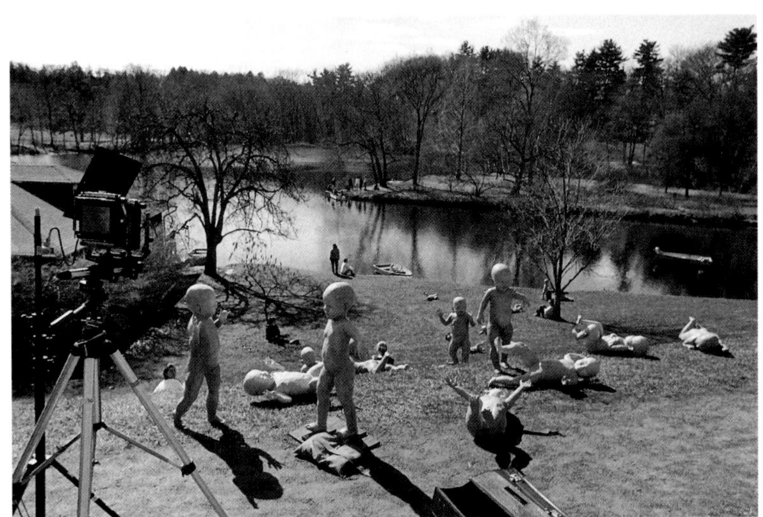

The camera setup for *Babies at Paradise Pond*, 1995

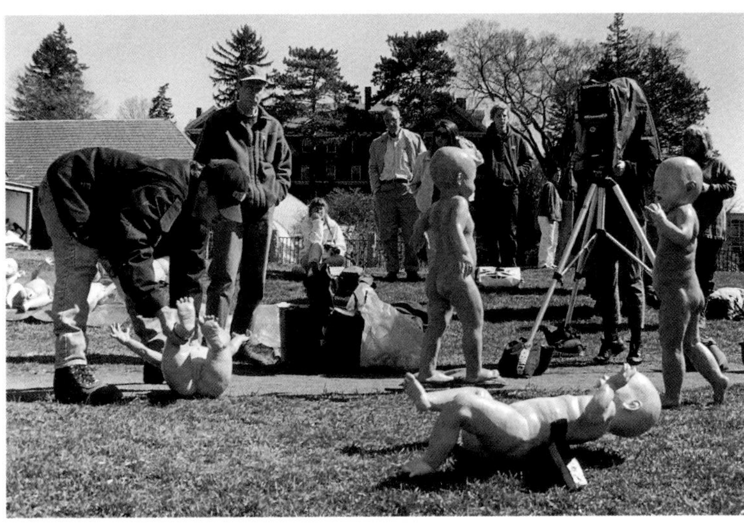

From her camera position Sandy Skoglund directs the placement of sculptures.

Paris, the artist took as her point of departure the warm tones she had tried out in her Cibachromes for *Arrêt sur Viaduc*,[18] deciding to move to the cooler blue of the final lithograph. First proofs for *Babies at Paradise Pond* were run in New York based on a set of color overlays that corresponded to the six lithographic plates, one for each of the four process colors, plus a plate that had been masked to include only the babies, and a high-contrast "punch" plate to strengthen the shadows. The two days of the Smith College Print Workshop were used to work from the initial proofs toward a bluer green and an effect of hyperreality and luminosity by making the inks more transparent and experimenting with the order of printing the plates. The final proofing in New York moved the print further toward black and white and a more moody feeling. *Squirrels at the Drive-In* is similarly monochromatic and sharply detailed, although here the note is lighter, thanks to the warm, rosy tone of the print.

The paper on which these highly detailed lithographs are printed is coated, and, therefore, extremely smooth. For her first two prints, in a conceit intended as a comment on paper, Skoglund bordered the image with a photolithographic reproduction of a highly textured art paper, colored to the dominant tone of the print and printed to the edge of the sheet. She has since abandoned this as being too self-reflexive, and her more recent images now float on the pristine white of a hand-torn sheet.

Often asked about the relative importance of her installations and the related photographs, Skoglund stresses their interdependence and equal status. She considers photography "the ultimate organizing tool" with which she can first compose the installa-

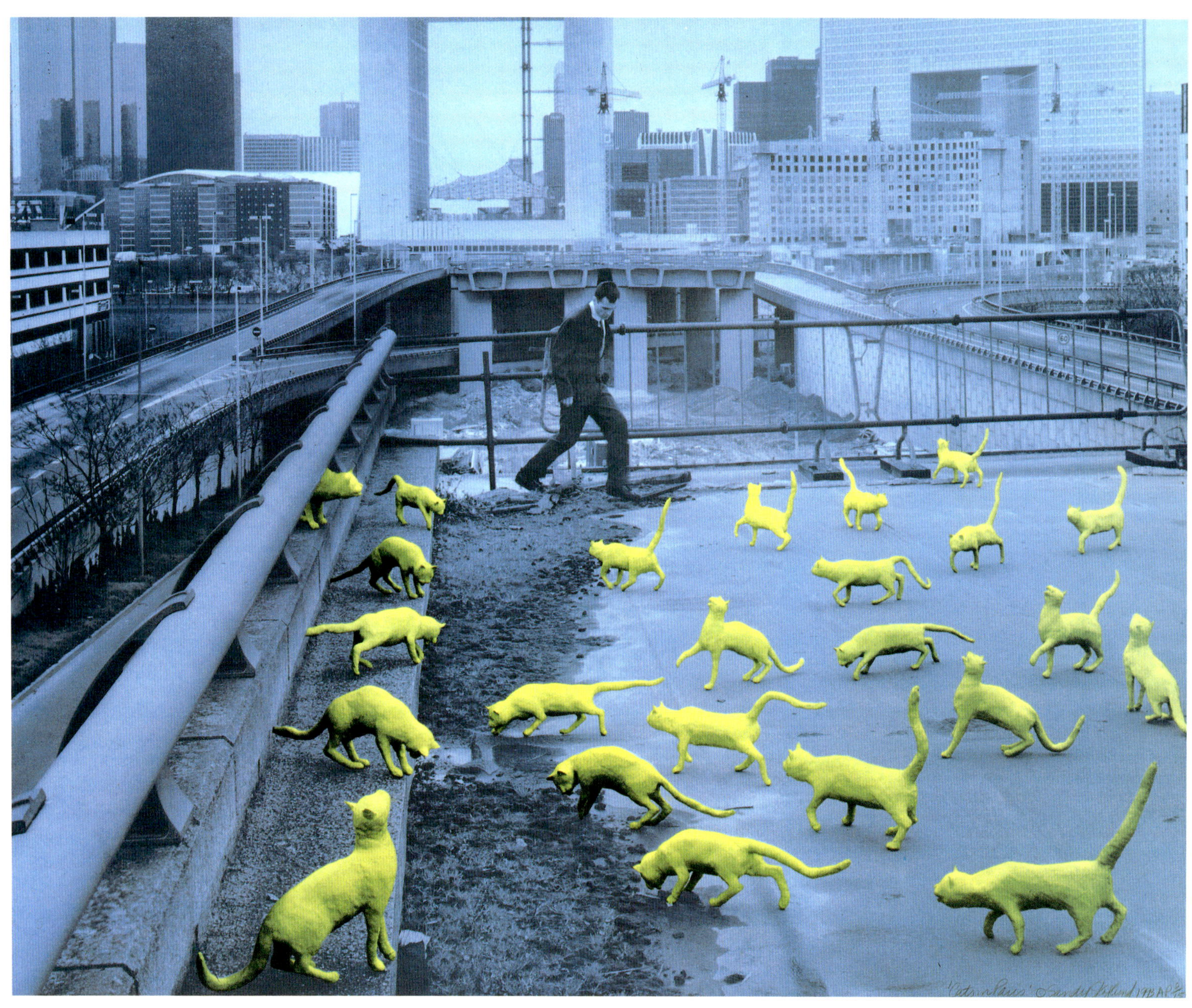

Cats in Paris, 1993 (cat. 50)

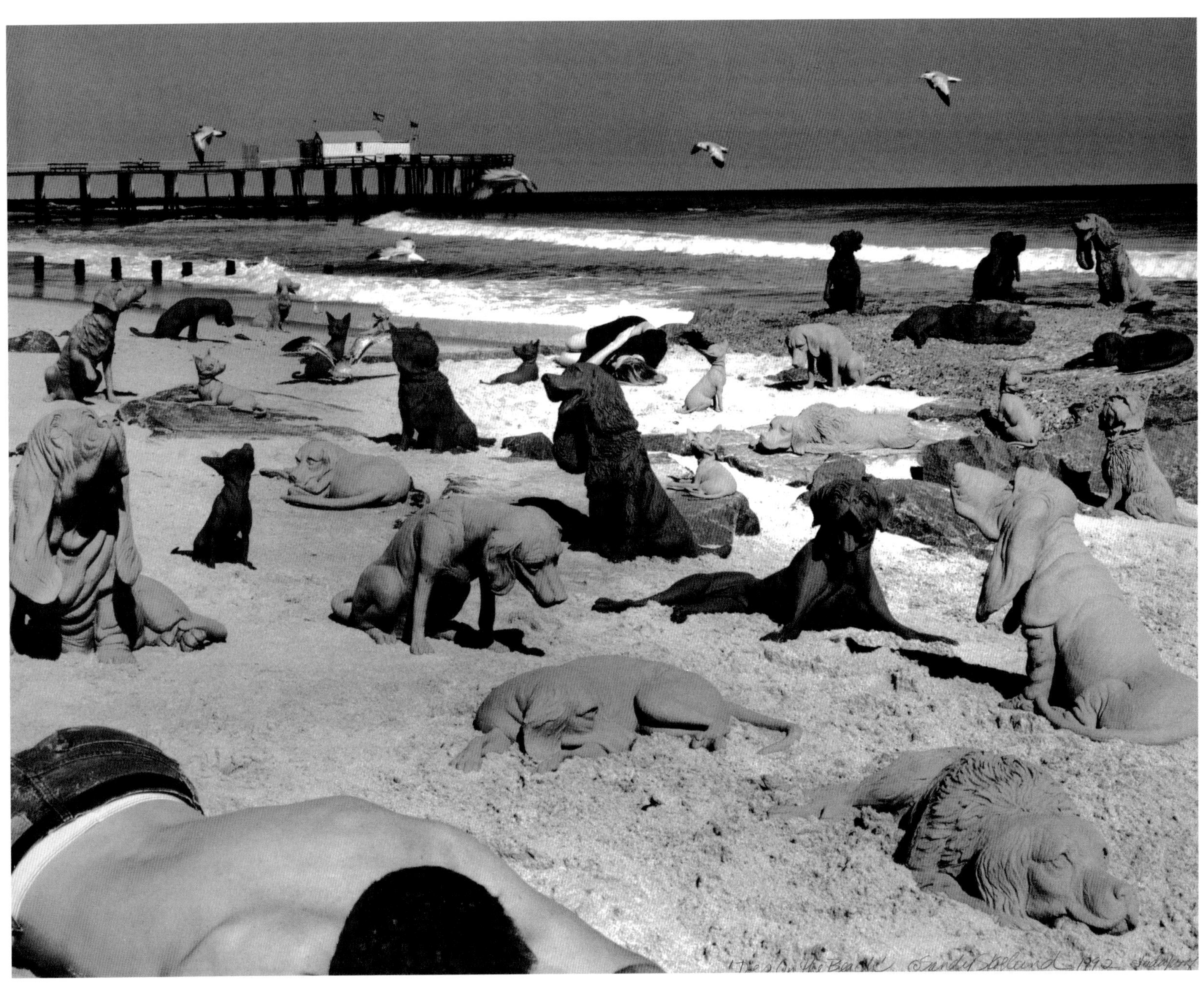

Dogs on the Beach, 1992 (cat. 49)

tion in her studio and then present it to the viewer from the single vantage point she has chosen.[19] She notes, however, that the installation is not just an artifact of this process, but rather contains "ingredients to be reassembled." Reconfiguring the installation in each new exhibition space becomes an ongoing process of reconsidering its meaning and revisiting her earlier ideas. Similarly, Skoglund's lithographs offer further possibilities for meaning by introducing the sculptures from these installations into completely new environments.

The titles Skoglund has assigned her prints are straightforward and descriptive, naming the sculpture and the site depicted, but offering no clue to the image's meaning, unlike her titles for some of the installations (*Radioactive Cats* or *Gathering Paradise*, for example) or for the series *True Fiction*, in which they suggest one way of reading the work. The lithographs are left entirely open to interpretation at the same time that their incorporation of sculptures created for other contexts invites comparison to the original works.

Because Skoglund's prints have in common with her installation photographs the inclusion of human models, the viewer inevitably attempts to interpret the images by analyzing the relationship between the people and the sculptures that surround them. But Skoglund characteristically thwarts simple answers. The faces of her human actors are usually impassive or are turned away from the viewer, almost never engaging us by looking directly out of the picture. In *Radioactive Cats* (page 10), *The Green House*, and *Gathering Paradise*, the humans' apparent emotional distance from the overabundant animal life that surrounds them—and therefore the ambiguity of their relationship to these "others"—contributes to our sense of unease and allows us to project our own emotions onto the photograph. Are we looking at scenes of peaceful coexistence or apocalyptic menace? Implicit in both the photographs and the lithographs are narratives that we attempt to explicate by answering such questions. When, however, confronting the installations themselves (which Skoglund always shows together with the related photographs), the viewer is compelled to explain the human absence. This instinct to seek a narrative connection between the installation and the photograph—a before and after—is encouraged not only by the fact that the spaces Skoglund chooses to construct (the living room, the kitchen, the patio) are sites of everyday human activity, but also by the concrete vestiges of human presence they contain: the carpet slippers in *The Green House*, the bowls of ice cream in *Gathering Paradise*. Is it then surprising that so many critics have suggested dark scenarios; for example, that the dogs in *The Green House* have finally devoured their "best friends"?

Skoglund's lithographs not only give new life to her individual sculptures, but also extend the performance aspect of her work. If the initial creation of an installation is "a way of actually performing for the camera in the studio,"[20] and the photograph is a document of that event, the exhibited installations continue the performances as they are reconfigured for new spaces. The audience's participation extends this aspect of the pieces, especially in those installations through which visitors are allowed to walk (*Gathering Paradise*, *Fox Games*).[21] In the case of Skoglund's lithographs, the setup for her photoshoots has been not only a performance for the camera, but often for an audience as well—whether they be the homeless people nearby or the police officers who came to investigate the strange off-season basking of *Dogs on the Beach*; the French commuters who passed by the scavenging *Cats in Paris*, or the members of the Smith College community who were stopped in their tracks by the spectacle of oversize bluish *Babies at Paradise Pond*. Sometimes, a fortuitous performance is captured in the final print—the curious dog that lopes over to sniff eagerly at a baby, or the sea gulls that soar above the sunbathing dogs. Although initially the setting of *Dogs on the Beach* might suggest a more familiar reality, Skoglund continues to frustrate our expectations by placing her human models in ambiguous poses. Are they sunbathing (and if so,why does the woman wear a dress)? Are they even alive?

The artist's monochromatic approach in the prints, her attempt to preserve, in color, the feel of black and white, lends a sensibility to the lithographs that is reminiscent of 1950s black-and-white films. Nowhere is this more evident than in *Babies at Paradise Pond.* Particularly close in mood to the science-fiction and horror movies of the 1950s, this lithograph, like the installation *Maybe Babies,* was partially inspired by the artist's recollection of the screen's eerie "children of the damned" (a detail that lends an ironic note to the print's title).[22] Whereas the unusually expressive face of the man who looks from his window in *Maybe Babies* makes that image particularly unsettling, and contributes significantly to the dark readings of the work, the models in *Babies at Paradise Pond* are Skoglund's more typical, impassive actors. Nevertheless, the lithograph remains disturbing to many viewers, for whom the "babies" trigger a strong emotional response.

An awareness of the important role a sense of place plays in human consciousness underlies all of Skoglund's lithographs, where, in every case, the location lends a powerful resonance of its own to the final image. The very commission that engendered *Cats in Paris* belongs to a long photographic tradition of documenting and memorializing a vanishing landscape—Atget's photographs of Paris come to mind. The structure recorded by Skoglund is a particularly familiar aspect of modern urban blight. Visible in the background, however, is the Grande Arche of La Défense, one of Paris's "Grands Projets" completed under President François Mitterrand, a triumphal arch configured as a huge open cube that rises on the vast concrete podium of La Défense, continuing the ceremonial axis that runs from the Louvre, along the Champs-Elysées, and across the Seine. A key monument in what has been called "the most lavish state-sponsored building program since the remaking of Paris by Baron Haussmann,"[23] the Grande Arche stands as an ironic counterpoint to the chaotic environment of abandoned highway and construction site in the foreground of Skoglund's lithograph. Given the bleak environment in which the green cats forage among scraps of vegetation growing from the cracked pavement, one can interpret the cranes that rise amid the background skyscrapers as instruments either of construction or of demolition. Skoglund's use of blue as the dominant color in her lithograph suggests both the cold and rainy weather of the photoshoot and the traditional black and white of reportage photography. The lone figure who hurries on his way across the wet pavement may remind some viewers of Henri Cartier-Bresson's famous photograph *Behind the Gare Saint-Lazare.* But Skoglund's print is a "decisive moment" created, not captured. In liberating her radioactive cats from domesticity, she circles back to the original idea for the installation in which they appeared—the representation of a threatening urban scene.[24]

Squirrels at the Drive-In presents a landscape of a different sort, but one of equal iconographic power. Here, however, we have returned to the realm of American popular culture. Skoglund's own recollections of going to a drive-in with her parents in the 1950s feature the snack bar rather than the movies. Indeed, the films seem to have been the least important part of the drive-in experience for many Americans (and, fittingly, the screen in this lithograph is blank). For an artist so devoted to investigating sites of ritualistic human behaviors, and to exploring both the light and dark sides of American culture, it is hard to imagine a more appropriate setting. The squirrels that populate this print originally foraged on a patio furnished with lounge chairs, picnic table, and barbecue, in *Gathering Paradise.* For the artist, that piece was about "paradise and vacation and time and space that is set aside in human imagination specifically for pleasure as opposed to work," but many critics have seen in it an indictment of suburbia.[25] The ambiguity that is a source of both the horror and the humor in Skoglund's work is less apparent in the lithograph *Squirrels at the Drive-In.* Suffused with the rosy glow of late afternoon, as the sun backlights the blank screen, and couples kiss or embrace, the scene has a nostalgic feel. Despite the air of strangeness lent by the derelict drive-in and its horde of squirrels, both humans and animals seem at ease, and the world, if not a terrestrial paradise, appears nonetheless to be a serene and peaceful place, if only for the moment.

NOTES

Entertainment and Distress: The Photographs of Sandy Skoglund by Carol Squiers

1. Roland Barthes, *Camera Lucida: Reflections on Photography* (New York: Hill and Wang, 1981), pp. 76–77.
2. All biographical information and direct quotes, unless otherwise noted, are from interviews conducted with Skoglund on October 15, 1996; November 29, 1996; and January 13, 1997.
3. John Szarkowski, then director of photography at the Museum of Modern Art in New York, had fueled the controversy about color photography when he gave the relatively unknown William Eggleston a one-man show of his color images in 1976; in the photography world, color was one of the main critical issues of the latter 1970s.
4. A. D. Coleman, "The Directorial Mode: Notes Toward a Definition," *Artforum* 15, no. 1 (September 1976), pp. 55–61.
5. Coleman also identified portraits, nudes, and other genres as being directorial, but in this essay I am interested in a more limited definition.
6. The ghost was created by a figure that entered the picture for a brief time while the exposure was being made, according to Helmut Gernsheim in *The Rise of Photography 1850–1880: The Age of Collodion* (New York: Thames and Hudson, 1988), p. 67.
7. Coleman, 1976, p. 58.
8. Barthes, 1981, p. 32.

Walking on Eggshells by Linda Muehlig

1. See, for example, the exhibition catalogue *Cross References: Sculpture into Photography* (Walker Art Center, Minneapolis, Minnesota, 1987), which includes the work of Sandy Skoglund and five international artists who create tableau-based photographs. As noted in the catalogue introduction, all of the artists in the exhibition—James Casebere, Bruce Charlesworth, Bernard Faucon, Ron O'Donnell, Boyd Webb, and Skoglund—"make large-scale constructions, which they usually destroy after their photographs are made."
2. See Sandy Skoglund, "Spirituality in the Flesh, A Project for Artforum," *Artforum* 30, no. 6 (February 1992), pp. 76–77, and Arlene Raven, "In the Last Hour: Sandy Skoglund: Photography/Sculpture, 1979–1992," in *In the Last Hour* (exh. cat.), The Fred Jones Jr. Museum of Art, The University of Oklahoma, 1992 (unpaginated).
3. See Jude Schwendenwien, "Cravings: Food into Sculpture," *Sculpture* 11, no. 6 (November–December 1992), pp. 44–49. In addition to Janine Antoni and Skoglund, Schwendenwien discusses other "food" artists, including Lynn Aldrich, Doug Hammette, Laura Foreman, Julie Bozzi, and Megan Marlatt.
4. Studio conversation with the artist, May 20, 1997.
5. See Anne H. Hoy, *Fabrications: Staged, Altered and Appropriated Photographs* (New York: Abbeville Press, 1987), pp. 8–61 ("Narrative Tableaux"). As Hoy points out (pp. 8–9), the history of staged or tableau photography dates almost to the inception of the medium itself. She traces its development from John Edwin Mayall's 1843 photo-illustrations of the Lord's Prayer and the calo-

types of the Scottish photographers David Octavius Hill and Robert Adamson, through the American Photo Secessionists and the Linked Ring of Great Britain at the turn of the century, the Surrealists in the second quarter of the century, and Hollywood film stills. She identifies two current generations of tableaux artists: the "forerunners," such as Ralph Eugene Meatyard and Duane Michals, and those whose work matured in the 1970s and later, such as Bernard Faucon, David Levinthal, Laurie Simmons, and Sandy Skoglund.

6. See Pontus Hulten, ed., with Jennifer Gough-Cooper and Jacques Caumont, *Marcel Duchamp, Work and Life: Ephemerides on and about Marcel Duchamp and Rrose Selavy 1887–1968* (Cambridge, Mass.: MIT Press, 1993), unpaginated (see under 17 January 1938). At the Galerie Beaux-Arts, 140 rue Faubourg Saint-Honoré, "ravishing life size mannequins" contributed by various artists lined a corridor leading to a grotto, where Marcel Duchamp had suspended 1,200 coal sacks from the ceiling. Dalí created a pond, while Wolfgang Paalen provided "a mossy, leaf-strewn carpet." Beds included in the installation were lent from a shop. A brazier provided the only light.
7. See Dickran Tashjian, *A Boatload of Madmen: Surrealism and the American Avant-Garde 1920–1950* (New York and London: Thames and Hudson, 1995), pp. 66–90 (chapter 3, "Surrealism in the Service of Fashion").
8. See John Perrault, "Through A Glass Darkly," *Artforum* 27, no. 7 (March 1989), pp. 106–12 (*Sock Situation* reproduced p. 108, discussed p. 111).
9. See William A. Camfield, "Marcel Duchamp's *Fountain*, Its History and Aesthetics in the Context of 1917," in Rudolf Kuenzli and Francis M. Naumann, eds., *Marcel Duchamp, Artist of the Century* (Cambridge, Mass. and London, England: MIT Press, 1989), pp. 64–94. In a defense of the *Fountain*, printed as an unsigned editorial in the issue of *The Blind Man* (no. 2, May 1917) that reproduced the Stieglitz photograph as a frontispiece, the writer emphasized the importance of choice in making a common bathroom fixture a work of art: "He CHOSE it. He took an ordinary article of life, placed it so that its useful significance disappeared under the new title and point of view—created a new thought for that object" (reprinted in Camfield, 1989, p. 76).

   In light of Skoglund's practice of developing her installations with reference to the camera's point of view, it is also interesting to note that Duchamp's installation *Etant Donnés: 1 la chute d'eau, 2 le gas d'eclairage (Given: 1 The Waterfall 2 The Illuminating Gas)*, 1946–1966, was constructed with only one possible vantage point, a voyeuristic peephole in an outer door, which directed the gaze through a hole in a brick wall to the disturbing scene of a nude figure sprawled in grass, holding a lamp, with a backdrop of a waterfall. This scene, almost impossible to photograph, ironically depended on a stationary, camera-eye view. See Dalia Judovitz, "Rendezvous with Marcel Duchamp: Given," in Kuenzli and Naumann, eds., 1989, pp. 184–202.
10. Thomas McEvilley, "Location and Space in the Kienholz World," in Walter Hopps et al., *Kienholz: A Retrospective*, exh. cat. (New York: Whitney Museum of American Art, in association with DAP, 1996), pp. 48–53.
11. Skoglund originally allowed two of her installations, *Fox Games* and *Gathering Paradise*, to be entered by viewers. She has since decided against this option with *Gathering Paradise*; it is still possible to configure the *Fox Games* installation in such a way that viewers can walk through.
12. Jude Schwendenwien, "Sandy Skoglund (Interview)," *Journal of Contemporary Art* 6, no. 1, (summer 1993), pp. 87–98 (see p. 98).
13. See Walter Hopps et al., 1996, pp. 138–39.
14. See Germano Celant et al., *Claes Oldenburg: An Anthology* (New York: The Solomon R. Guggenheim Museum in association with Harry N. Abrams, Inc., 1995), p. 204, and fig. 112.
15. Oldenburg, quoted in Celant et al., 1995, p. 223. The *Bathroom* objects are reproduced in figs. 128–32.
16. Jan van der Marck, *George Segal* (New York: Harry N. Abrams, Inc., 1975), pl. 29 and accompanying description, opposite page (*Woman Shaving Her Leg*, 1963), and fig. 131 (*Girl Washing Her Hair at a Sink*, 1971).
17. Studio conversation with the artist, May 20, 1997
18. Studio conversation with the artist, October 15, 1996.
19 See Matthew Rose, "Playing a Round in Tribeca," *New York Times*, Arts and Leisure section, July 26, 1992.

20. Studio conversation with the artist, May 20, 1997.
21. Schwendenwien, 1993, p. 96.
22. Mircea Eliade, *A History of Religious Ideas*, trans. Willard R. Trask, (Chicago: University of Chicago Press, 1975). Skoglund was reading the first volume, "From the Stone Age to the Eleusinian Mysteries," while she was working on the cast-paper tiles for *Walking on Eggshells*.
23. Carol Andrews, introduction to *The Ancient Egyptian Book of the Dead*, trans. R. O. Faulkner (Austin: University of Texas Press, rev. ed., 1985), pp. 11–16.
24. Andrews, 1985, p. 84.
25. Alison Roberts, *Hathor Rising: The Serpent Power of Ancient Egypt* (Devon: Northgate Publishers, 1995), p. 111, pl. 117.
26. Patrick R. Houlihan, *The Animal World of the Pharaohs* (London and New York: Thames and Hudson, 1996), pp. 86–87, fig. 62.
27. The author is grateful to Professor Barbara Kellum, of the Smith College art department, for sharing her expertise on Etruscan and Roman art (discussion May 28, 1997). In addition to the information on the little-represented deity Tages, Professor Kellum explained the serpent symbolism in tile 17, after a detail from a wall fresco in a Lararium from the Casa dei Vettii, Pompeii. The central figure is the pater familias of the house, flanked at either side by rustic deities. The snake below their feet is a ubiquitous symbol in this setting, one of two that approach to lick an egg on the altar. Ancestors were thought to take the form of snakes, which are also sometimes shown bearded.
28. Esther Pasztory, *Aztec Art* (New York: Harry N. Abrams, Inc., 1983), pp. 82–83, pl. 41 and pl. 273 (carved greenstone box with relief of the feathered serpent on its lid, collection of the Hamburgisches Museum für Volkerkunde und Vorgeschichte), and pl. 3 (the "Fair Bearded Ruler Quetzalcoatl" from Durán's *Historia de las Indias de Nueva España y Islas de la Tierra Firme*, Bk. I, ch. 1, fol. 228r). In tile 31, Skoglund has moved the double-coiled snakes beneath Queztalcoatl's litter (as shown in Durán's manuscript) to the upper left of the tile.
29. A. T. Mann and Jane Lyle, *Sacred Sexuality* (New York: Barnes & Noble Books, 1995), pp. 18, 20, and repro. on p. 20.
30. Marilyn Nissenson and Susan Jonas, *Snake Charm* (New York: Harry N. Abrams, Inc., 1995), p. 76 and repro.
31. See Bram Dijkstra, *Idols of Perversity* (Oxford and New York: Oxford University Press, 1986), pp. 305–13.
32. Allen F. Roberts, *Animals in African Art: From the Familiar to the Marvelous* (New York: The Museum of African Art in association with Prestel, Munich, 1995), pp. 62–65, pls. 30 and 33.
33. Marie McLaughlin, *Myths and Legends of the Sioux* (1916, reprint, Lincoln: University of Nebraska Press, 1990), pp. 31–33.
34. Hans Biedermann, *Dictionary of Symbolism: Cultural Icons and the Meaning Behind Them*, James Hulbert trans. (New York: Meridian, 1994), p. 165.
35. Jacobus Boschius, *Symbolographia, sive, De arte symbolica sermones septem* (Augsburg: J. C.Benard, 1701), 3:623, pl. 3:33 (engraving by Johann Georg Wolfgang, after a drawing by J. C. Schalk). See also Biederman, 1994, p. 164.
36. Pasztory, 1983, pp. 253–54, color pl. 45.
37. Carol Andrews, *Amulets of Ancient Egypt* (Austin: University of Texas Press, 1994), pp. 63–64, fig. 60.
38. R. T. Rundle Clark, *Myth and Symbol in Ancient Egypt* (New York and London: Thames and Hudson, 1959), pp. 52–57, fig. 8.
39. Schwendenwien, 1993, p. 96.

On Location in Paradise (and Elsewhere): The Lithographs of Sandy Skoglund by Ann H. Sievers

1. All artist quotations are from conversations between Skoglund and the author (spring 1997) unless otherwise noted.
2. See cat. nos. 22–24.
3. Among the variables she cites are paper shrinkage and registration problems.
4. The project and resulting exhibition were sponsored by L'Etablissement Public pour L'Aménagement de la Région de La Défense (EPAD).
5. The installation *Radioactive Cats* was in storage in Germany at the time, having been exhibited there recently (see Solo Exhibitions).

6. Held June 25–September 7, 1992, at L'Espace Art Défense. The installation *Radioactive Cats* was also exhibited in Paris that summer (July 10–August 2) at L'Espace Photographique de la Ville de Paris.
7. The Smith College Print Workshop, organized by the College's Department of Art with the collaboration of the Smith College Museum of Art, annually brings a prominent artist and a master printer together for two to five days to produce a limited edition print in the Art Department's Harnish Graphics Studio.
8. Paradise Pond derives its name from a local legend that the singer Jenny Lind, the "Swedish Nightingale," exclaimed of Northampton, "Oh, what a paradise!"
9. Skoglund held the Richard Koopman Distinguished Chair in the Visual Arts.
10. This site was proposed by Jerry Mocarsky.
11. In 1993 the Photographic Resource Center (Boston, Massachusetts) included a limited edition of Skoglund's photograph as part of its Members Print Program, which offers a selection of photographs to members in each of several membership categories. *The Hartford Drive-In* (1992, a limited edition of 10) was specially printed as an 11- by 14-inch color coupler print for the PRC by Gus Kayafas and Boston Photo Lab. The photograph was offered to members at the highest level of membership. One print of the photograph was offered for sale in the PRC benefit auction.
12. ArtsEdNet mail for March 1996, Re: Questions to Sandy Skoglund.
13. For example, the artist's first attempt to photograph *Dogs at the Beach* was canceled by a massive rainstorm.
14. Skoglund usually uses friends or acquaintances as models, as in *Dogs on the Beach*, where crew members (husband and wife) posed; *Squirrels at the Drive-In*, which featured friends of the artist from New York; or *Cats in Paris*, where the model was an American collector of Skoglund's work who wanted to be in one of her pieces. For *Babies at Paradise Pond*, models included Smith students (and one male Hampshire College student who was studying photography at Smith), as well as Smith College Museum of Art curators Muehlig and Sievers, and curatorial intern Kristen Erickson.
15. For succinct descriptions of the printing processes see Bamber Gascoigne, *How to Identify Prints* (New York: Thames and Hudson, 1986).
16. This source proved to be a high-quality 8-by 10-inch black-and-white positive film (transparency).
17. These are qualities she had observed in recent high-end black-and-white commercial printing.
18. Retaining the original green of the cats in both photographs, Skoglund chose an acid yellow for the scene under the viaduct and a rosy red for that on top of the structure.
19. Cate McQuaid, "Close-Up: Sandy Skoglund," *PRC Newsletter* 17, no. 2 (March 1993), p. 2.
20. Darcy Deal, "Sandy Skoglund," *Q: A Journal of Art* (spring 1993), p. 22. Sometimes, most notably, perhaps, in *Spirituality in the Flesh*, all that remains of the performance is the Cibachrome photograph.
21. This experience has occasionally been extended in other cases by the artist's allowing visitors to be photographed in the installation as a fund-raiser for the exhibiting museum (for example, the Lakeview Museum when it showed *The Green House*).
22. From the movies *The Village of the Damned* (1960) and the sequel *Children of the Damned* (1963), in which extraterrestrial radiation spawns child look-alikes who threaten Earth.
23. [M.F.S.] introduction to William R. Curtis, "Grands Projets," *Architectural Record* (March 1990), p.76.
24. See "Who's New? USA: Sandy Skoglund," *Amateur Photographer* (July 4, 1981), p. 84.
25. Owen McNally, "Still-Life Patio Scene Invites Viewers to Test Perceptions," *The Hartford Courant*, November 24, 1991.

EXHIBITION CHECKLIST

Key to abbreviations:
AP: Artist's Proof; BAT: *Bon à tirer*; HC: *Hors commerce*;
PP: Printer's Proof; RTP: Right to Print
Unless otherwise noted, all works are from the collection of the artist

Early Conceptual and Process Works: 1973–1976

1. *Crumpled and Copied*, 1973
(1997 reconstruction)
Xerox process
Size: 88 x 161" (223.6 x 408.8 cm)

2. *Resemblance and Difference*, 1974
Three Cibachrome prints
Each image: 9 x 13 5/8" (22.9 x 34.3 cm)
Each sheet: 14 x 11" (35.5 x 27.9 cm)

3. *Resemblance and Difference*, 1974
Two Cibachrome prints
Each image: 9 x 13 5/8" (22.9 x 34.3 cm)
Each sheet: 14 x 11" (35.5 x 27.9 cm)

4. *Starting with a Pencil Sharpened Once*, 1975
Graphite on gessoed canvas
60 x 60" (152.4 x 152.4 cm)

5. *Starting with Two Lines*, 1975
Black ink on gessoed canvas
60 x 60" (152.4 x 152.4 cm)

6. *One Line Crossing Itself*, 1975
Black ink on gessoed canvas
60 x 60" (152.4 x 152.4 cm)

7. *Starting with the Letter A*, 1975
Ink on white wove paper
13 3/4 x 17" (34.9 x 43.2 cm)

8. *Starting with a Square*, 1975
Ink on white wove paper
14 x 17" (35.5 x 43.2 cm)

Working in a House Trailer, Utica, New York: 1976–1978

9. *Pink Sink*, 1977
Cibachrome print
Image: 10 1/2 x 10 3/4" (26.7 x 27.3 cm)
Sheet: 11 x 14" (27.9 x 35.5 cm)

10. *Peaches in a Toaster*, 1977
Cibachrome print
Image: 10 3/8 x 9 5/8" (26.4 x 24.2 cm)
Sheet: 11 x 14" (27.9 x 35.5 cm)

11. *Iron*, 1977
Cibachrome print
Image: 10 3/8 x 13 1/2" (26.4 x 34.3 cm)
Sheet: 11 x 14" (27.9 x 35.5 cm)

12. *Toaster*, 1977
Cibachrome print
Image: 10 3/8 x 13 1/2" (26.4 x 34.3 cm)
Sheet: 11 x 14" (27.9 x 35.5 cm)

13. *Pots and Knobs*, 1978
Charcoal on white wove paper
24 x 19" (60.9 x 48.2 cm)

14. *Salt and Pepper Shakers Shaped Like Milk Cans*, 1978
Charcoal on white wove paper
19 x 25 1/4" (48.2 x 64.1 cm)

Food Still Life Series: 1978

15. *Luncheon Meat on a Counter*, 1978
Cibachrome print
Image: 22 1/2 x 28 1/2" (57.1 x 72.4 cm)
Edition: 25, plus 5 AP, 2 HC

16. *Cookies on a Plate*, 1978
Cibachrome print
Image: 22 x 27 1/2" (55.9 x 69.8 cm)
Edition: 25, plus 5 AP, 2 HC

17. *Peas on a Plate*, 1978
Cibachrome print
Image: 21 7/8 x 27 7/8" (55.6 x 70.8 cm)
Edition: 25, plus 5 AP, 2 HC

18. *Nine Slices of Marblecake*, 1978
Cibachrome print
Image: 21 7/8 x 27 1/2" (55.6 x 69.8 cm)
Edition: 25, plus 5 AP, 2 HC

19. *Two Boxes*, 1978
Cibachrome print
Image: 25 1/4 x 32 1/4" (64.1 x 81.9 cm)
Edition: 15, plus 3 AP, 1 HC

True Fiction: Paintings and Dye Transfer Prints: 1984–1987

The True Fiction photographs form a portfolio consisting of twenty different dye transfer prints.

20. *Tools of Expression*, 1986
Airbrush with acrylic on canvas
72 x 108" (183 x 274.6 cm)
Smith College Museum of Art, Northampton, Massachusetts. Gift of Castelli Graphics, 1991

21. *Life After Death*, 1986
Airbrush with acrylic on canvas
48 x 72" (121.9 x 182.9 cm)
Collection of Lita Hornick, New York

22. *Possibilities of Trash*, 1986
Dye transfer print
Image: 11 3/8 x 22 1/4" (28.9 x 56.5 cm)
Sheet: 20 x 24" (50.8 x 60.9 cm)
Edition: 25, plus 10 AP, 5 HC, 1 RTP

23. *Parallel Thinking*, 1986
Dye transfer print
Image: 13 7/8 x 22 1/8" (35.3 x 56.5 cm)
Sheet: 20 x 24" (50.8 x 60.9 cm)
Edition: 25, plus 10 AP, 5 HC, 1 RTP

24. *Laws of Interior Design*, 1986
Dye transfer print
Image: 12 x 22 1/2" (30.5 x 57.2 cm)
Sheet: 20 x 24" (50.8 x 60.9 cm)
Edition: 25, plus 10 AP, 5 HC, 1 RTP

Installations and Photographs: 1979–Present

25. *Spoons*, 1979
Cibachrome print
Image: 26 1/2 x 34" (67.3 x 86.4 cm)
Edition: 20, plus 10 AP, 5 HC, 1 RTP

26. *Hangers*, 1979
Cibachrome print
Image: 25 1/4 x 32 1/4" (64.2 x 81.9 cm)
Edition: 20, plus 10 AP, 5 HC, 1 RTP

27. *Radioactive Cats*, 1980
Cibachrome print
Image: 25 1/2 x 33" (64.7 x 83.8 cm)
Edition: 20, plus 10 AP, 5 HC, 1 RTP
Smith College Museum of Art, Northampton, Massachusetts. Purchased, 1987

28. *Revenge of the Goldfish*, 1981
Low-fired clay sculpture with acrylic paint, bedroom furniture (bed, bedclothes, pillows, lamps, bedside tables, bureau mirror); interior walls reconstructed at each venue
15 x 15' (4.6 x 4.6 m) floor space (variable)

29. *Revenge of the Goldfish*, 1981
Cibachrome print
Image: 27 1/4 x 35" (69.2 x 88.9 cm)
Edition: 30, plus 10 AP, 5 HC, 1 RTP

30. *Maybe Babies*, 1983
Dye transfer print
Image: 29 3/4 x 37 1/8" (75.6 x 94.3 cm)
Edition: 30, plus 10 AP, 9 HC, 1 RTP
Smith College Museum of Art, Northampton, Massachusetts. Gift of J. Michael Parish, 1993

31. *Germs Are Everywhere*, 1984
Cibachrome print
Image: 25 5/8 x 31 1/2" (65.1 x 80 cm)
Edition: 20, plus 10 AP, 5 HC, 1 RTP

32. *Sock Situation*, 1986
Cibachrome print
Image: 21 1/4 x 37 1/2" (54 x 95.2 cm)
Edition: 30, plus 10 AP, 5 HC, 1 RTP

33. *The Lost and Found*, 1986
Cibachrome print
Image: 26 1/2 x 38" (67.3 x 96.5 cm)
Edition: 30, plus 10 AP, 5 HC, 1 RTP

34. *A Breeze at Work*, 1987
Cibachrome print
Image: 38 x 54" (96.5 x 137.2 cm)
Edition: 30, plus 12 AP, 5 HC, 1 RTP

35. *Fox Games*, 1989
Cast polyester resin sculpture, restaurant furniture (tables and chairs, chandelier, salt and pepper shakers, breadbaskets with bread and napkins, bud vases); interior walls reconstructed at each venue
25 x 25' (7.6 x 7.6 m) floor space (variable)
Collection of The Denver Art Museum

36. *Fox Games*, 1989
Cibachrome print
Image: 46 1/4 x 63" (117.5 x 160 cm)
Edition: 30, plus 10 AP, 5 HC, 1 RTP

37. *The Green House*, 1990
Cibachrome print
Image: 46 1/4 x 59 1/4" (117.5 x 150.5 cm)
Edition: 30, plus 10 AP, 5 HC, 1 RTP

38. *Gathering Paradise*, 1991
Cibachrome print
Image: 47 1/4 x 61" (120 x 153.9 cm)
Edition: 30, plus 10 AP, 5 HC, 1 RTP
Mead Art Museum, Amherst College. Museum Purchase, Allan Albert (Class of 1967) Contemporary Photography Fund

39. *Spirituality in the Flesh*, 1992
Cibachrome print
Image: 36 x 28 3/16" (91.4 x 71.6 cm)
Edition: 20, plus 4 AP, 2 HC, 1 RTP

40. *Body Limits*, 1992
Cibachrome print
Image: 35 3/4 x 28" (90.8 x 71.1 cm)
Edition: 20, plus 4 AP, 2 HC, 1 RTP

41. *Atomic Love*, 1992
Cibachrome print
Image: 47 3/4 x 62 1/2" (121.3 x 158.7 cm)
Edition: 30, plus 7 AP, 4 HC, 1 RTP
Collection of Jenette Kahn, New York

42. *The Cocktail Party*, 1992
Epoxied cheese-flavored snack food, stationary figures and mechanized mannequins, furniture (lamps, chairs, table with cups), painted floor and wall panels (covered with cheese-flavored snacks)
15 x 15' (4.6 x 4.6 m) floor space (variable)

43. *The Cocktail Party*, 1992
Cibachrome print
Image: 48 x 65" (121.9 x 165.1 cm)
Edition: 30, plus 7 AP, 4 HC, 1 RTP

44. *The Wedding*, 1994
Cibachrome print
Image: 38 1/4 x 48" (97.1 x 121.9 cm)
Edition: 30, plus 7 AP, 4 HC, 1 RTP
Collection of Alvin D. Hall, New York

45. *Walking on Eggshells*, 1996–97
Whole, empty eggshells (some filled with plaster), cast paper bathroom fixtures (sink, bathtub, toilet, and mirror), cast paper wall tiles with relief-printed images, cold-cast (bonded-bronze) sculptures of snakes and rabbits
30 x 30' (9.1 x 9.1 m) floor space (variable)

46. *Walking on Eggshells*, 1997
Cibachrome print
Image: 47 3/8 x 60" (120.4 x 152.4 cm)
Edition: 30, plus 7 AP, 4 HC, 1 RTP

Other Photographs: 1990s

47. *At the Shore*, 1994
Cibachrome print
Image: 10 5/8 x 13 5/8" (27 x 34.6 cm)
Sheet: 11 x 14" (27.9 x 35.5 cm)
Edition: 30, plus 7 AP, 4 HC, 1 RTP

48. *Thirty Burgers with Mustard*, 1995
Cibachrome print
Image: 13 1/2 x 10 1/2" (34.3 x 26.7 cm)
Sheet: 14 x 11" (35.5 x 27.9 cm)
Edition: 30, plus 7 AP, 4 HC, 1 RTP

Prints: 1992–Present

49. *Dogs on the Beach*, 1992
Lithograph printed in color on Ragcote paper (AP 15/15)
Printer: Maurice Sanchez, Derrière l'Etoile Studios, with Joseph Petruzelli, James Miller, and Linda Gray
Image (including border): 24 3/4 x 22 3/8" (62.8 x 56.8 cm)
Sheet: 24 3/4 x 28 3/4" (62.2 x 73 cm)
Edition: 65, plus 15 AP, 5 PP, 1 BAT
Smith College Museum of Art, Northampton, Massachusetts. Gift of Sandy Skoglund (1968) and Janet Borden (1973), 1995

50. *Cats in Paris*, 1993
Lithograph printed in color on Ragcote paper (AP 15/15)
Printer: Maurice Sanchez, Derrière L'Etoile Studios, with Joseph Petruzelli, James Miller, and Linda Gray
Image (including border): 24 x 28 1/2" (61 x 72.3 cm)
Sheet: 24 x 28 1/2" (61 x 72.3 cm)
Edition: 50, plus 15 AP, 5 PP, 1 BAT
Smith College Museum of Art, Northampton, Massachusetts. Gift of Sandy Skoglund (1968) and Janet Borden (1973), 1995

51. *Babies at Paradise Pond*, 1996
Lithograph printed in color on Ragcote paper (1/75)
Printer: Maurice Sanchez, Derrière L'Etoile Studios, with James Miller
Image: 20 x 25 1/2" (50.8 x 64.9 cm)
Sheet: 26 1/2 x 31 1/2" (67.3 x 80 cm)
Edition: 75, plus 15 AP, 5 PP, 2 workshop proofs, 1 BAT
Smith College Museum of Art, Northampton, Massachusetts. Gift of the artist through the Smith College Print Workshop, 1996

52. *Squirrels at the Drive-In*, 1996
Lithograph printed in color on paper
Printer: Maurice Sanchez, Derrière L'Etoile Studios, with James Miller
Image: 20 x 25 1/2" (50.8 x 64.9 cm)
Sheet: 26 5/8 x 31 5/8" (67.6 x 80.3 cm)
Edition: 75, plus 15 AP, 5 PP, 1 BAT
Smith College Museum of Art, Northampton, Massachusetts. Gift of Sandy Skoglund (1968), 1997

EXHIBITION HISTORY

Sandy Skoglund

1946: Born in Quincy, Massachusetts
1968: B.A. Smith College, Northampton, Massachusetts
1971: M.A. University of Iowa, Iowa City, Iowa
1972: M.F.A. University of Iowa, Iowa City, Iowa

Solo Exhibitions and Major Catalogues

1998

Light as a Feather (installation, working title), commissioned by Robeson Gallery, Rutgers University, Newark, New Jersey, September–November 1998

1996

Sandy Skoglund. Manezh Exhibition Hall, Moscow, Russia, March–June 1996. Curators: Olga Sviblova and Yvonamor Palix.

Sandy Skoglund: Teaching Contemporary Art. ArtsEdNet, The Getty Education Institute for the Arts: http://www.artsednet.getty.edu/. On-line discussion with the artist, January–May 1996; on-line exhibition with archived discussions and curriculum materials, January 1996–present.

1995

Sandy Skoglund: The Subject of Food (photographs). Ehlers Caudill Gallery, Chicago, Illinois, April 21–May 27, 1995.

Sandy Skoglund (photographs). Galeria Spectrum, Zaragoza, Spain, February 24–March 22, 1995, organized with the collaboration of Espace d'Art Yvonamor Palix, Paris, France.

1994

The Wedding (installation). Janet Borden, Inc., New York, New York, September 10–October 22, 1994.

Sandy Skoglund. Tarazonafoto 1994. Veruela Monastery, Tarazona, Spain, July 1–September 5, 1994. Catalogue. Curator: Yvonamor Palix.

The Cocktail Party (installation). Allene LaPides Gallery, Santa Fe, New Mexico, April 15–August 31, 1994.

1993

The Cocktail Party (installation). Manchester Craftsmen's Guild, Pittsburgh, Pennsylvania, November 8–December 3, 1993.

Sandy Skoglund: A Breeze at Work and Other Works (installation and photographs). Sawhill Gallery, James Madison University, Harrisonburg, Virginia, September 28–October 24, 1993.

Pour la Vie. Musée d'art contemporain (CAPC), Bordeaux, France, September 24–November 21, 1993.

In the Last Hour. Espace d'Art Yvonamor Palix, Paris, France, September 16–November 6, 1993.

Photographs. Salama-Caro Gallery, London, England, September 14–October 20, 1993.

Photographs. Allene LaPides Gallery, Santa Fe, New Mexico, August 27–October 1, 1993.

Sandy Skoglund (*A Breeze at Work* installation and photographs). Southeastern Center for Contemporary Art, Winston-Salem, North Carolina, July 17–September 19, 1993.

The Green House (installation). Madison Art Center, Madison, Wisconsin, June 26–August 22, 1993.

Sandy Skoglund: A Survey of Works from 1979 to 1992. Installations, Photographs, Sculpture. (The Cocktail Party and *Body Limits* installations). Bernard Toale Gallery, Boston, Massachusetts, March 30–May 1, 1993.

1992

The Green House (installation with photographs). DiverseWorks Artspace, Houston, Texas, December 12, 1992–January 17, 1993.

Sandy Skoglund. Beard Greenhouse Gallery, New York, New York, November–December 1992.

Atomic Love, Body Limits, The Cocktail Party (three installations). Janet Borden, Inc., New York, New York, October 1–31, 1992.

In the Last Hour: Sandy Skoglund Photographs and Sculpture 1979–1992. Fred Jones, Jr., Museum of Art (organizer), University of Oklahoma, Norman, Oklahoma, September 27–November 8, 1992 (also shown: *The Green House* installation); Blue Star Artspace, San Antonio, Texas, February 12–April 14, 1993 (also shown: *A Breeze at Work* and *Gathering Paradise* installations); University of North Texas Art Gallery, Denton, Texas, February 10–March 13, 1993 (also shown: *The Green House* installation); The Morris Museum, Morristown, New Jersey, October 3—November 21, 1993; The Edwin A. Ulrich Museum, Wichita State University, Wichita, Kansas, January 21–March 6, 1994 (also shown: *The Cocktail Party* installation); Columbus Museum of Art, Columbus, Ohio, March 20–June 12, 1994 (also shown: *The Wedding* installation, commissioned by the Columbus Museum of Art); The Amarillo Art Museum, Amarillo, Texas, September 10–November 6, 1994; Lakeview Museum, Peoria, Illinois, December 5, 1994–January 29, 1995 (also shown: *The Green House* installation); Art Museum of South Texas, Corpus Christi, Texas, March 3–May 1, 1995; Scottsdale Center for the Arts, Scottsdale, Arizona, June 2–August 20, 1995 (also shown: *The Cocktail Party* installation); Huntington Museum of Art, Huntington, West Virginia, September 9–October 29, 1995 (also shown: *The Green House* installation). Catalogue, with essays by Arlene Raven and Glòria Picazo (Picazo essay reprinted from catalogue for Fundació "la Caixa" exhibition, 1992; trans. Lorenza Panero).

The Greenhouse (installation). Aspen Art Museum, Aspen, Colorado, June 25–September 7, 1992.

Art Basel 23 '92 mit Sandy Skoglund Photographien 1978–1992. Galerie Zur Stockeregg, Zurich, Switzerland, June 17–22, 1992.

Sandy Skoglund (retrospective of photographs). L'Espace Photographique de la Ville de Paris, Paris, France, June 10–August 2, 1992, organized in collaboration with Jean Luc Monterosso of Paris Audiovisuel. Catalogue, with texts by Glòria Picazo and Patrick Roegiers (essays reprinted from catalogue for Fundació "la Caixa" exhibition, 1992).

Sandy Skoglund: Food Still Life Series. Janet Borden, Inc., New York, New York, May 15–June 19, 1992.

Sandy Skoglund (*Radioactive Cats* installation and retrospective of photographs). Sala Catalunya, Fundació "la Caixa," Barcelona, Spain, April 28–May 31, 1992. Catalogue, with essays by Glòria Picazo and Patrick Roegiers.

The Green House Installation and Photographs by Sandy Skoglund. The Lowe Art Museum, Coral Gables, Florida, April 9–May 24, 1992.

Photographs. Gallery K, Washington, D.C., March 14–April 11, 1992.

The Green House: Sandy Skoglund. The Tampa Museum of Art, Tampa, Florida, January 19–March 2, 1992.

1991

Sandy Skoglund. Kyle Roberts Gallery, San Francisco, California, September 21, 1991–November 2, 1992.

Sandy Skoglund: The Green House. Memphis Brooks Museum, Memphis, Tennessee, September 13, 1991–January 5, 1992.

Gathering Paradise (installation). P.P.O.W. Gallery, New York, New York, September 5–28, 1991.

Sandy Skoglund Foto-Inszenierungen 1986–1991 (*Radioactive Cats* installation and survey of photographs). Städtische Galerie, Erlangen, Germany, August 3–September 1, 1991; Nikon Galerie, Zurich, Switzerland, November 30, 1991–January 14, 1992; Fotografie Forum Frankfurt, Frankfurt, Germany, January 18–February 23, 1992; Fotoforum, Bremen, Germany, February 28–April 1, 1992. Curator: Michael Köhler.

The Green House: Installation and Photographs. The Morgan Gallery, Kansas City, Missouri, June 21–July 27, 1991.

Gathering Paradise (installation and retrospective of photographs). Carl Solway Gallery, Cincinnati, Ohio, June 7–July 31, 1991.

Photographs. Ehlers Caudill Gallery, Chicago, Illinois, April 19–May 30, 1991.

Sandy Skoglund: The Green House Installation and Photographs. Fay Gold Gallery, Atlanta, Georgia, February 8–March 6, 1991.

1990

The Green House (installation). Temple Gallery, Tyler School of Art, Temple University, Philadelphia, Pennsylvania, November 16, 1990–January 26, 1991.

The Green House (installation). Janet Borden, Inc., New York, New York, September 4–29, 1990.

Sandy Skoglund (*Radioactive Cats* installation and retrospective of photographs). Parco Corporation Gallery, Tokyo, Japan, August 3–22, 1990.

Fox Games (installation). The Denver Art Museum, Denver, Colorado, June 2–August 5, 1990.

The Green House (installation). G. H. Dalsheimer Gallery, Baltimore, Maryland, April 28–June 16, 1990.

Sandy Skoglund: True Fiction and Fox Games (photographs). The International Museum of Photography, George Eastman House, Rochester, New York, January 18–February 18, 1990.

1989

Sandy Skoglund: Rétrospective (photographs and sculpture). Galerie Urbi et Orbi, Paris, France, October 14–November 20, 1989.

Sandy Skoglund. Bronze Sculpture: A Breeze at Work and Photographs: 1980–1988. Stephen Wirtz Gallery, San Francisco, California, February 28–April 1, 1989.

1988

A Breeze at Work (photographs). Hollins Art Gallery, Hollins College, Roanoke, Virginia, October 16–November 11, 1988.

Sandy Skoglund: A Sculpture Installation. Lorence-Monk Gallery, New York, New York, September 17–October 15, 1988.

A Breeze at Work (installation). Damon Brandt Gallery, New York, New York, September 10–October 1, 1988.

1987

True Fiction (photographs). Real Art Ways, Hartford, Connecticut, October 16–November 7, 1987.

Hard Work. Fay Gold Gallery, Atlanta, Georgia, October 9–November 4, 1987.

Photographs, Selected Works, and True Fiction Portfolio. Fahey/Klein Gallery, Los Angeles, California, August 11–September 12, 1987.

Neo Auto (installation). Sharpe Gallery, New York, New York, January 11–February 8, 1987.

True Fiction. Castelli Uptown Gallery, New York, New York, January 9–31, 1987.

1986

Sock Situation (installation). Christmas window for Barneys department store, New York, New York, December 1986.

1984

Maybe Babies/Sandy Skoglund. Galerie Watari, Tokyo, Japan, April 13–May 4, 1984.

1983

Maybe Babies (installation). Greenberg Gallery, St. Louis, Missouri, October 22–November 26, 1983.

Maybe Babies (installation). Leo Castelli Gallery, New York, New York, March 5–26, 1983.

1982

Maybe Babies (installation). Art Across the Park. Prospect Park, Brooklyn, New York, August 24–31, 1982. Curators: Gylbert Coker and Horace Brockington.

Matrix 71: Sandy Skoglund (Revenge of the Goldfish installation). Wadsworth Atheneum, Hartford, Connecticut, April 24–August 15, 1982. Curator: Andrea Miller-Keller.

1981

Revenge of the Goldfish and *Radioactive Cats* (installations). Minneapolis Institute of Art, Minneapolis, Minnesota, December 19, 1981–January 24, 1982.

Revenge of the Goldfish (installation). Greenberg Gallery, St. Louis, Missouri, November 1981.

Focus: Revenge of the Goldfish (installation and photographs). Fort Worth Art Museum, Fort Worth, Texas, September 18–October 18, 1981. Curator: Susan Freudenheim.

Radioactive Cats (installation). Addison Gallery of American Art, Phillips Academy, Andover, Massachusetts, May 9–June 14, 1981.

Revenge of the Goldfish (installation and photographs). Castelli Graphics, New York, New York, January 6–31, 1981.

1980

Radioactive Cats (installation and photographs). Real Art Ways, Hartford, Connecticut, March 1–14, 1980.

1979

University of Connecticut, Torrington, Connecticut.

1974

Camera Obscura 74. Joseloff Gallery, Hartford Art School, University of Hartford, West Hartford, Connecticut, September 4–13, 1974.

Group Exhibitions and Major Catalogues

1997

Making It Real. Organized by Independent Curators, Inc. Aldrich Museum of Contemporary Art, Ridgefield, Connecticut, January

19–April 20, 1997; Reykjavík Municipal Art Museum, Reykjavík, Iceland, October 18–November 23, 1997; Portland Museum of Art, Portland, Maine, January 22–March 22, 1998; Bayly Art Museum, University of Virginia, Charlottesville, Virginia, September 18–November 15, 1998. Catalogue, with introduction by Luc Sante and essay by Vik Muniz, guest curator.

1996

Color and Humor. A Gallery for Fine Photography, New Orleans, Louisiana, November 15, 1995–January 21, 1996.

This Is a Set-Up: Fab Photo Fictions. Dorothy Uber Bryan Gallery, Bowling Green State University, Bowling Green, Ohio, October 4–November 8, 1996. Curators: Jacqueline S. Nathan and Lynn Whitney.

Art & The Law, 1996. Organized by West Publishing Company. Indiana Convention Center and RCA Dome, Indianapolis, Indiana, July 20–23, 1996; Hyatt Regency Grand Cypress, Orlando, Florida, August 1–7, 1996; Kresge Art Museum, Michigan State University, East Lansing, Michigan, September 3–October 20, 1996; The University of Tulsa College of Law and School of Art, Alexandre Hogue Gallery, University of Tulsa, Tulsa, Oklahoma, November 14–December 20, 1996; Miami University Art Museum, Oxford, Ohio, January 21–March 18, 1997. Catalogue.

Decathlon. Fay Gold Gallery, Atlanta, Georgia, June 7–July 7, 1996.

Telling Stories. Jacksonville Museum of Contemporary Art, Jacksonville, Florida, March 14–April 29, 1996. Curator: Paul Karabinis.

Feast for the Eyes. Austin Museum of Art at Laguna Gloria, Austin, Texas, February 17–April 7, 1996.

Photography in the 1990s. Wright State University, Dayton, Ohio, February 11–March 17, 1996. Curator: Ron Geibert.

1995

Biennale internationale d'art de groupe. Cargo Marseille, Centre international d'arts visuels, Marseilles, France, September 21–October 26, 1995. Curator: Marianne Sarraílh.

Portrait of My Mother, in conjunction with *Signals*, the first UK-wide Festival of Women Photographers. Institut Français d'Ecosse, Edinburgh, Scotland, September 9–October 8, 1995; Institut Français du Royaume Uni, London, England, October 14–November 19, 1995. Catalogue, with essay by Viviane Esders.

Work in Progress. Mississippi Museum of Art, Jackson, Mississippi, May 19–July 29, 1995. Curator: René-Paul Barilleaux.

L'Immagine Riflessa (una selezioni di fotografia contemporanea dalla Collezione LAC, Svizzera). Museo Pecci (Centro per l'Arte Contemporanea Luigi Pecci and Museo d'Arte Contemporaneo), Prato, Italy, April 1–May 28, 1995. Curator: Paolo Colombo. Catalogue by Antonella Soldaini.

Photography Today. Sonje Museum of Contemporary Art, Seoul, South Korea, March 31–May 31, 1995. Catalogue, with essay by Sun Jung Kim.

Fotoinszenierungen: Sandy Skoglund/Arthur Tress (retrospective of photographs). Museumsverein Arolsen, Arolsen, Germany, February 11–March 26, 1995.

Women in Photography. Light Impressions Spectrum Gallery, Rochester, New York, January 13–February 12, 1995.

1994

An American Century of Photography, from Dry-Plate to Digital. The Hallmark Photographic Collection. Nelson-Atkins Museum of Art, Kansas City, Missouri, December 15, 1994–February 19, 1995; Mead Art Museum, Amherst College, Amherst, Massachusetts, March 10–May 7, 1995; International Center of Photography—Midtown, New York, New York, June 2–September 10, 1995; Auckland City Art Gallery, Auckland, New Zealand, November 15, 1995–February 5, 1996; National Gallery of Victoria, Melbourne, Victoria, Australia, March 8–May 6, 1996; Art Gallery of New South Wales, Sydney, New South Wales, Australia, May 17–July 7, 1996; Museum of Photographic Arts, San Diego, California, October 16–December 1, 1996; Terra Museum of American Art, Chicago, Illinois, January 17–March 30, 1997. Curator: Keith F. Davis. Catalogue.

La Chair Promise. Musée de l'Abbaye Sainte-Croix, Les Sables-d'Olonne, France, June 18–September 30, 1994.

Around the House: An Invitational Exhibition of Paintings, Drawings, Sculptures of Domestic Themes. Frumkin/Adams Gallery, New York, New York, June 16–August 5, 1994.

La Faune et la Flore. Mois de l'Image, Maison des Jeunes et de la Culture, Dieppe, France, April 6–May 7, 1994.

Babies and Bambies. Maatschappij Arti et Amicitiae, Amsterdam, The Netherlands, January 30–February 27, 1994. Catalogue, with essays by Nina Folkersma, Frank Reijnders, and Leontine Coelewi.

1993

Ten by Ten by Ten (a Testwall exhibition). TZ Art & Co., New York, New York, November 30, 1993–January 15, 1994. Curator: Barbara Sahlman.

Sonsbeek 93. Gemeentemuseum Arnhem, Arnhem, The Netherlands, June 5–September 26, 1993. Catalogue (*The Uncanny*), with essay by Mike Kelley.

American-Made: The New Still Life. Isetan Museum of Art (organizer), Tokyo, Japan, June 3–15, 1993; Hokkaido Obihiro Museum of Art, Hokkaido, Japan, November 13–December 19, 1993. Catalogue, with essay by Patty Carroll.

Vivid: Intense Images by American Photographers. Raab Galerie, Berlin, Germany, May 19–July 31, 1993; Raab Boukamel Galleries Ltd., London, England, September 14–October 23, 1993; Gian Ferrari Arte Contemporanea, Milan, Italy, September 15–November 13, 1994. Curator: Victoria Espy Burns. Catalogue.

From the Gallery to the Museum, Photographic Discoveries: Extracts of the Paris Audiovisuel Collection. Grand Palais, Paris, France, February 3–8, 1993.

1992

Putt-Modernism. Artists Space (organizer), New York, New York, July 30–September 27, 1992; Southeastern Center for Contemporary Art, Winston-Salem, North Carolina, August 7–September 30, 1993; Artists' Space, New York, New York, October 23, 1993–February 27, 1994; Allentown Art Museum, Allentown, Pennsylvania, March 20–August 15, 1994; Cleveland Center for Contemporary Art, Cleveland, Ohio, September 9–October 31, 1994; Salt Lake Art Center, Salt Lake City, Utah, July 14—September 3, 1995; Kemper Art Museum, Kansas City, Missouri, February 4–April 21, 1996; The Hyde Collection, Glens Falls, New York, May 25–August 4, 1996; Palm Beach Community College Museum of Art, Lake Worth, Florida, November 16–December 20, 1996.

Installations & Constructions. Tavelli Williams Gallery, Aspen, Colorado, July 7–August 1, 1992.

Arrêt sur Viaduc. Organized by L'Etablissement Public pour l'Aménagement de la Région de la Défense. Espace Art Défense, Paris, France, June 25–September 7, 1992. Curator: Alain Sayag. Catalogue.

Unclear and Present Danger. The National Arts Club, New York, New York, March 5–29, 1992.

Points of View—Photography Today. Champion Gallery, Stamford, Connecticut, February 26–June 10, 1992.

1991

Investigations in Perception. Joseloff Gallery, Hartford Art School, University of Hartford, West Hartford, Connecticut, November 24, 1991–January 10, 1992.

The Intuitive Eye: Photographs from the David C. and Sarajean Ruttenberg Collection. The Art Institute of Chicago, Chicago, Illinois, October 12, 1991–January 12, 1992.

Photography 1980–1990. Ginny Williams Gallery, Denver, Colorado, June 7–July 1991.

The American Scene: Contemporary Photographs. Rena Bransten Gallery, San Francisco, California, June 4–July 6, 1991.

Visions/Revisions: Selections from the Contemporary Collection. Denver Art Museum, Denver, Colorado, April 27–August 25, 1991.

Fotografía Americana del Siglo XX. Fundació "la Caixa," Barcelona, Spain, April 16–May 26, 1991. Catalogue.

Lo Specchio/In/Fedele: evoluzione dell'immagine nella fotografia contemporanea. Padiglione d'Arte Contemporanea di Milano, Milan, Italy, February 14–March 10, 1991. Curator: Giuliana Scime. Catalogue.

1990

Constructed Reality. New Jersey Center for Visual Arts, Summit, New Jersey, April 8–May 20, 1990. Catalogue, with an introduction by Anne H. Hoy.

Biennale Internationale de Marseille. Musées de Marseille, Marseilles, France, April–June 1990. Curator: Bernard Millet. Catalogue, with essay by Patrick Roegiers.

To Be and Not to Be. Centre d'Art Santa Monica, Barcelona, Spain, April–May 1990. Curators: V. Altaio and C. Grande. Catalogue.

The Indomitable Spirit. Sponsored by Photographers + Friends United Against AIDS. International Center of Photography, New York, New York, February 8–April 17, 1990; The Los Angeles Municipal Art Gallery, Barnsdall Art Park, Los Angeles, California, May 13–June 17, 1990. Curator: Marvin Heiferman. Catalogue.

1989

Das Konstruierte Bild. Fotografie-arrangiert und inszeniert [Constructed Realities]. Kunstverein, Munich, Germany, October

28–December 3, 1989; Kunsthalle, Nuremberg, Germany, February 23–March 25, 1990; Forum Bottcherstrasse, Bremen, Germany, April 25–June 13, 1990; Badischer Kunstverein, Karlsruhe, Germany, June 17–July 20, 1990. Catalogue, with essay by Michael Köhler.

L'Invention d'un Art (Cent-cinquantième anniversaire de la photographie). Centre Georges Pompidou, Paris, France, October 12, 1989–January 1, 1990. Curators: Alain Sayag and Jean-Claude Lemagny. Catalogue, with essays by Jean-Claude Lemagny, Alain Sayag, and Michel Nuredsany.

A Decade of Collecting: The Liberated Image: Fabricated Photography Since 1970. Tampa Museum of Art, Tampa, Florida. September 10–November 26, 1989. Curator: Genevieve Linnehan. Exhibition checklist.

Fragments of History. Albany Museum of Art, Albany, Georgia, July 21–September 3, 1989. Catalogue by Peter Doroshenko.

Made Not Taken: The Expansion of Photography. Locks Gallery, Philadelphia, Pennsylvania, July 10–August 25, 1989.

Lines of Vision: Drawings by Contemporary Women. Blum-Helman Warehouse, New York, New York, July 6–August 17, 1989.

Fantasies, Fables, and Fabrications. Delaware Art Museum, Wilmington, Delaware, May 12–July 2, 1989; Herter Art Gallery (organizer), University of Massachusetts, Amherst, Massachusetts, September 22–November 3, 1989; Lamont Gallery, Phillips-Exeter Academy, Exeter, New Hampshire, January 3–February 14, 1990; University of Missouri Gallery of Art, Kansas City, Missouri, March 18–April 29, 1990; Provinciaal Museum voor Moderne Kunst, Ostend, Belgium, June 17–July 28, 1990; Museum at the Palazzo Mangarni, Fiesole, Italy, September 1–October 14, 1990; Provinciaal Museum voor Fotografie, Antwerp, Belgium, November 8–December 16, 1990. Curators: Trevor Richardson and Michael Coblyn. Catalogue.

New Acquisitions/New Work/NewDirections: 1981–1989. The International Museum of Photography, George Eastman House, Rochester, New York, May 12–July 16, 1989.

Suburban Home Life: Tracking the American Dream. Whitney Museum of American Art, Downtown at Federal Reserve Plaza, New York, New York, May 3–June 28, 1989; Whitney Museum of American Art at Champion, Stamford, Connecticut, July 13–September 6, 1989. Curators: Sarah Bayliss, Amy Michael Homes, Christopher Robert Hoover, and Miwon Kwan. Catalogue, with essays by Miwon Kwan and Sarah Bayliss.

The Photography of Invention: American Pictures of the 1980s. National Museum of American Art, Washington, D.C., April 28–September 10, 1989; Museum of Contemporary Art, Chicago, Illinois, November 4, 1989–January 28, 1990; The Walker Art Center, Minneapolis, Minnesota, June 10–August 26, 1990. Curator: Joshua Smith. Catalogue.

Artists of the 80s: Selected Works from the Maslow Collection. Sordoni Art Gallery, Wilkes College, Wilkes-Barre, Pennsylvania, April 9–May 7, 1989. Catalogue.

Fictive Strategies: Actuality and Originality in Contemporary Photography. Squibb Gallery, Princeton, New Jersey, February 26–April 2, 1989. Curator: Joseph B. Rauch.

Making Their Mark: Women Artists Move into the Mainstream, 1970–85. Cincinnati Art Museum, Cincinnati, Ohio, February 22–April 2, 1989; New Orleans Museum of Art, New Orleans, Louisiana, May 6–June 18, 1989; Denver Art Museum, Denver, Colorado, July 15–September 10, 1989; Pennsylvania Academy of Fine Arts, Philadelphia, Pennsylvania, October 18–January 3, 1990. Curators: Catherine Coleman Brawer and Randy Rosen. Catalogue.

Science Projects. The Gallery, Williams Center for the Arts, Lafayette College, Easton, Pennsylvania, February 15–March 31, 1989. Catalogue, with essay by Janet Borden.

Decade by Decade. Twentieth-Century American Photography from the Collection of the Center for Creative Photography. Center for Creative Photography, University of Arizona, Tucson, Arizona, February 10–June 9, 1989. Catalogue.

Art of the 80s from the Collection of Chemical Bank. The Montclair Art Museum, Montclair, New Jersey, January 29–April 9, 1989. Catalogue, with essay by Janice C. Oresman.

F.N.A.C. 88. *Une exposition des oeuvres photographiques acquises en 1988 par le Fond National d'Art Contemporain.* Centre national de la photographie, Palais de Tokyo, Paris, France, January 26–March 27, 1989.

International Contemporary Women. Galerie für Kunstphotographie Zur Stockeregg, Zurich, Switzerland, January 25–March 9, 1989.

Photography Expanded. G. H. Dalsheimer Gallery, Baltimore, Maryland, January 24–February 23, 1989.

Visiting Artists. Meyerhoff Gallery, The Maryland Institute, College of Art, Baltimore, Maryland, January 20–February 19, 1989.

1988

The Nature of Things. Cydney Payton Gallery, Denver, Colorado, November 4–December 9, 1988.

Forecasts: Visions of Technology in Contemporary Painting and Sculpture. Nerlino Gallery, Inc., New York, New York, September 24–October 25, 1988. Catalogue, with essays by Gail Levin and Sandy Skoglund.

Objects. Lorence-Monk Gallery, New York, New York, July 7–29, 1988.

Lifelike. Lorence-Monk Gallery, New York, New York, June 4–25, 1988. Curator: Marvin Heiferman.

Photography on the Edge. The Haggarty Museum of Art, Marquette University, Milwaukee, Wisconsin, March 24–June 8, 1988.

Fabricated Photographs. The Carpenter Center, Harvard University, Cambridge, Massachusetts, March 3–April 10, 1988. Curator: Anne H. Hoy.

Perceptual Subversion. Bruno Facchetti Gallery, New York, New York, February 6–March 2, 1988.

Castelli Graphics 1969–1988, Castelli Graphics, New York, New York, 1988. Catalogue with essay by Pat Caporaso.

8 Visions: Works by 8 Contemporary American Women. Parco Corporation Art Gallery, Tokyo, Japan, 1988. Catalogue, with essay by Gyoh Suzuki.

1987

Cross-References: Sculpture into Photography. The Walker Art Center, Minneapolis, Minnesota, September 26–December 13, 1987; Museum of Contemporary Art, Chicago, Illinois, January 29–April 3, 1988. Curators: Marge Goldwater, Adam Weinberg, and Elizabeth Armstrong. Catalogue.

Photography and Art: Interactions Since 1946. The Los Angeles County Museum of Art (organizer), Los Angeles, California, June 4–August 30, 1987; The Museum of Art, Fort Lauderdale, Florida, October 15, 1987–January 24, 1988; Queens Museum, Flushing, New York, February 13–April 3, 1988; Des Moines Art Center, Des Moines, Iowa, May 6–June 26, 1988. Curators: Kathleen Gauss and Andy Grundberg. Catalogue.

Greater Than or Equal to 30" x 40": Large-Format Photography. Jayne H. Baum Gallery, New York, New York, March 19–April 18, 1987.

This Is Not a Photograph: Twenty Years of Large-Scale Photography, 1966–1986. The John and Mable Ringling Museum of Art (organizer), Sarasota, Florida, March 7–May 31, 1987; Akron Art Museum, Akron, Ohio, October 31, 1987–January 10, 1988; The Chrysler Museum, Norfolk, Virginia, February 26–May 1, 1988. Catalogue, with essays by Joseph Jacobs and Marvin Heiferman, introduction by Gordon Lewis.

Arrangements for the Camera: A View of Contemporary Photography. Baltimore Museum of Art, Baltimore, Maryland, February 10–April 19, 1987. Curator: Janice Howard.

1986

Fifty Years of Modern Color Photography 1936–1986. Photokina, Cologne, Germany, September 3–9, 1986. Curator: Manfred Heiting.

La Magie de l'image. Musée d'Art Contemporain de Montréal, Montreal, Canada, June 1–August 31, 1986. Catalogue, with essay by Paulette Gagnon.

Short Stories. One Penn Plaza, New York, New York, May 19–September 5, 1986. Curators: Judd Tully and Carola van den Houten.

Photographic Fictions. Whitney Museum of American Art, Fairfield County, Stamford, Connecticut, April 4–May 28, 1986. Curator: Roni Feinstein.

Contemporary Issues II: Works from the Collection of Robert and Nancy Kaye. Holman Hall Art Gallery, Trenton State College, Trenton, New Jersey, April 2–25, 1986. Catalogue.

Théâtre des Réalités. Metz pour la Photographie (organizer), Caves Sainte-Croix, Metz, France, March 1986; presented by le Centre National de la Photographie, Palais de Tokyo, Paris, France, October 1986. Catalogue, with essays by Philippe Lacoue-Labarthe, Christopher Meatyard, and Patrick Roegiers.

Figurations. Organized by the Museum of Modern Art's Art Lending Service/Art Advisory Service, New York, New York. American Express Co., December 13, 1986–April 25, 1987; Gannett Co., Inc., November 2, 1987–March 14, 1988; General Electric, May 9–July 25, 1988; Pfizer, Inc., October 10, 1991–February 4, 1992.

1985

Psychodrama Restructured. Philadelphia Art Alliance, Philadelphia, Pennsylvania, December 1985–January 1986. Curator: Saul Ostrow.

Correspondences New York Art Now. Laforet Museum Harajuku, Tokyo, Japan, December 20, 1985–January 19, 1986; Tochigi Prefectural Museum of Fine Arts, Utsunomiya, Japan, February 8–March 23, 1986. Curator: Nicolas Moufarrege. Catalogue, with essays by Nicolas Moufarrege and Alan Jones.

Illuminating Color: Four Approaches in Contemporary Painting and Photography. Pratt Institute Gallery, Brooklyn, New York, October 16–November 7, 1985. Curators: Nina Prantis, Donna Stein, and Lynn Zelevansky.

Imagemakers: Eight Contemporary Photographers. College Art Gallery, State University of New York, New Paltz, New York, October 2–November 6, 1985. Curator: François Deschamps.

Group Show. Myers Gallery, State University of New York, Plattsburgh, New York, September 25–October 30, 1985.

Two Photographers: Skoglund and Pfahl. Museum of Art, Science, and Industry, Bridgeport, Connecticut, July 12–September 8, 1985.

Real Surreal. Lorence-Monk Gallery, New York, New York, May 1985.

Still Life in Photography. Rotterdam Arts Council, Rotterdam, The Netherlands, March 30–June 30, 1985.

1984

Situations. Organized by the Museum of Modern Art's Art Lending Service/Art Advisory Service, New York, New York. Dancer Fitzgerald, Sample, December 15, 1984–May 9, 1985; Freeport-McMoRan, Inc., May 12–August 12, 1985; General Electric, January 9–April 9, 1988; Pfizer, Inc., September 7–December 7, 1988.

Sculpture from Rutgers. Robeson Center Gallery, Rutgers University, Newark, New Jersey, November 29–December 21, 1984.

New Talent/New York. Sioux City Art Center, Sioux City, Iowa, November 17, 1984–January 13, 1985; University of Wisconsin-Stout, Menomonie, Wisconsin, March 11–April 11, 1985; Luther College, Decorah, Iowa, June 1–July 31, 1985; University of Northern Iowa, Cedar Falls, Iowa, September 9–October 13, 1985; Fort Hays Kansas State College, Hays, Kansas, October 28, 1985–January 5, 1986; University of Wisconsin, Green Bay, Wisconsin, February 7–March 15, 1986. Curator: Tom Butler. Catalogue, with essays by Lisa Liberian and Tom Butler.

New Drawings by Castelli Artists. Castelli Uptown Gallery, New York, New York, October 13–November 3, 1984.

Disarming Images: Art for Nuclear Disarmament. Organized by Bread and Roses, the cultural project of the National Union of Hospital and Health Care Employees, AFL-CIO, and Physicians for Social Responsibility, New York, New York. Contemporary Art Center, Cincinnati, Ohio, September 14–October 27, 1984; University Art Gallery, San Diego State University, San Diego, California, November 23–December 22, 1984; Museum of Art, Washington State University, Pullman, Washington, February 11–March 3, 1985; New York State Museum, Albany, New York, March 24–June 2, 1985; University Art Museum, University of California, Santa Barbara, California, June 25–August 4, 1985; Munson-Williams-Proctor Institute Museum of Art, Utica, New York, September 1–29, 1985; Fine Arts Gallery, University of Nevada, Las Vegas, Nevada, January 5–February 2, 1986; Baxter Art Gallery, California Institute of Technology, Pasadena, California, March 2–30, 1986; Yellowstone Art Center, Billings, Montana, April 28–June 9, 1986; Bronx Museum of the Arts, New York, New York, September 11–November 20, 1986. Curator: Nina Felshin. Catalogue.

Large-Scale Photography. Dart Gallery, Chicago, Illinois, September 14–October 10, 1984.

American Style: Faces and Places. Liberty House, Honolulu, Hawaii, September 9–22, 1984. Curator: Marvin Heiferman.

The Contemporary Photograph 1980s: Toward a New Development. Fukuoka Art Museum, Fukuoka, Japan, September 4–October 14, 1984. Catalogue.

Photographic Narration. The Rotunda Gallery, Brooklyn, New York, April 5–May 5, 1984.

Visions of Childhood: A Contemporary Iconography. Whitney Museum of American Art, Downtown Branch at Federal Hall National Memorial, New York, New York, March 28–May 11, 1984. Catalogue.

Castelli Graphics Fifteenth Anniversary Exhibition. Castelli Graphics, New York, New York, March 10–31, 1984.

Art as Social Conscience. Edith C. Blum Art Institute, Bard College, Annandale-on-Hudson, New York, February 9–March 28, 1984. Curator: Linda Weintraub.

Anxious Interiors: An Exhibition of Tableau Photography and Sculpture. Laguna Beach Museum of Art (organizer), Laguna Beach, California, January 6–February 19, 1984; Alaska State Museum, Juneau, Alaska, March 31–May 6, 1984; Alaska Association for the Arts, Fairbanks, Alaska, May 19–June 24, 1984; Visual Arts Center of Alaska, Anchorage, Alaska, July 9–August 3, 1984; Walter Phillips Gallery, Banff Center for the Arts, Banff, Alberta, Canada, September 21–October 14, 1984; The Visual Arts Gallery, Florida International University, Miami, Florida, November 4–December 9, 1984; University of South Florida Art Galleries, Tampa, Florida, January 6–February 10, 1985; The Munson-Williams-Proctor Institute, Utica, New York, March 3–April 7, 1985. Curator: Elaine Dines. Catalogue.

1983

Images Fabriquées. Galerie Viviane Esders, Paris, France, December 10, 1983–January 17, 1984.

New New York Generation. Origrafica, Malmö, Sweden, October 16–November 27, 1983.

Sculpture Now: Recent Figurative Works. Institute of Contemporary Art of the Virginia Museum, Richmond, Virginia, October 12–November 13, 1983. Curator: Julia Boyd.

New Work: New York. Newcastle Polytechnic Gallery, Newcastle Polytechnic, Newcastle upon Tyne, England, October 8–November 4, 1983. Curator: Ellen Price. Catalogue, with essay by William Varley.

Arranged Image Photography. Boise Gallery of Art, Boise, Idaho, October 1–November 6, 1983; Cheney Cowles Memorial Art Museum, Eastern Washington State Historical Society, Spokane, Washington, May 24–June 24, 1984; Yellowstone Art Center, Billings, Montana, September 1–October 30, 1984. Curator: Sandy Harthorn. Catalogue.

Invention and Allegory. Daniel Wolf Gallery, New York, New York, September 8–October 1, 1983.

Photography in America: 1910 to 1983. The Tampa Museum of Art, Tampa, Florida, September 4–November 6, 1983. Curator: Julie M. Saul. Catalogue.

Figurative Contexts. Turman Gallery, Indiana State University, Terre Haute, Indiana, September 3–October 2, 1983. Catalogue by Frances Lattanzio and Bert Brouwer.

Phototypes: The Development of Photography in New York City. Whitney Museum of American Art, Downtown Branch at Federal Hall National Memorial, New York, New York, May 4–June 3, 1983. Catalogue, with essays by Philip Hotchkiss Walsh, Lauren Baker, and Jennifer Dowd.

Reordered Realities: The Photograph as Fiction. The Arts Center of the Portsmouth Museums, Portsmouth, Virginia, April 10–May 22, 1983.

Habitats. The Clocktower, New York, New York, March 9–April 9, 1983. Curator: Robert Littman.

Printed by Women: A National Exhibition of Prints and Photographs. Organized by The Print Club and the Women's Caucus for Art, Philadelphia, Pennsylvania; The Port of History Museum at Penn's Landing, Philadelphia, Pennsylvania, February 17–May 8, 1983. Catalogue by Judith K. Brodsky and Ofelia Garcia.

Drawings/Photographs. Leo Castelli Gallery, New York, New York, 1983.

Photography: The Constructed Image. The Castle Gallery, The College of New Rochelle, New Rochelle, New York, 1983. Curators: Barbara Lipton and Robert Worth.

Three-Dimensional Photographs. Castelli Graphics (organizer), New York, New York; Grapestake Gallery, San Francisco, California; Hermann Wunsche Gallery, Bonn, Germany, 1983.

1982

Inside Spaces. Organized by the Museum of Modern Art's Art Lending Service/Art Advisory Service, New York, New York. Dancer Fitzgerald, Sample, October 31, 1982–March 12, 1983; Freeport-McMoRan, Inc., April 6–June 21, 1983; General Electric, June 26–August 23, 1983; Pfizer, Inc., June 9–September 9, 1992.

Staged Photo Events. Rotterdam Arts Council (organizer), Lijnbaancenter, Rotterdam, The Netherlands, September 3–November 4, 1982; Neue Galerie–Sammlung Ludwig, Aachen, Germany, December 12, 1982–January 24, 1983; Van Reekum Museum, Apeldoorn, The Netherlands, January 1983; Antwerp Museum of Contemporary Art, Antwerp, Belgium, April–May 1983.

Color as Form, A History of Color Photography. The International Museum of Photography, George Eastman House (organizer), Rochester, New York, July 2–September 5, 1982; Corcoran Gallery of Art, Washington, D.C., April 10–May 6, 1982. Catalogue, with essay by Robert A. Sobieszek.

The Atomic Salon. Ronald Feldman Fine Arts, New York, New York, June 9–July 2, 1982.

Visions of Reality. Goddard Riverside Community Art Center, New York, New York, April 29–May 16, 1982.

Points of View 1982. Fred C. Jones Museum of Art, University of Oklahoma, Norman, Oklahoma, January 17–February 21, 1982. Catalogue.

Beyond Photography: The Fabricated Image. Delahunty Gallery, New York, New York, 1982.

1981

Artists Photographs. University of South Florida Art Galleries, Tampa, Florida, November 7, 1981–January 6, 1982.

New American Color Photography. Institute of Contemporary Art, London, England, September 25–November 8, 1981.

Selections from the Chase Manhattan Bank Art Collection. University Gallery, University of Massachusetts, Amherst,

Massachusetts, September 19–December 20, 1981; Robert Hull Fleming Museum, Burlington, Vermont, January 22–March 21, 1982; David Winton Bell Gallery, Brown University, Providence, Rhode Island, October 16–November 11, 1982. Curator: Helaine Posner.

Coastal Currents: A California/New York Exhibition. South Texas Artmobile, September 4–December 18, 1981. Catalogue.

Photography: A Personal View. Morris Museum of Arts and Sciences, Morristown, New Jersey, July 11–September 6, 1981.

Ellen Carey, Nancy Dwyer, Laurie Simmons, and Sandy Skoglund. Texas Gallery, Houston, Texas, June 25–July 31, 1981.

The New Color: A Decade of Color Photography. Everson Museum of Art, Syracuse, New York, May 15–July 26, 1981; International Center of Photography, New York, New York, October 15–November 13, 1981; Columbus Museum of Art, Columbus, Ohio, January 8–February 14, 1982; Gibbes Art Gallery, Charleston, South Carolina, September 10–November 7, 1982; Art Gallery of Hamilton, Ontario, Canada, February 4–April 4, 1983. Curator: Sally Eauclaire.

Staged Shots: Photographs of Fabricated Images. Delahunty Gallery, Dallas, Texas, April 11–May 6, 1981.

10 Years of Women Artists at Douglass College, 1971–1981. Douglass Library, Rutgers University, New Brunswick, New Jersey, March 13–April 8, 1981.

Animals in the Arsenal. Department of Parks and Recreation, The Arsenal Gallery, New York, New York, March 4–April 28, 1981. Curators: Angela Fremont and Betty Tompkins. Catalogue.

1981 Whitney Biennial Exhibition. Whitney Museum of American Art, New York, New York, February 4–April 5, 1981. Curators: John G. Hanhardt, Barbara Haskell, Richard Marshall, and Patterson Sims. Catalogue.

New American Art. Göteborgs Konstmuseum, Göteborg, Sweden, 1981.

Schemes: A Decade of Installation Drawing. Elise Meyer Gallery (organizer), New York, New York; Emily Lowe Gallery, Hofstra University, Hempstead, New York; Musée d'Art Contemporain, Cité du Havre, Montreal, Canada; Lehigh University Art Galleries, Bethlehem, Pennsylvania, 1981. Curator: Shelley Rice. Catalogue.

1980

Group Show. CEPA Gallery, Buffalo, New York, October 18–November 24, 1980.

Contemporary Photographs. Fogg Art Museum, Harvard University, Cambridge, Massachusetts, October 1–November 12, 1980.

Three Photographers at Rutgers. Douglass Library, Rutgers University, New Brunswick, New Jersey, August 28–September 23, 1980.

Ten Photographers. Texas Gallery, Houston, Texas, July 12–August 9, 1980. Curator: Marvin Heiferman.

Likely Stories. Castelli Graphics, New York, New York, July 7–September 13, 1980.

Interiors. Barbara Gladstone Gallery, New York, New York, May 7–June 6, 1980.

1979

Pictures: Photographs. Castelli Graphics, New York, New York, June 23–July 27, 1979. Curator: Marvin Heiferman.

First Move. Interactive Arts Foundation, New York, New York, March 13–29, 1979.

1978

Drawings. Dreyfus Gallery, New York, New York, March 30–April 22, 1978.

Drawings II. Touchstone Gallery, New York, New York, February 14–March 1, 1978.

1977

Invitational. 55 Mercer Gallery, New York, New York, December 20, 1977–January 7, 1978.

SELECTED BIBLIOGRAPHY

"Art Babies/Boathouse Babies." *Daily Hampshire Gazette* (Northampton, Massachusetts), March 29, 1995.

Artner, Alan G. "Cross References." *Chicago Tribune*, February 14, 1988.

"Aus den Fugen: Sandy Skoglund's Installationen." *Frankfurter Allgemeine Zeitung*, January 29, 1992.

Badia, Montse. "La Realitat Amenacada." *Avui Art Supplement: Primavera Fotografica 1992* (Barcelona), April 15, 1992.

Bastin, Pierre. "Installez-vous. Les fictions de la realité de Sandy Skoglund." *La Wallone* (Namur, Belgium), July 3, 1992.

Becker, Michael. "Wahn im Wohnzimmes." *Erlanger Nachrichten Tagblatt*, August 2, 1991.

Bell, Tiffany. "Reviews." *Arts* 52, no. 7 (March 1978): 22–23.

"Benefit Print." *The Print Collector's Newsletter* 27, no. 1 (March–April 1996): 25.

Brandenburg, John. "Chronicle of Photographer/Sculptor's Work Arresting." *The Daily Oklahoman*, October 16, 1992.

Burnside, Mary Wade. "Another World: Sandy Skoglund's Glimpses of Eerie and Amusing Parallel Places." *Charleston Gazette*, October 12, 1995.

Butterfield, Jan, and Susan Rush. *The Art Collection of Pacific Enterprises*. Los Angeles: Pacific Enterprises Corporation, 1991.

Calderón, Manuel. "Criticos en Busca de la Nueva Imagen." *El Guia* (Barcelona), April–May 1992.

Caldwell, John. "Show, *The Constructed Image*, Has Eight Distinct Visions." *New York Times*, July 31, 1983.

"Camera at Work: Sandy Skoglund." *Life*, October 1987, 122–23.

Casas, Enric. "Contactar i Interferir la Realitat." *Regio* (Barcelona), May 17, 1992.

"Challenging Traditions: Into the Third Dimension." *The Art of Photography*. Revised edition. New York: Time-Life Books, Inc., 1981.

Collins, James. "Reviews." *Artforum* 12, no. 5 (January 1974): 73–74.

Contrada, Fred. "Giant Babies Invade College Pond: Smith College Alumna Exhibits Apocalyptic Work." *Hampshire Union-News* (Northampton, Massachusetts), March 29, 1995.

Cornand, Brigitte. "Images." *Actuel* (Paris), November 1989.

Curtiss, Deborah. *Introduction to Visual Literacy*. New York: Prentice-Hall, Inc., 1985.

Cyphers, Peggy. "New York Review: Sandy Skoglund." *Arts Magazine* 65, no. 4 (December 1990): 99.

Davis, Douglas. "Worlds of Color, A Call to the Colors." *Newsweek*, November 23, 1981, 115–16.

Davis, Keith F. *1991 Acquisitions: The Hallmark Photographic Collection*. Kansas City, Missouri: Hallmark, Inc., 1991.

Deal, Darcy. "Sandy Skoglund: Interview." *Q: A Journal of Art* (Department of Art, College of Architecture, Art, and Planning, Cornell University, Ithaca, New York, spring 1993): 21–23.

DeBell, Jeff. "Accessible Avant-Garde." *Roanoke Times and World News*, November 5, 1988.

Degener, Patricia. "Reviews: Midwest. Sandy Skoglund at Greenberg Gallery." *The New Art Examiner* (Chicago), February 1982.

DiGrappa, Carol. "Close Quarters." *Camera Arts* 1, no. 3 (May–June 1981): 86–93, 95. Reprinted in *Fotografi* 11 (November 1981): 46–49.

Dister, Alain. "Au Pays des Merveilles de Sandy Skoglund." *Le Nouvel Observateur* 350 (June 4–10, 1992): 1.

Dorsey, John. "The Confusion of Illusion in Photography." *Baltimore Sun*, February 10, 1987.

Dusein, Gilles. "Sandy Skoglund." *Clichés* 58 (1989): 24–31.

Eauclaire, Sally. *The New Color Photography.* New York: Abbeville Press, 1981.

Edwards, Owen. "Maybe Babies: Sandy Skoglund's Toys in Babeland." *American Photographer,* August 1983, 59–61.

Entrekin, Millie. "In the Last Hour." *Columbus (Ohio) Alive,* March 30–April 6, 1994.

Estevez, Isidre. "Sandy Skoglund: L'Art ha de crear sempre una certa intranquillitat." *Diari de Barcelona,* April 28, 1992.

Eyguesier, Jean-Luc. "Requiem Pour un Viaduc." *Le Figaro Défense* (Paris), June 30, 1992.

Feran, Tim. "The Arts: A Moment in Jam." *Columbus (Ohio) Dispatch,* March 24, 1994.

Filler, Martin. "Living Color." *TWA Ambassador Magazine,* January 1983, 25–31.

Foerstner, Abigail. "Skoglund Fills Complex Spaces with Detailed Fantasies." *Chicago Tribune,* April 26, 1991.

Fontova, Rosario. "Sandy Skoglund utiliza la fotogràfia como medio de crítica social." *El Periodico* (Barcelona), April 30, 1992.

Fontrodona, Oscar. "Sandy Skoglund: Mis personajes son visitantes temporales de su proprio mundo." *ABC* (Barcelona), April 26, 1992.

Fox, Catherine. "Sandy Skoglund's Grand Illusions." *Atlanta Journal Constitution,* February 17, 1991.

Frisach, Montse. "L'artista Sandy Skoglund presenta les seves fotografies inquietants a Barcelona." *Avui* (Barcelona), April 28, 1992.

Gaessler, Dominique. "Sandy Skoglund: des bestioles et des hommes." *Photographies* (Paris) 53 (November 1993): 28–31.

Gimelson, Deborah. "The Green House." *Aspen Magazine,* midsummer 1992, 67–68, 99.

Glueck, Grace. "Art That Comments on the Fate of the Earth." *New York Times,* March 13, 1983.

Goddard, Dan. "Skoglund Explores Fears of Middle Class." *San Antonio Express News,* February 25, 1993.

Goldberger, Corine. "Bureaux: la guerre de l'espace." *Biba* 179 (January 1995): 74–76.

"Goldfische im Schlafzimmer." *Nachrichten Zeitung Erlanger,* August 8, 1991.

Gralnik, Herbert. "Maybe Surrealism." *St. Louis Magazine,* November 1983.

Grundberg, Andy. "Fairy Tales." *SoHo News,* September 17, 1980.

———. "Fish on a Line." *SoHo News,* January 14, 1981.

———. "A Revival of Interest in a World Gone Awry." *New York Times,* December 4, 1988.

———. "Weekend Reviews: Sandy Skoglund, The Green House." *New York Times,* September 14, 1990.

Grundberg, Andy, and Carol Squiers. "Family Fables." *Modern Photography* 47, no. 6 (June 1983): 78–83.

Guerrin, Michel. "Photographie: L'Intrusion du fantastique. Retrospective d'un auteur inclassable: Sandy Skoglund." *Le Monde,* July 6, 1992.

Hagen, Charles. "Reviews." *Artforum* 21, no. 9 (May 1983): 95.

———. "Reviews: Sandy Skoglund. Sharpe Gallery, Castelli Uptown." *Artforum* 25, no. 8 (April 1987): 127–28.

———. "Sandy Skoglund." *New York Times,* October 23, 1992.

———. "Around the House." *New York Times,* August 5, 1994.

———. "Sandy Skoglund at Janet Borden Gallery." *New York Times,* September 23, 1994.

Handy, Ellen. "Sandy Skoglund." *Arts Magazine* 63, no. 4 (December 1988): 83.

———. "Sandy Skoglund at P.P.O.W." *Art in America* 79, no. 11 (November 1991): 153.

Hanson, Bernard. "A Plunge into the Surreal." *Hartford Courant,* May 23, 1982.

Haus, Mary. "Reviews: Sandy Skoglund." *Art News* 88, no. 2 (February 1989): 135–36.

———. "A Little Bit Normal." *Mirabella,* September 1991, 64.

Heimrath, Gerhard. "Nervenkitzel im Horror-Disneyland." *Abendzeitung/Nürnberg,* August 3–4, 1991.

Heiting, Manfred. *50 Jahre moderne Farbfotografie, 1936–1986.* Cologne and Amsterdam: Messe-und Austellungs-Ges.m.b.H., 1986.

Hirsch, Robert. *Exploring Color Photography.* Dubuque, Iowa: William C. Brown College Division, 1989.

Hobbs, Jack A. *Art in Context.* 4th ed. San Diego: Harcourt Brace Jovanovich, Inc., 1991.

Holg, Garrett. "Cross-References: Sculpture into Photography." *The New Art Examiner* (Chicago), April 1988.
Horner, Carol. "The Call of the Suburbs." *Philadelphia Inquirer,* May 28, 1989.
Howe, Jennifer. "A Frozen Slice of Imagination." *Kansas City (Missouri) Star,* July 15, 1991.
Howe, Peter. "The World's Best Photographers 1980–1990." *Life* Collector's Edition, winter 1990, 35, 123.
Hoy, Anne H. *Fabrications: Staged, Altered, and Appropriated Photographs.* New York: Abbeville Press, 1987.
Indiana, Gary. "Home." *Aperture* 127 (spring 1992): 56–63.
"Invasion der Gipskatzen." *Darmstadter Echo,* January 28, 1992.
Johnson, Chris, and Ted Hedgepeth. "Interview with Sandy Skoglund." *San Francisco Camerawork Quarterly Magazine* 10, no. 3 (autumn 1983): 4–5, 10–11.
Johnson, Ken. "Sandy Skoglund at Damon Brandt and Lorence-Monk." *Art in America* 76, no. 12 (December 1988): 147–48.
Johnson, Patricia C. "While Not a Photography Show, Exhibit Uses Medium as Art Form." *Houston Chronicle,* July 9, 1981.
———. "Dogged Fun: Nonchalance, Exaggeration Give Images Bite and Appeal." *Houston Chronicle,* January 8, 1993.
Jones, Richard, ed. "Sandy Skoglund: A Portfolio of Recent Work." *Poetry East Magazine* (DePaul University Press) 32 (fall 1991): 67–79, 171.
K., M. "Radioaktive Katzen." *Main-Echo* (Germany), January 20, 1992.
Kaindl, Kurt. "Sandy Skoglund: Fay Gold Gallery." *Art Papers* 12, no. 1 (January–February 1988).
Kalil, Susie. "New York Storytellers: Ambiguities and Obfuscations." *Artweek* 12, no. 25 (August 1, 1981): 1, 20.
———. "Pop Goes the Country: Two Diverse Works Installations Reflect on America's Consumer-Driven, Media-Soaked Culture." *Houston Press,* December 31, 1992.
Karabinis, Paul. "Five Tales." *Point of Contact* (winter/spring 1997): 18–24.
Keeran, James. "Woof Woof! Sandy Skoglund Is the Art World's Cat's Meow." *The Pantagraph* (Normal, Illinois), December 9, 1994.
Kent, Sarah. "Sandy Skoglund." *Time Out,* October 13–20, 1993, 49.
Kenyon, Theo Jean. "The Green House Arrives at Lakeview." *Journal Star* (Peoria), December 2, 1994.
King, Mary. "Windows Into a Surreal World." *St. Louis Post-Dispatch,* November 6, 1981.
Kino, Carol. "Sandy Skoglund." *Art News* 93, no. 10 (December 1994): 139.
Kirshenblatt-Gimblett, Barbara. "Who's Bad? Accounting for Taste." *Artforum* (November 1991): 120–25.
Koeppel, Fredric. "Broken Rules." *Commercial Appeal* (Memphis), September 12, 1991.
Koetzle, Michael. "Invasion der Eichhornchen." *Photo Technik International* (January–February 1992): 18–25. Reprinted as "Invasion of the Squirrels." *Photo Technique International* (February 1992): 44–51.
———. "Inszenierte Traume." *Max Magazine* 2 (February 1995): 230–37.
Kohen, Helen L. "Rooms with a View." *Miami Herald,* April 11, 1992.
Kozloff, Max. "Hapless Figures in an Artificial Storm." *Artforum* 28, no. 3 (November 1989): 131–36.
Kutner, Janet. "What the Camera Records Didn't Happen Naturally." *Dallas Morning News,* October 7, 1981.
Larrain, Christine. "Sandy Skoglund." *Zoom* 94 (1982): 42–53.
Levin, Kim. "Voice Choices." *Village Voice,* September 18, 1990.
Lewis, Diane. "Skoglund Works Explore Bizarre." *Wichita Eagle,* January 21, 1994.
Lyons, Channy. "Beyond Blue Dogs: Artist Studies Culture from One Step Back." *Observer* (Peoria), December 14, 1994.
Maatjes, Door Hennie. "Schilderen mit de Camera." *Nieuwe Revu Magazine* (Amsterdam), January 14–21, 1988.
Marco, Luis Miguel. "Sueños Fosforescentes." *El Periodico* (Barcelona), April 19, 1992, 20–23.
Martin, Mary Abbe. "Exhibit's Photos Lie—But Artfully." *Minneapolis Star Tribune,* September 27, 1987.
Mason, M. S. "The Quick (Gray) Fox Jumped Over the . . ." *Christian Science Monitor,* June 10, 1991.
Mason, Robert G. "Trends: Pictures That Tell the Truth by Making It Up." *Photography Year 1981.* New York: Time-Life, Inc, 1981.

Masters, Greg. "Displacing Sensory Expectations: Interview with Sandy Skoglund." *Cover Magazine* (September 1988): 14.

Maxfield, David. "Today's New 'Photoartists' Make, Not Take, Pictures." *St. Louis Post-Dispatch*, June 25, 1989.

"Maybe Babies, 1983, Galerie Leo Castelli NYC." *Actuel* (Paris) 85 (November 1986): 24, 44.

McKenzie, Barbara. "Art Review: Skoglund's Photographs Capture the True Fiction in Modern Life." *Atlanta Journal-Constitution*, October 18, 1987.

McNally, Owen. "Still-Life Patio Scene Invites Viewers to Test Perceptions." *Hartford Courant*, November 24, 1991.

McQuaid, Cate. "Close-Up: Sandy Skoglund." *PRC Newsletter* (Boston) 17, no. 2 (March 1993).

———. "Cheese It: Sandy Skoglund Throws the Cocktail Party of Your Dreams." *Boston Phoenix*, April 9, 1993.

Merritt, Robert. "Sculpture Now Unsettling." *Richmond Times Dispatch*, October 14, 1983.

Michner, Charles. "The Struggle to Live with Reality." *New Republic*, April 4, 1981, 27–30.

Millis, Christopher. "Material Worlds: Sandy Skoglund on Installation." *Boston Phoenix*, April 4, 1997.

Mitchell, Charles Dee. "Opening the Shutters: Skoglund Challenges Photographic Traditions." *Dallas Morning News*, February 18, 1993.

Naef, Weston. *New Trends, The Gallery of World Photography.* New York: Dai Nippon, 1984.

Nilsen, Richard. "An Uneasy Reality." *Arizona Republic*, June 21, 1995.

Olivares, Rosa. "Una Cuestión de Método." *Lapiz: Entre el Retrato y la Representación* (Barcelona) 68 (September 1991): 28–37.

Perreault, John. "Through a Glass Darkly." *Artforum* 27, no. 7 (March 1989): 106–12.

Pinto, Roberto. "To Be and Not To Be." *Flash Art International Magazine* 23, no. 157 (1990): 176–77.

Pinvol, Theresa. "Els Muntatges Fotografics de Sandy Skoglund." *Diari de Barcelona*, May 3, 1992, 25–27.

Plagens, Peter. "Into the Fun House." *Newsweek*, August 21, 1989.

Preble, Duane, and Sarah Preble. *Artforms: An Introduction to the Visual Arts.* 4th ed. New York: Harper & Row, 1988.

Radziewsky, Elke von. "Zuchersüsse Alpträume." *Architektur & Wohnen* (Hamburg) 4 (July 1994): 148–54.

Raven, Arlene. "Flood Tide." *Village Voice*, September 24, 1991.

Raynor, Vivien. "New Drawings by Castelli Artists." *New York Times*, November 2, 1984.

———. "The Indispensability of Surrealism." *New York Times*, May 6, 1990, New Jersey edition.

———. "Exhibitions Examine Human Anatomy and Human Folly." *New York Times*, December 15, 1991.

Reeve, Catharine. "Using Sculpture to Pose Some Photographic Questions." *Chicago Tribune*, January 29, 1988.

Rice, Shelley. "Reviews." *Artforum* 19, no. 7 (March 1981): 88.

———. "Photographic Installations." *San Francisco Camerawork* 12, no. 1 (spring 1984): 4, 5.

Richard, Paul. "The Shifting Shutter of Photography: Unsettling, Convincing American Pictures." *Washington Post*, April 28, 1989.

Richardson, Nan. "Sandy Skoglund: Wild at Heart." *Art News* (April 1991): 114–19.

Robins, Corrine. *The Pluralist Era: American Art, 1968–1981.* New York: Harper & Row, 1984.

Roegiers, Patrick. "Un autre monde." *Le Monde*, November 25, 1989.

———. "Sandy Skoglund: Un autre monde." *Photographies* (June 1992): 30–34.

———. "Sandy Skoglund: du syndrome de la sucromanie." *Art Press* 171 (July–August 1992): 43–45.

Rose, Matthew. "Playing a Round in TriBeCa." *New York Times*, July 26, 1992.

Rosen, Steven. "Fox Games Message Strong and Bright." *Denver Post*, June 2, 1990.

Rosenblum, Naomi. *A History of Women Photographers.* Paris/London/New York: Abbeville Press, 1994.

Russell, John. "In Connecticut . . . Reviews 'Stamford.'" *New York Times*, August 4, 1989.

Salway, Kate. "New American Color Photography." *The British Journal of Photography*, November 18, 1981.

"Sandy Skoglund, On-Line Artist. http://www.artsednet.getty.edu/."

The Getty Bulletin 10, no. 1 (summer 1996): 19.

"Sandy Skoglund: Erst Erlanger, dann Paris und Barcelona." *Erlanger Nachrichten*, August 14, 1991.

"Sandy Skoglund." *Marie Claire* (Tokyo) 57 (1987): 102–5.

"Sandy Skoglund." *Nikkei Art Magazine* (December 1991): 61–66.

Sayag, Alain. *De la photographie comme un des beaux-arts*. Paris: Centre National de la Photographie, Series Photo-Poche, 1989.

Schwabsky, Barry. "Reviews of Exhibitions." *Flash Art International Magazine* 133 (April 1987): 90.

Schwendenwein, Jude. "Regional Reviews: Connecticut. Investigations in Photography: Sandy Skoglund and John Coplans." *Art New England* 13, no. 4 (June–July 1992): 36.

———. "Cravings: Food into Sculpture." *Sculpture* 2, no. 6 (November–December 1992): 44–49.

———. "Sandy Skoglund: Interview." *Journal of Contemporary Art* 6, no. 1 (summer 1993): 87–98.

Shearin, Margaret. "Skoglund's Art Captivates on More Than One Level." *Triad* (Winston-Salem), July 28, 1993.

Sherman, Mary. "At MCA, Sculptors Affirm Reality with Photographs." *Chicago Sun-Times*, March 3, 1988.

Sischy, Ingrid. "Photography: Food for Thought." *The New Yorker*, October 19, 1992, 22.

"Skoglund: The Month of Photography in Paris." *Photo Magazine* 230 (November 1986): 114–17.

Skoglund, Sandy. "Spirituality in the Flesh. A Project for *Artforum*." *Artforum* 30, no. 6 (February 1992): 76–77.

———. "Self-Portrait." *The New Yorker*, October 3, 1994, 26.

Sladden, Mike. "Gallery Talk by Sandy Skoglund, February 14, 1990." In *RF & PC Info Update*. Rochester, New York: Eastman House International Center of Photography, March–April 1990, 1–8.

Smith, Lisa. "OU Art Museum Stretches the Visual Vocabulary: Skoglund, Gottlieb Shows Bring Unusual Art to Norman." *Oklahoma Gazette*, September 24, 1992.

Sozanski, Edward J. "Reviews: Sandy Skoglund at the Temple Gallery." *Philadelphia Inquirer*, December 6, 1990.

Staniszewski, Mary Anne. "New York Reviews." *Art News* 79, no. 9 (November 1980): 214.

Stapen, Nancy. "Fun with Bacon and Cheese Curls." *Boston Globe*, April 13, 1993.

Stein, Harvey, and others. *Artists Observed*. New York: Harry N. Abrams, Inc., 1986.

Steinbrok, Sarah. "Printed by Women." *Philadelphia Photo Review* 7, no. 3 (fall 1983): 2–4.

Stolt, Veronica. "Sandy Skoglund." *Nordst Jernan* (New York), June 17, 1993.

Sullivan, Constance, and Eugenia Parry Janis. *Women Photographers*. New York: Harry N. Abrams, Inc., 1990.

Tallmer, Jerry. "Mini Art in a Maxi Way." *New York Post*, January 9, 1987.

Tanaka, Hiroko. *Art Is Beautiful: Interviews with New York Artists*. Tokyo: Kawade Shobo Shinsha, 1990.

Tibbetts, John C. "Framing a Century of American Change." *Christian Science Monitor*, January 18, 1995.

Trebay, Guy. "The Fish Knows the Way." *Village Voice*, January 7, 1981.

Tully, Judd. "Reviews of Exhibitions." *Flash Art International Magazine* 103 (summer 1981): 55.

———. "Reviews of Exhibitions: New York." *The New Art Examiner* (Chicago), May 1987.

———. "Off the Wall." *Taxi Magazine* (October 1988): 120–24.

———. "Blasting Out of the Darkroom." *Taxi Magazine* (July 1989): 30.

Turcat, Raphaël. "Food Environments." *Technikart* (October–November 1993): 54.

Tyson, Janet. "Worlds Overrun by Animals and Food." *Fort Worth Star-Telegram*, February 23, 1993.

"Une Exposition Parmi d'Autres. Art 23: Sandy Skoglund à la galerie Zur Stockeregg." *Schweizerische Photorundschau* (July 1992): 29.

Vallongo, Sally. "Columbus Exhibits Show. How Two Artists Carved Their Niches." *Toledo (Ohio) Blade*, March 27, 1994.

Visani, Virginia. "Sognando S'Impara." *Anna bella Magazine*, April 1988, 3, 56–62.

"*Walking on Eggshells*: A Collaboration." *Pulp: Dieu Donné Newsletter*, no. 23 (June–August 1997): 1.

Wallach, Amei. "The Thinking Person's Link: Golf or Art? Putt-Modernism Is Both." *New York Newsday*, July 31, 1992.

———. "Rooms with Views. Putting Yourself in Artist's Places." *New York Newsday*, October 14, 1994.

Watts, James D. "Crunch Time." *Tulsa World*, March 3, 1995.

Weber, Bruce. "Outfoxing the Viewer." *New York Times Magazine*, October 8, 1989.

Weinstein, Ann. "Skoglund Always Pushes Photography to Limit." *Roanoke Times & World News*, October 30, 1988.

Weinstein, Michael. "Sandy Skoglund." *Chicago News and Art Weekly*, May 16–22, 1991.

Williams, Kent. "Brain Teasers." *Isthmus*, July 9, 1993.

Wilson, Jane. "Skoglund Installations Meant to Jolt Us out of Our Normalcy." *The Aspen Times*, July 18–19, 1992.

Wise, Kelly. "Fantasies, Fables Kindle the Imagination." *Boston Globe*, March 23, 1991.

Wolf, Sylvia. *Focus: Five Women Photographers*. Morton Grove, Illinois: Albert Whitman & Co., 1994.

Wolff, Thomas A. "Heiter bis nervig: Sandy Skoglunds Bilderdramen im Fotografie Forum." *Frankfurter Rundschau*, January 18, 1992.

Wolin, Joseph R. "Sandy Skoglund: P.P.O.W., New York." *Artscribe* 89 (November–December 1991): 99.

Wood, S. D. "Reviews: Sandy Skoglund at Real Art Ways." *Art New England* 1, no. 5 (April 1980).

Yau, John. "Review: Sandy Skoglund at Damon Brandt Gallery and Lorence-Monk Gallery." *Artforum* 27, no. 3 (November 1988): 141.

Yoe, Craig. *The Art of Barbie. Artists Celebrate the World's Favorite Doll.* Mattel, Inc., and Workman Publishing Co., Inc., 1994.

Yuan, Angie. "Photos of Fantasies, Fables, and Fabrications Explores Style of 80s." *Boston Daily News*, March 6, 1991.

Zimmer, William. "Home on the Strange." *SoHo News*, May 21, 1980.

INDEX